Life's Riddle

Life's Riddle

Nils A. Amnéus

Author of
Does Chance or Justice Rule Our Lives?

THEOSOPHICAL UNIVERSITY PRESS
PASADENA, CALIFORNIA

Theosophical University Press
Post Office Box C
Pasadena, California 91109-7107
1998

Library of Congress Cataloging-in-Publication Data

Amnéus, Nils A. (Nils August), 1878–1952.
   Life's riddle / by Nils A. Amnéus.
     p.   cm.
   Originally published: Los Angeles : T. Amnéus, 1954.
   Includes bibliographical references.
   ISBN 1-55700-130-8 (pbk. : alk. paper)
   ISBN 1-55700-131-6 (Internet)
    1. Theosophy.   I. Title.
BP565.A44L54   1998
299'.934—dc21   98-10510
                                      CIP

Printed at Theosophical University Press
Pasadena, California

TABLE OF CONTENTS

Chapter I

THE ANCIENT WISDOM

Life's Riddle is a compound of many problems such as the following:

Why is there so much suffering in the world?

Why so much injustice?

What is the purpose of life?

Is there a life after death?

Have we free will or are we the puppets of destiny?

Are we responsible for our acts—shall we reap what we sow?

Is this a haphazard universe, governed by blind forces, or is there a plan behind it?

THE ANCIENT WISDOM

The writer has found an answer to these and many other questions regarding life in a system of ancient teachings which has existed from time immemorial. These teachings, that have been known under the name of the "Ancient Wisdom," or the "Wisdom Religion," have existed in all ages and in all countries, but have often and for long periods of time been obscured from the world. Yet they have always been preserved and have at intervals been reissued to illumine and guide mankind on its upward journey.

After each new presentation these teachings remain pure for a period, but gradually they become warped by manmade dogmas and opinions and their true inner meaning is lost. They must then be given out anew in language suited to the new time in which they are issued. The latest such restatement of the ancient teachings was begun by Helena Petrovna Blavatsky, who founded the Theosophical Society for this purpose in 1875. The Ancient Wisdom, clothed in modern language, is known today under the name *Theosophy*.

In the following will be presented some of the ancient teachings that furnish a solution to many of the problems of life and show that Man is not a helpless pawn ruled by blind forces, but that he has the power of choice and freedom of action, and is therefore responsible for his acts, in due time reaping all that he has sown. They show also that there is a purpose in life, and that Man faces a glorious destiny.

A brief outline of some of the Ancient Teachings will first be presented; later some of these will be taken up for further discussion.

THE ONE LIFE

The first proposition of the Ancient Teachings is the most difficult to present, for it deals with something infinite and there-

1

fore not easily grasped by our finite minds, and still less easily expressed in words. The general teaching is, however, that back of the material, visible universe that we know, there is an Omnipresent, Eternal, Boundless and Unchanging Principle: a Divine Life-Essence, that is the unseen cause of the visible universe and all life in it.*

This Universal Divine Essence is eternal and unchanging. But when a Material Universe comes into manifestation, then this Universal Life emanates or differentiates individualized units from its own essence, and every such life-unit, or "Monad" as it is called, enters upon a Pilgrimage of Evolution in the new universe that is just coming into being.

The Universal Divine Essence, then, is the fountain and origin of all life. Every evolving Monad has at its innermost core a ray of this Divine Essence, just as a sunbeam has its origin in the sun and carries with it some of the sun's essence. The ancient Hindu scriptures express this idea:

> As a single sun illumines the whole world
> even so the One Spirit illumines every body.†

THE UNIVERSE A LIVING ORGANISM

The ancient teachings state that the Universe as a whole is a living organism and that every individual life within that Universe is linked with the Universal Life, is in fact an inseparable part of that life.

The various forms of life that we see in Nature appear to be separate from and quite independent of one another, but the Ancient Wisdom tells us that this independence exists only in the outward, material form, vehicle or body in which the Monad is embodied for the time being. Behind this outward form they are not independent of each other, but simply different manifestations, different expressions of the same Universal Life, inwardly united with one another on the invisible planes of Nature.

---

*The Secret Doctrine, Vol. I, pp. 14-17.
†The Bhagavad-Gîtâ, Chap. 13 (one of the Hindu sacred scriptures.)

As a group of islands seem to exist independently, yet are all outcroppings of the same Mother Earth hidden but connected beneath the water; as the fingers of one hand, though free to some extent, are yet united in the same hand; as the leaves of one tree, though leading their separate existences are yet parts of the greater unit, the tree, so also is every life in the Universe part of the One Universal Life. The link that binds the individual to the Universal Life and therefore to all other individual lives, "the stem of the leaf," is the ray of Divinity at the core of every being.

This doctrine that all beings are emanations from the One Universal Life is found everywhere in the world and is recognized in such expressions as: "God is everywhere," "God is in all things." It is the "One in all," the One Life expressing itself through the vast variety of forms that we see in the Universe.

But since the Universal Divine Essence extends throughout infinite space and the whole must embrace all its parts, it is equally true that we are "All in One," or as St. Paul puts it in speaking to the Athenians:

> ". . . . in him we live, and move and have our being:
> as certain also of your own poets have said, For we are
> also his offspring."   —*Acts* XVII, 28

In parentheses St. Paul admits that the doctrine was already known among the Greeks. The fact that all life-units have emanated from the same Universal Source is the basis for the ancient teaching that "Brotherhood is a fact in Nature."

To sum up: Everything in the Universe is alive and "All are... parts of one stupendous whole, whose body Nature is and God the Soul."*

DUALITY OF SPIRIT AND MATTER

When a period for manifestation of an outward, visible Universe is at hand, the One Life Essence appears under two contrasting aspects: Spirit or Consciousness on one hand, and matter

---

*Alexander Pope.

or vehicle on the other. Spirit and Matter, however, are not independent realities, but are the opposite poles of the One Reality,
so that even matter is not without life and consciousness of a
lower order; and Consciousness must have a vehicle of matter,
whether gross or ethereal, in order to express itself as individual
Consciousness. In more evolved entities Spirit dominates, while
Matter dominates in those less evolved. But in every case, as the
Hindu scriptures express it:

> There is no matter without spirit and there is no spirit without
> matter.

As a lens is necessary to focus diffused sunlight into a bright,
active center, so is a body or vehicle of matter necessary to focus
a ray of the Universal Mind as individual Consciousness. A large,
perfectly transparent lens will produce a much stronger concentra-
tion of light than a small lens of uneven transparency or rough
surface. So also will a highly evolved body or instrument admit
a more perfect manifestation of the indwelling Consciousness
than a less perfect instrument.

All through the manifested Universe we see this duality of
Spirit and Matter. Spirit or Consciousness cannot, however, act
directly on gross matter, and the Ancient Teachings tell us that
there are many intermediate forces and energies that form the
connecting links between these two, thus enabling Spirit to control
the body in which it functions. This will be discussed further on.

INVOLUTION AND EVOLUTION

The Teachings regarding Evolution and Involution can best be
understood by tracing the origin of these two words. They both
come from the Latin verb *volvere*, "to turn, to roll." The prefix
"e" means "out, or away from," while the prefix "in" has the
same meaning as in English. Evolution therefore means to unroll
or unwrap something that is wrapped up or rolled up, while Involution means the process of wrapping or rolling up something
that has been unrolled. The following illustration may help to
explain.

In ancient times books were not printed on flat sheets of paper and bound into volumes such as we have today. The information was inscribed on rolls of parchment, called *scrolls,* and when these were read, they had to be unrolled so as to expose the writing. As the reading proceeded, the lower end of the scroll was unrolled, or evolved, exposing the hidden writing, while at the same time the upper end of the scroll was rolled up, thus involving, and hiding what had so far been read.

When the One Life manifests a portion of itself as a visible Universe, it does so by alternately evolving its two aspects of Matter and Spirit. In the beginning of a cycle of manifestation, Matter is evolved, as there must be a sub-stratum or foundation provided for the higher evolution that is to follow. This is exemplified in the early stages of a planet's existence when Matter dominates the scene and no higher life is discernible. Yet the Ancient Teaching tells us that even in the rock there exists a form of life—of a very low order, not life as we ordinarily think of it, but still life of a kind. In this case Matter dominates and Spirit is almost completely dormant or involved. This is Evolution of Matter and Involution of Spirit.

As the process unfolds and Life and Spirit have had time to exert their influence on Matter; the latter loses some of its grossness and becomes more complex, as matter in the bodies of plants, animals and humans is more refined than matter in the rock. In the Animal and Human Kingdoms, Life and Spirit gradually gain the ascendency as Matter loses some of its retarding influence on Spirit. This is Evolution of Spirit and Involution or recession of the gross aspect of Matter.

The Evolution of Spirit, then, is always accompanied by a simultaneous Involution of Matter. In the same way the Evolution of Matter is accompanied by an Involution of Spirit, just as the unrolling of one end of the scroll is accompanied by the simultaneous inrolling of the opposite end. The purpose of life is growth, development, expansion of Consciousness, the rising from lower states of being to higher ones, and this advancement is accomplished through the process of Evolution.

The innermost center or core of every life-unit or Monad is a

Ray or emanation from the One Universal Life. It is this Ray
that originates and vitalizes every form in Nature. Through its
inner connection with the Universal Life it has within itself latent
possibilities for infinite growth and development. From this Ray
comes the upward urge, the driving and impelling force that is
the hidden cause of all evolution.

Every individual Monad must, in the course of its evolutionary
pilgrimage, inhabit all the various forms of Nature beginning with
the lowest, gradually advancing through eternities of time and
the various kingdoms, until it is ready to inhabit the higher forms.
In each embodiment the Monad gains the experience and learns
the lessons which that particular embodiment has to offer. When
the lessons of that embodiment have been learned and there is no
longer any need for experience in that type of body, the upward
urge within the Monad causes it to seek higher forms in order to
continue its evolution. In its new embodiment with its altered environment, the Monad has different experiences and develops different faculties, until these faculties operate in relative perfection.
Then another forward step is taken, and so on, *ad infinitum.*

The various forms of Nature in which the Monad embodies itself may be likened to the rungs of a ladder, up which the evolving Monad climbs. Figuratively, the highest rung of one ladder
takes the climber to an imaginary platform, a temporary goal,
where he may rest and recuperate from his effort. But the urge
from within allows him no long respite and he soon discovers
that his platform supports another "evolutionary ladder" which
he now begins to climb to reach the greater heights he dimly per-
ceives above him.

We see below us on the Ladder of Life, Monads in an ever
ascending scale of Evolution, reaching from the atom and the
minerals to Man. All these Monads are heading towards the Human stage in an upward march that embraces time periods of in-
comprehensible duration. The Ancient Teachings tell us that there
are above Man other Ladders, leading to heights inconceivable,
which some day, in ages to come, Man shall begin to climb. The
possibilities for growth are infinite, and Man's destiny is far
greater than he can picture.

Evolution, then, is endless, but it is not one continuous, un-interrupted climb. There are temporary stopping places, relative beginnings and relative endings, but there never was a first beginning and there never will be a final end.

It will be noted that the subject of Evolution as presented by the Ancient Wisdom differs from the Darwinian Theory. According to the latter it is the *forms* of Nature that change, through a process of "natural selection" and "the survival of the fittest," by im-perceptible degrees from one form into another. The Ancient Wisdom, on the other hand, states that the forms of Nature are relatively stable, although they do undergo some exceeding slow changes. But the real actor in the drama of Evolution is the in-dwelling Monad, and a distinction is made between this Monad and the vehicle or body it inhabits.

The Monad "migrates" through the ages, from lower to higher forms, up through the Kingdoms of Nature, until after aeons it reaches the Human Kingdom.

To summarize: The Ancient Wisdom looks upon Evolution as an unwrapping or unfolding process by which latent possibilities, inherent in the Monad, gradually find expression. As the Monad advances and inhabits higher forms, a greater unfoldment of its latent faculties becomes possible.

Chapter II

THE UNIVERSE: A SCHOOL OF EXPERIENCE

"The Universe, including the visible and the invisible . . . .
exists for the sake of the soul's experience and emancipation."

—Patañjali (Ancient Hindu philosopher)

THE SCHOOLHOUSE OF NATURE

The Universe is a vast school of experience for the unfoldment
of a greater Consciousness in all life-units, which compose the
Universe. Material Nature is one of the schoolhouses in which
certain courses of instruction are given. The Monads that gain
their experience in the great school of Nature all began their
evolution for this cycle at various times in the far distant past,
and therefore show vast differences in development. Therefore they
cannot all profit by having the same experiences at this time, and
Nature provides for this great diversity of development by offer-
ing opportunities for embodiment in a vast variety of different
forms: in the Mineral, Plant, Animal and Human Kingdoms; and
an almost infinite number of sub-grades or sub-divisions within
these.

The less evolved Monads embody themselves in the Mineral
Kingdom; those that have advanced farther in their evolution
embody in the Plant Kingdom and those still more advanced, in
the Animal Kingdom. The Monads that have learned all that can
be gained from an existence in the Animal Kingdom advance beyond it and begin their evolution in the Human Kingdom.

Since the Monads, now embodied in human form, started on
their evolutionary journey at different times in the far distant past
and therefore "arrived" at the Human stage at different times,
it is but natural that human beings should show vast differences
in their development. Those who arrived at the Human stage
ages ago, and hence had many opportunities to incarnate, have
advanced quite far in their human evolution, and embody themselves in one of the more highly civilized races of mankind. Those

11

Monads, on the other hand, who more recently arrived at the Human stage, embody themselves in one of the more primitive races to begin their human evolution. As their advancement proceeds they embody in more highly developed races. Within the race the Monads are attracted to and incarnate in that nation and that family which most closely correspond to their own development.

Thus there is passing up through Nature a vast army, an immense aggregate of Monads successively inhabiting various forms in the lower kingdoms, then migrating to higher and higher forms, ever learning and advancing by means of such experiences as their various embodiments offer.

An ordinary school has classrooms and courses of instruction for children of kindergarten up to graduation age. Every year a new group enters kindergarten, and every year the children in one grade complete their courses and advance into the next higher one. After each semester there is a vacation period before the new term begins, and each year one class graduates from the highest grade and leaves the school for other fields of activity, or perhaps to enter the lowest grade in the next higher school. There is then a continuous stream of children gaining instruction in this school by working up through its various grades, "migrating," as it were, from classroom to classroom, after having gained suitable proficiency in the preceding grade.

The classrooms and courses of instruction in the school remain unchanged, as in the Kingdoms of Nature, but the children, like the Monads, form a constant stream of new and advancing entities. The time-periods consumed in these migrations of the Monads up through the Kingdoms of Nature are of such immense duration as to stagger the imagination and far exceed anything that would seem acceptable today.

THE LAW OF CAUSE AND EFFECT

It has been said that the Universe is a School of Experience. In order to learn by experience, it is necessary to repeat an act over and over again. It is also necessary that Nature should be consistent in her reactions. If we bounce a ball against the floor it rebounds in a direction that depends entirely on how it was thrown. It is because the forces of Nature obey definite and invariable laws that the ball thrower can profit by experience and produce certain desired results. If the forces of Nature were not constant, the ball might react differently each time and it would be impossible to predict what might happen. Under such conditions there would be nothing to base experience on and all progress would be impossible.

The Ancient Teachings state that everything in the Universe is subject to an absolute and unerring Law of Cause and Effect that brings to every action an equal and opposite reaction. This law governs all actions involving atoms and universes and everything between these, whether visible or invisible, physical, psychic, mental or spiritual.

In an ordinary school the teacher is an individual. In the "School of Experience" the teacher is no individual, but is this law of Cause and Effect, that is inherent in Nature. This law is referred to in the Ancient Teachings by the name *Karma,* and will be discussed in greater detail under this heading.

REIMBODIMENT

No child can learn all that its school has to teach in one single day. The time would be too short and the labor too strenuous. Hence he returns day after day to his studies. The child cannot stay in school 24 hours a day, month after month, without interruption. If he is to retain his health and capacity for learning, his study periods must be alternated with periods for play, refreshment and rest, and our school systems are arranged in accord with these requirements. Neither can a Monad learn all that may be experienced in a certain form of body during a single embodiment, any more than a child can absorb all its schooling in a single day.

Evolution of the Monad would be impossible if it were limited to a single life in any one form of body. In order to accomplish the purpose of Evolution, the Monad must have time and more time. And Nature provides the necessary time by giving the Monad new opportunities for repeated embodiments in any particular form, so long as such reimbodiment is needed.

The doctrine of Reimbodiment, says the Ancient Wisdom, applies to every individual life-unit within the Universe. All assume bodies or vehicles of various types; all have their periods of activity of various lengths; all discard their outworn garments and enter into their periods of assimilation and rest, and all reimbody to continue their evolution.

When the reimbodiment takes place in a body of flesh it is called *Reincarnation,* from the three Latin words: *re,* "again," *in,* "in," and *carnis,* "flesh," which therefore gives the word the meaning of "again in flesh." All life-units reimbody. Only those whose bodies are of flesh reincarnate. Reincarnation therefore is a "special case" of reimbodiment.

CYCLES

According to the Ancient Teachings, all activity in Nature is cyclic. That is, it repeats itself, and consists of periods of activity alternated with periods of rest. On a small time scale we see this law of Periodicity, or law of Cycles, operating in such phenomena as the return of the seasons, the ebb and flow of the tides, day and night, sleeping and waking, etc. On a larger time-scale, the same principle operates by means of repeated embodiments, life-periods, broken by death, and followed by rest-periods in other states of being, followed in their turn by new embodiments in the material world.

MAN'S CLASSROOM

In the Human kingdom our evolution is advanced both by outer and inner experiences. Outwardly we learn our lessons from contact with Nature and with our fellow men. Sometimes we learn pleasantly, but often through suffering and struggle. We "brush up against life"; we find ourselves in varying circumstances that call forth our ingenuity, draw out our latent faculties and talents, and develop courage, fortitude and patience.

Inwardly Man finds himself enmeshed in a network of conflicting forces and energies at play within his own nature. On the one hand are his desires and his "tumultuous senses and organs which impel to action in every direction", to borrow an expression from *The Bhagavad-Gîtâ*. These are stimulated into activity by the needs, temptations and allurements presented by the material world. On the other hand is Man's divine nature from which he receives impulses to do unselfish, altruistic acts, to serve, to give, to build a better world. To strengthen him in his efforts, he has also the ethical teachings of religion that urge him to love his neighbor, to "seek the Kingdom of Heaven," and to do unto others as he would be done by.

The average man oscillates between these two sides of his nature, sometimes obeying one and then the other. He stands, as it were, between two opposite poles that attract his being, but he is not a helpless pawn of either side. He has free will, and can follow his higher impulses or yield to the lower, just as he chooses. By his repeated thoughts and deeds Man has it in his own power to alter his character and thereby determine his own destiny.

When we realize that the Law of Cause and Effect governs all our actions and will bring us a reaction of pain for every pain we inflict on others, as well as a benefit for every beneficial act, we begin to see the wisdom of doing good to others and the folly of doing them harm. We then realize that if we want to experience happiness and harmony, we must first sow seeds of happiness and harmony.

If, in spite of this knowledge, we persist in wrong-doing and bring unhappiness and sorrow to others, we thereby bring a reaction of suffering on ourselves. This suffering, however, is not without its compensation, for it teaches us lessons that we were unwilling to learn any other way. It turns our attention to the important issues in life, that might otherwise have been overlooked. It brings out compassion, sympathy and understanding for the sorrows of others. If we do not repeat our wrong-doing, suffering will gradually cease, and if we listen to the voice of our Higher

Nature and live in accord with it, life will flow smoothly and harmoniously.

Thus we learn from the experiences of life and gradually become wiser and gentler, and better able to live in harmony with one another.

THE GOAL

"Theosophy considers Humanity as an emanation from Divinity on its return path thereto."   —H. P. Blavatsky

The Ancient Wisdom tells us that the goal of Man's existence on Earth is to become godlike, and to express actively and fully in his daily life the godlike qualities which, though dormant, are innate. It is Man's limited and self-centered *personality* that prevents these godlike qualities from finding expression. The purpose of Man's evolution is, therefore, to broaden, refine and raise the personality until it becomes a fit instrument to express the godlike qualities within him.

All great Teachers such as Christ and Buddha were at one time ordinary human beings. Compassion for their suffering fellow men aroused in their hearts a desire to bring relief and establish a happier and more harmonious relationship between men. To accomplish this they had to hasten their evolution by a *self-directed* effort, continued during many lives. Thus they forged ahead of their fellows, advancing in perfection until they reached union with their inner god. The attainment of this union made them the highly evolved, outstanding characters they were, with a far deeper understanding of Nature's Laws than ordinary men, hence a greater control over known and unknown forces in the Universe.

Christ and Buddha always taught that their attainment could be achieved by all. Jesus showed his belief in the perfectibility of Man when he admonished his listeners: "Be ye therefore perfect, even as your Father in Heaven is perfect" (*Matt.* V, 48). The "Father in Heaven," says the Ancient Wisdom, is the Divinity innate in every man. Jesus said also, in *John*, X, 30: "I and my Father are one," indicating thereby that his human self had been refined and raised into full and conscious union with his inner god.

The purpose of Man's existence—here on Earth—shall have been accomplished and the goal of evolution attained when, in the distant future, the human race as a whole has become Christlike. Then godlike men will walk the Earth, harmony will reign, and the Kingdom of Heaven will be a reality on Earth.

Chapter III

THE UNSEEN SIDE OF NATURE

SUPER SENSORY PLANES OF EXISTENCE

In the foregoing has been presented a brief outline of some of the Ancient Wisdom teachings in regard to Evolution and the Universe as a "school of experience," in order to show man's place in the general scheme. A number of questions naturally present themselves in this connection.

How can the Universe be a living organism? Where are the links that connect the individual lives with the One Life?

How are effects linked with their causes when there is no visible connection in the outer world?

How can the center of consciousness of each entity, the Monad, which dwells during earthlife in its physical body, survive after the death of this body, and what is the nature of its existence during the interval between two physical embodiments?

The answers to these questions, according to the Ancient Wisdom, is that the physical world in which we live is only one of many different "planes" or levels, or cross-sections of consciousness that exist in Nature. These other planes or worlds are co-existent with and interpenetrate our physical world as water penetrates a sponge, or as a gas can permeate and be absorbed by a liquid. There are other states of consciousness different from the one we are familiar with that correspond to these inner, invisible planes.

As man has a set of physical senses for contact with the physical plane, so also does he have other, inner senses for contact with the inner, invisible planes of nature. These inner senses, however, are as yet dormant or inactive in most men.

It is on these inner, invisible planes that the Monads exist when they are not embodied on the physical plane and it is in this inner, invisible world that we must look for the forces, energies and "mechanisms" that are necessary to explain so much that happens in the outer visible world.

21

These inner worlds are the worlds of causes, while the outer world is one of effects.

The idea of such invisible worlds is unfamiliar in the Occident, and those who hold that nothing exists that cannot be examined by our five senses will reject the idea at once and classify it as superstition or a belief in the "Supernatural."

The Ancient Wisdom admits of no "miracles" and nothing "supernatural," but states that on the contrary everything in Nature whether visible or invisible is subject to definite natural laws. But it affirms that there are, on the invisible side of Nature, other worlds or planes of existence that are as yet unknown to man. Since the matter of which these worlds are composed is more ethereal than ordinary gross matter and since it vibrates at different rates from such known matter, it is naturally out of tune with our senses and cannot be "picked up" by them any more than we can pick up a radio station that is beyond the capacity of our receiving set.

We can therefore neither prove nor disprove the existence of such planes on the basis of evidence furnished by our senses. An attempt to do this would be like trying to prove the presence or absence of a gas by passing a wire screen through it. These worlds, being beyond the reach of man's ordinary senses, may be called "extra-sensory" or "super-sensory" but they are not supernatural.

The idea of Invisible Worlds will seem less strange when we stop to realize that there are invisibles in our own nature and that every day of our lives we are dealing with and making use of faculties and forces that are invisible and intangible, but none the less real.

The center of consciousness in us which recognizes itself as "I am myself and not someone else," the learning and evolving entity, is invisible. It is associated with the body during physical life; it expresses itself through the body, yet this center of consciousness is itself unseen.

How much can we tell about a man's character, intelligence or abilities by observing his outward appearance? In most cases very little, and if we judge a man solely on this, we are apt to make very serious mistakes. If it were possible to determine a man's character by his exterior, we should be able to spot a criminal before he has committed his crime. This cannot be done however, for the Character belongs to the unseen part of man.

Thoughts and ideas are realities, for they affect individuals and the whole of humanity, yet no one has ever seen a thought. Understanding, sympathy, love, hatred, are all potent powers that cause men to act for weal or woe; yet they are invisible.

We do not see the life that animates a tree, but we know it must be there, for we notice the difference when the tree has died. We do not see the process by which a plant takes material from the dark coarse soil of the earth and changes it into the delicate fabric of a beautiful flower, but we see the result of this process unfolding before our eyes. We cannot see air, and many other gases are also invisible. The forces of gravity, magnetism and electricity have never been seen, but are known only through their effects.

OUR SENSES LIMITED

We also often overlook the fact that our senses have only a limited range and give us a very incomplete picture even of the physical world around us. This is strikingly illustrated by an examination of the electro-magnetic spectrum.

When sunlight is made to pass through a glass prism it is broken up into seven different colors, each one caused by radiations of different wave lengths from the others. At one end of this spectrum or color band is the violet light, with relatively short wave lengths; at the other end is the red light with wave lengths almost twice the length of the violet light; and between these two extremes are the other colors, each with its own intermediate wave length. All of these radiations can be seen by the human eye.

But the electromagnetic spectrum extends far beyond the visible light-spectrum, both on the side of longer and shorter wave lengths. Radiations are known that vary all the way from those with wave lengths just a little too long for the human eye to see, up to those that are many millions of times longer. Likewise radiations are known with wave lengths so short that it requires millions of them to equal the shortest one visible to the human eye. As scientific knowledge increases, the electro-magnetic spectrum is extended. For all we know it may extend indefinitely in both directions, and among this almost infinite variety of radiations, the little group that can be seen by the human eye forms but an infinitesimally small part.

Some radiations that cannot be detected by the eye can be perceived by our sense of touch, since they generate heat. If we were absolutely blind we would still be aware of these heat radiations, but would be unable to sense the light with which we might be flooded. If our eyes were normal but we lacked the sense of touch, we would recognize the light, but we would be unaware of the existence of the heat radiations that might be pouring in on us.

Common photographic plates are sensitive to ordinary light, but plates have been made with chemicals that are sensitive to invisible radiant heat. An audience seated in a room from which all light had been excluded was photographed by means of these invisible rays, sometimes called "black light." The audience saw nothing and felt nothing, and could not detect the presence or absence of these rays, but the resulting photograph, which looked to all appearances like an ordinary photo, demonstrated their presence.

X-rays have the ability to penetrate material bodies. Pictures have been taken of objects through a plate of four-inch solid steel. But perhaps this is not so surprising when we are told by our scientists that there is no such thing as "solid matter," but that what appears to us as solid is mostly empty space, and that the atoms in matter are relatively as far apart as are the stars in space. And further, we are told that the atoms themselves are not solid, but consist of various energy charges moving around one another at incredible velocities. Matter then, which to our touch and our sight seems solid, is in reality mostly empty space, and what little "substance" there is in matter is electrical in nature. This is something about which our unaided senses failed to inform us.

Certain rocks, which in daylight appear no different from those found in any field or gravel pit, are sensitive to ultra-violet radiation. If these rocks are placed in a darkroom and subjected to ultra-violet rays, which are also invisible, the rocks, although not hot, seem to glow and become translucent, apparently exposing the interior of the rocks, and this becomes illuminated in different and most beautiful colors. These radiations seem capable of penetrating to the interior of the solid rock and in their passage through the rock produce a change in this or are themselves transformed into radiations that come within the range of human vision. Illuminated by this invisible light these drab-looking rocks display an aspect of unsuspected beauty.

One cannot help speculating on what fairyland of beauty this world might present if our eyes were tuned to see by ultra-violet radiations instead of by ordinary sunlight.

The cat and the owl have eyes with a different range of vision from those of man. They "see in the dark." In other words, their eyes are sensitive to some of the radiations that are invisible to us. Hence, what is darkness to us is light to them. This shows how even eyes of physical matter can be constructed so as to embrace different ranges of visibility.

X-rays and cosmic rays as well as ultra-violet rays can penetrate and pass through solid matter. May there not be eyes constructed that can follow these rays and thus see through physical substance as though it were empty space, just as our eyes can see through air and water?

Scores of telephone messages can be sent over the same wire at the same time without interfering with one another, simply by using different wave lengths in transmitting them. As we talk we are unaware of other conversations mingling with ours, yet in the end they are all separated and reach their destination as though the others did not exist.

The air is constantly filled with radio waves of various lengths and yet we are entirely unaware of their presence until we turn on our radio. As we shift from station to station around the dial, we hear the most diverse programs being broadcast all at once, yet not interfering with one another if the apparatus is properly adjusted.

Ether vibrations of many different wave-lengths can thus interpenetrate each other and co-exist in the same space without interfering with one another and without making any impression on the human senses.

Vibrations in the air reach us as sound waves, but our ears, like our eyes, are limited in their capacity to register these. There are sound waves of too low a pitch and others of too high a pitch for the human ear to record.

Our senses of touch, taste and smell seem relatively less evolved that those of sight and hearing and tell us very little of the world in which we live.

Our senses, on which we depend for contact with the physical world, are like windows through which we can look out and observe the world around us, but they are very small windows, narrow slots, little "periscopes" that only permit us to see a small part of the phenomenal world in which we live. By means of various mechanical and electrical devices we have been able to extend our field of vision considerably. Even with these aids, however, the picture our senses give us is very incomplete. What may lie beyond the reach of these devices is unknown territory to us.

Our present knowledge, nevertheless, is sufficient to demonstrate that there exists an unseen side in nature. It is unseen because of the limitations of our senses and not because it does not exist.

A THOUGHT WORLD

There is one invisible world that we are conscious of every moment of the day, but it is so close to us that we overlook its existence. We are here and now leading a dual existence, an outer physical one, as well as an inner, invisible one of thoughts and feelings. The outer visible life we share with our fellows, but our interior thought-life is lived behind a curtain, as it were, and is known only to ourselves.

We know that many of our thoughts are stimulated by events in the outer world that attract our attention, but we also know that thoughts often "come to us" without any external stimulus. The same is true of moods and feelings.

Where could these come from unless we live in an atmosphere of thought and feeling as well as in an atmosphere of air, and how could we become aware of them unless we have an inner "receiving set" that responds to this type of vibration? And how do we know but that our own thoughts, unknown to us, are being broadcast into this same atmosphere to be picked up by some other individual, to whom they may be attracted?

We may thus send out and receive thoughts, but this is done unconsciously. We have not yet learned how to communicate directly from our own thought-sphere to that of another. If we want to exchange ideas with others, we must make use of the physical body for this purpose, and express ourselves in speech or writing.

We must admit that although we are all active in this thought-world, yet we understand very little about it, but the proposition fits in well with our knowledge of other aspects of nature. Physical energies exist and have a world of physical matter in which they operate. Thought energies exist; why should not these have a thought-world, with its appropriate thought-substance in which to operate?

Everything in nature is energy in some form. Physical energies have their "spectrum" or scale of vibration within which they are recorded. May there not be another spectrum embracing energies of a more refined nature with vibrational rates entirely different from anything that we know of, perhaps in some other "dimension" or through some other medium? May it not be possible that some day thought-energies will be found to have their place somewhere in this "spectrum"?

Scientists have already discovered that the organs of the human body, and especially the heart and brain, emit radiations that can be recorded by means of suitable apparatus. The radiations emitted by the brain are known to vary with sleep, consciousness, mental activity, etc. These discoveries may be the fore-runners of others that may reveal the existence of still more refined energies within the human organism. But the probability is that thought-energies are too subtle to be detected by any apparatus that we could construct. We may have to wait for final proof until we ourselves have developed our inner senses and learned how to use them.

It is known that man, even of the intellectual type, uses only a minute fraction of his brain capacity. It is therefore well within the range of possibility that man may have inner senses that could have their counterpart or seat in the unused part of his brain.

We seem to have a subconscious recognition of using such senses, for when an idea is explained to us and we do not at first understand, we say, "I don't get you," as though we were groping in the dark trying to feel the contact of someone or something. When we finally do understand, we say "I see," as though we were using an inner eye for this purpose.

EXTRA-SENSORY PERCEPTION

The phenomena of mind-reading and telepathy, or thought-transference at a distance without physical means cannot be satisfactorily explained unless we recognize that man is endowed with an inner set of senses or organs that are to some extent controlled by man's will and can be directed to send and receive thoughts. The power to use these faculties consciously and at will is not possessed by the ordinary individual, hence the natural tendency to deny their existence. It is no longer considered a sign of intelligence to ridicule a belief in mind-reading and telepathy, for these phenomena are too well authenticated to be brushed aside or "laughed off," as anyone who wishes to inform himself can easily ascertain.

The individuals who possess these faculties are said to be endowed with "extra-sensory perception" since their impressions are received without the aid of the physical sense-organs. We feel instinctively, however, that they must be using senses of some sort, for we often refer to them as "sensitives." Since these faculties are not possessed by the average individual they are extra-ordinary or supernormal, but they are not supernatural.

A striking example of successful thought-transference over long distances is presented by the experiment conducted between Sir Hubert Wilkins, the arctic explorer, as sender, and his friend, Mr. Harold Sherman, as receiver. The former was engaged in an expedition in northwestern Canada and Alaska, while the latter was located in New York City 2000 to 3000 miles away. Most of Sherman's impressions of Wilkins' activities in the arctic were received and recorded on the very day that they happened, and weeks before Wilkins could be reached for verification. The experiments were conducted three times a week during a period of six months in the winter of 1937-38. The records were kept in such a way as to exclude all possibility of fraud, and were later arranged in parallel columns comparing item for item the experiences of Wilkins with the impressions recorded by Sherman. Although the result is not 100 per cent perfect, it shows a truly remarkable percentage of correct readings. In one instance Mr. Sherman records seeing a fire in an Alaskan community at the very moment it took place. Another time he "sees" that an accident has happened to one of the propellers of Wilkins' plane, and that the new propeller ordered does not have the correct pitch on the blades. Many other similar instances are recorded. The experiment, which is fully documented, is described in a book entitled, *Thought Through Space** that should be read by anyone who has the slightest doubt as to the actuality of thought transference.

Other experiments in thought transference have been conducted by Dr. J. B. Rhine at Duke University, under strictly supervised conditions, extending over a period of many years. The outcome varied with the individual subjects tested, but as a result of many thousands of tests, the average number of hits for all subjects, good and poor, was 6.5 when the straight chance-result would have been 5. With more gifted subjects, the score repeatedly ran as high as 8, 9, 10, or 11, when 5 would have been a chance result and 25 a perfect score.

One individual made the perfect score of 25 hits in 25 trials. These tests, described by Dr. Rhine in *New Frontiers of the Mind*, should be read by those inclined to doubt the reality of thought transference.

Success or failure in experiments with extra-sensory perception depend on the degree to which the inner senses of the individual ex-

---

*Creative Age Press, Inc., 11 East 44th St., New York City.

perimented on are developed. Even in the best these are just beginning to function, and it is surprising that so many experiments
have proved successful. That many mistakes are made should be
expected. An infant does not learn to walk with his first attempt.

How can we explain telepathy, and how can we explain the fact
that "thoughts come to us," seemingly out of the atmosphere, unless we have some kind of "receiving set" with some sort of an-
tenna, some internal, unseen organ to pick them up and convey
them to our consciousness?

Does the mind-reader, unknown to himself, use an inner set
of "eyes" or other organs, not made of gross, physical substance,
but of matter appropriate to the field in which it operates?

The ordinary five senses cannot operate without their corresponding physical organs. Is it not reasonable, then, to assume that
our inner faculties must also have some sort of inner organs in
order to operate. And if we have internal organs, must they not be
part of an internal body?

Is our relationship to our inner body like that of an infant to
his small body? He lies in his crib and moves his arms and legs
and uses his eyes to watch his surroundings. He is too immature
to reflect upon his situation. He has a body and is using it to a
limited extent, but is himself unaware of the fact that he has
and uses this body.

Are we in exercising our inner faculties, similarly making use
of an inner body and sense-apparatus before we are aware of its
existence? We do not know what may exist in the unexplored
depths of nature. Almost anything lies within the range of possibility. In view of scientific discoveries already made, it does not
seem wise to put limits on the possibilities of the future. What is
commonplace knowledge to us today would have seemed like wild
speculation to our forefathers.

There is nothing in our present knowledge that conflicts with
the idea of invisible sides to Nature. For all we know to the contrary, there might very well exist whole worlds or planes of different rates of vibration from our own, in which might exist, live
and move other sets of beings, whom we could not cognize, and
who might be unaware of our existence.

A denial of the possible existence of invisible planes because they are invisible, has no better basis than the blind man's denial of the light, or a deaf man's denial of sound.

MANY CROSS-SECTIONS OF CONSCIOUSNESS

The Teachers of the Ancient Wisdom, men whose evolution has proceeded beyond that of ordinary humans, tell us that our plane of consciousness is like a single "cross-section" in the middle of an imaginary log of infinite length; or like an octave in the middle of an infinite scale of consciousness, just as the octave of radiations that appear to us as light constitutes an infinitesimally small fraction of the electromagnetic spectrum.

They also tell us that on both sides of our "cross-section" there are other cross-sections of consciousness, higher and lower than ours, and that it is possible for those who have developed their inner faculties to step across the border into those other planes. To them these inner worlds are more real than the outer, physical world that we know. They call this outer world an "illusion", in the sense that it is not what it seems to be. To them it is a "shadow-world" with its matter that seems so solid, but is so porous it is almost non-existent.

The Teachers also tell us that it is in these inner, invisible worlds that Man's consciousness is acting, observing and experiencing, while to our knowledge he is unconscious in sleep or death.

The fact that some can to a limited extent use their inner faculties, as is done in thought-transference, indicates that these faculties are beginning to awaken from their dormant state, in the case of a few individuals. When these faculties are fully developed in us, we shall see thoughts as clearly as we now see physical objects.

The present phase of man's evolution requires his existence chiefly on the physical and mental planes, and his first lesson is to learn how to live in harmony with his fellow men. When we notice the greed, the jealousies and self-interests that cause individuals and groups to fight one another, it becomes apparent that man is far from having learned the lesson that his present existence should have taught him. When we see how new inventions, meant for the benefit of mankind, such as the submarine, the airplane, atomic energy, etc., are instead turned to destructive purposes, it should be plain to us that what man needs is not new forces and new faculties, but the ability to use the faculties he already possesses for the benefit of himself and his fellow men.

A premature development by a few individuals of their inner faculties would give these individuals an advantage over their fellow men. With our knowledge of the inherent selfishness of man's *lower* nature, it is safe to predict that these faculties would sooner or later be made use of by selfish individuals for their own gain and to the detriment of others.

There are also very real dangers connected with a premature and artificial development of man's psychic faculties, including insanity, and a serious unbalancing of the psychic and moral nature.

It is for this reason that true Spiritual Teachers have always insisted that man should first cultivate his spiritual faculties: Forgiveness, compassion, love, etc., and apply them in daily life.

When man has learned to live in harmony with his fellows and practices Brotherhood in his daily life, his inner, psychic faculties will develop safely and normally as our physical and mental faculties do today.

Chapter IV

MAN'S COMPLEX NATURE

SELF-ANALYSIS DIFFICULT

In order to understand what happens to Man in sleep and after death it is necessary to have an understanding of Man's constitution.

A subject of this nature can not be treated like Mathematics or Chemistry where ideas can be expressed in formulas and words mean definite things. When we consider that we can not from our own observations describe the appearance and functions of the organs in our body, we should not be surprised at the difficulty we experience in trying to understand such intangibles as mind and consciousness and we must not expect a clear-cut presentation such as might be possible if we were dealing with physical objects.

One difficulty is that we can not get far enough away from the objects we are trying to understand to get a perspective view of them, for they are in one sense parts of ourselves. In another sense they are tools of ours and the description of their functions varies according to the view-point we take at the moment. Another difficulty is that the various elements or principles of Man's constitution overlap, interblend and merge one into another and some of them are entirely above the understanding of the human mind in its present stage of development. In studying this subject, therefore, we must make use of our intuition as well as our mind.

ONE RAY—VARIOUS ASPECTS

Man is not a single, indivisible homogeneous unit, but is a composite entity made up of many different elements and principles, under normal conditions operating harmoniously together during Man's life on Earth. Besides his visible, physical body, he is endowed with an *inner*, invisible, complex constitution, part of which is inferior to his ordinary mental Consciousness, and part superior to this Consciousness.

The essential part of Man is a Ray or stream of consciousness, a part of the Universal Consciousness, the Divine Source of all life. This Ray is inseparable from the One Universal Life, just as a sunbeam is inseparable from the sun, but while embodied it appears as a separate unit.

This Ray is the core around which Man's composite nature is built. The various principles of his constitution are all different aspects or manifestations of this Ray, and all are vitalized into activity by its presence.

As this Ray descends through the various planes or levels of Nature, it focuses its essence into active centers at each of these levels and builds for itself vehicles suitable for existence thereon. In each case the vehicle is built from the materials and energies of the plane in which it is to operate, and each such vehicle enables the Ray to evolve and progress by experience on one or another of these planes.

The idea of a stream of consciousness using different vehicles or appearing under different aspects, might be illustrated by comparing the stream of consciousness to a ray of sunlight. This appears as a single ray, but is in reality a combination of different radiations and can be made to appear under different aspects as the seven prismatic colors .

The descent of the Ray of Consciousness through the planes of Nature might be compared to the passage of a sunbeam through several layers of glass. There are varieties of glass that will permit the passage of certain radiations from the sun, while excluding others. Let us imagine a sunbeam passing through seven different grades of glass, of which the first one will allow all the radiations to pass; the next one will be impervious to one wave-length with its corresponding color, but lets the other six pass through, and so on down through the different strata or layers of glass until finally, in the last instance only a single color penetrates and illumines the objects under the lowest glass. Even though the light, that penetrates to the lowest level, is feeble and gives an inadequate idea of the brilliance of its source, yet it is a part of the original ray and carries with it a faint glimmer from the highest to the lowest level.

In a similar manner the Ray of Consciousness that forms the core of Man's nature, finds full expression only on the higher planes of being, while on the lower, only a minute portion is able to manifest.

The Ray of Consciousness thus expresses itself through various vehicles, each acting on its own plane and all apparently more or less independent of one another, but since all these vehicles are vitalized by the same Ray they are in reality only different aspects of this one Ray, just as the seven prismatic colors are different aspects of the one sunbeam.

Whereas the one Ray of Consciousness vitalizes all the principles that go to make up Man's constitution, it can only center its dominant activity in any one of these at a time, and while it is fully active in this one principle, the others remain inactive.

In each case the consciousness of one plane receives its vitality from the next higher plane and in its turn vitalizes the consciousness on the next lower plane. When the vitalizing current withdraws from one plane into its source on the next higher plane, the vehicle on the lower plane becomes dormant.

The vehicle produces a limiting effect on the Ray of Consciousness, which causes the portion of the Ray thus encompassed to identify itself with its vehicle and thus gives to this fraction of the Ray a feeling of separate and independent existence.

When the Ray vitalizes its vehicle it transforms some of its consciousness to the latter and this, together with the limiting effect of the vehicle, gives to the combination of Ray and vehicle a feeling of self-hood, or Ego-ship belonging to the plane in which the Ray functions for the time being.

There is in Man, therefore, only one Ray or stream of Consciousness, but more than one Ego. Only one of the latter, however, is active at any one time.

The relationship between the Ray of consciousness and its vehicles might be compared to the relationship between an individual and his different activities in daily life.

A man working in the basement of his house, dressed in over-alls, shoveling coal into the furnace, sifting ashes, cleaning up rubbish or tinkering in his basement shop seems like a different individual from the same man, when, dressed in his business suit, he is engaged in his daily work, perhaps meeting and conversing with customers, advising clients or mixing with his business as-sociates at dinner. And again, we might hardly recognize him if we visited him in his home on a Sunday afternoon when, with his family, he enjoys some music, listens to the radio or perhaps re-laxes by the fireplace or in his hobby-room.

We might say that this individual expresses himself and func-tions through three different "egos," the Basement ego, the Busi-ness ego and the Family ego. While he functions as one he is for the time being identical with it and the other "egos" are dormant. He has, as it were, a "sliding scale of egos" through which he expresses himself and his consciousness moves up and down this scale as conditions require.

In the illustration used, the difference between the various "egos" is not so great but that the individual knows perfectly well of his identity through them all, for his experiences all take place on the same plane and he does not lose consciousness in changing from one "ego" to another.

The different egos in Man's constitution on the other hand are separated by a greater gulf and usually a loss of conciousness in-tervenes in changing from one vehicle to another, hence the con-tinuity of identity is not so apparent in this case.

THE HUMAN EGO

When we come to study Man's constitution in greater detail, it will be convenient to "begin at the middle" or with the part that is most familiar to us. Let us therefore start by trying to de-termine what our ordinary, everyday consciousness is, and where it fits into the scale of Man's complex nature.

Every individual is aware of a center of consciousness within, which he recognizes as "himself." This individualized consciousness feels its separateness from other entities and thinks of itself as "I-AM-I" and not someone else. This "I-AM-I" or Ego has the power to direct the mind to any object it chooses. The mind in that case acts like a mirror that reflects the light of consciousness on the object and thus enables the Ego to learn about it.

When the Ego uses the mirror of the mind to reflect the light of consciousness back upon itself, The Ego becomes aware of its own existence. It is then what we call "self-conscious." It exists and it knows that it exists. This faculty belongs to the evolutionary stage of Man, but is lacking in the animals. The latter are conscious, but not yet self-conscious.

What is this "I-AM-I," this center of self-conscious existence, this "YOU" or "I," this entity or "Ego," that presides over our nature during the waking hours of the day?

It is a portion of the central core of man's being, focussed or individualized by working through a physical-mental vehicle. It is the Ray of Consciousness expressing itself through the Human Constitution and may therefore be referred to as the "Human Ego."

When we go to sleep, the Ray withdraws its projection from the physical body which it inhabited during the waking state.

The Human Ego then loses consciousness of the physical plane, for it abandons the body, its only means of contact with this plane. It is then reabsorbed into its source on the next higher plane of being. This source is the Ego or focus of the Ray on the next plane above the ordinary mental. This higher center of consciousness is the real and enduring principle in man. It functions in and through a higher, mental-spiritual vehicle independent of the physical body and will be referred to in the following as the "Higher Ego" or "Reincarnating Ego."

In going to sleep, then, the Human Ego leaves the physical plane behind and takes up its existence on the mental-spiritual plane of the Higher Ego, but, since it is here deprived of its usual vehicle, it can not retain full self-consciousness on this higher plane and it therefore lapses into a dormant or dreamlike existence.

When morning comes, the body, rested and refreshed, is again ready to receive its tenant-master. Then the Higher Ego again sends out its projection, the Human Ego, into its waiting vehicle, the physical body, and a new day of learning and experience begins for the observing consciousness.

There are planes intermediate between the physical and the mental-spiritual where the Higher Ego exists and these must be traversed by the Human Ego before it can return to its source. It frequently happens that the Human Ego lingers on one of these in the course of its journey. Some memories of this may be retained as dreams and on rare occasions it may even have some recollection of existence on the plane of the Higher Ego.

Just as the foliage of a "perennial" flower has its origin in its enduring root, so does the Human Ego have its origin in the Higher Ego, the undying part of man. And as the visible part of the plant wilts and dies in the fall, when its vitality is re-absorbed into the root, so is the Human Ego re-absorbed into its root, the Higher Ego, both in sleep and after death. In sleep, the return is incomplete, perhaps more like the closing of the petals of some flowers at night. At death the "foliage," the body with its brain and lower mind dies, and the return of the Human Ego to its "Father," the Higher Ego, is complete.

The Human Ego itself is not a "fixed quantity" for it has its octaves of consciousness running all the way from our highest aspirations at the upper pole down through intermediate states to purely personal concerns of bodily comforts and pleasures at the lower pole. The lowest octave of the human consciousness, which is only concerned with its own personal welfare may be referred to as the "Personal Ego."

In view of this variable scale of consciousness, this interblending and overlapping of the higher and the lower, it will not always be possible to specify just what shade of meaning should be applied to the term "Ego."

Since it seems easier to visualize the idea of an "Ego" rather that that of a Ray or Stream of Consciousness, and since any Ego is in fact always a product of the Ray, it is felt that the term Ego may safely be applied in a general sense and sometimes interchanged with the term Ray and that the reader's intuition will guide him in interpreting the correct meaning.

The Human Ego might be said to be the midpoint of man's

complex nature. It is, as it were, a spectator, an observer of the drama of life. It feels the impulses from the organs of the body. It takes note of events that occur in the outer world around it. It watches the thought-stream that flows through the mind as a spectator in a theater would watch the pictures on the screen. It experiences the tides of emotion and feeling that sometimes lift it on wings of hope and other times drop it into the depths of despair. It may identify itself with the experiences it undergoes or it may stand apart from these, viewing them like a panorama seen from an observation post. In the former case it is being whirled around at "the rim of the wheel of life." In the latter case its observation post is at the calm and unmoving "hub." It weighs and considers the experiences of life and passes judgment on them, approving or disapproving as the case may be. It extracts from these experiences lessons for the future. By its choice of good or bad, it modifies and remolds its character, using the Will for its instrument of control.

This is the Human Ego, the I-AM-I, the YOU or I of everyday life. This is the Ray of Consciousness as it shuttles back and forth every twenty-four hours between activity on the physical and the inner planes of being.

From its first conscious memory in early childhood, up through youth, maturity and old age, the Human Ego has passed through many and varied experiences. It has changed its outlook on life many times, but at the end of life it knows itself to be the same, identical entity that awoke to consciousness in early childhood.

MAN'S INNER GOD

Above the Human Ego in man's constitution stands the Higher or Reincarnating Ego, already referred to. This, however, is not the summit, for the core of man, the Ray of Consciousness, has its origin in the Universal Divine Essence—the One Life—and there are other and higher foci between the Higher Ego and its ultimate source. These higher foci, which may be grouped together and referred to collectively as "Man's Inner God," are as yet dormant in the ordinary individual.

The Ancient Wisdom tells us that the only way Man can learn about his Inner God is to gradually evolve the faculties necessary for a conscious existence on the planes where this god functions, and this means for the Human Ego to ascend along the Ray of Consciousness and become one with its Inner God.

Since the Inner God is beyond the comprehension of the human mind and since the latter is prone to deny the existence of what it can not understand, it is not surprising that the idea should seem strange and unacceptable to many. The inability of the human mind to understand something is, however, not a valid reason for denying its existence. Compassion and self-sacrificing love can never be explained by the mind, for they belong to a higher plane of consciousness, yet we know that they are realities and exert a powerful influence in the world.

All great religions teach us that there is something divine within Man. The Bible tells us that Man was created in the image of God (*Gen*, I, 26, 27) and refers to his innate divinity in *I Cor.* III, 16, where St. Paul asks: "Know ye not that ye are the temple of God, and that the spirit of God dwells in you?"

The ancient Scriptures of the Hindus refer to Man as a "reflection in matter" of his Inner God and their literature teems with references to this subject. The entire *Bhagavad-Gîtâ* for instance is a dialog between man's Inner God "Krishna" and the Human Ego here called "Arjuna." In the following quotations Krishna speaking to Arjuna says:

It is even a portion of myself which, having assumed life in this world of conditioned existence, draws together the five senses and the mind in order that it may obtain a body and may leave it again. And these are carried by the Sovereign Lord to and from whatever body he enters or quits, even as the breeeze bears the fragrance from the flowers. Presiding over the eye, the ear, the touch, the taste and the power of smelling, and also over the mind, he experiences the objects of sense.—Chap. XV

And in Chapter XVIII Krishna says:

"There dwelleth in the heart of every creature, O Arjuna, the

Master,—Ishwara*—who by his magic power causeth all things and creatures to revolve mounted upon the universal wheel of time. Take sanctuary with him alone . . ."

Although our awareness of the Divinity within us is vague and incomplete, it is not altogether lacking. From where come Man's impulses toward noble and generous deeds, to self-sacrifice, kindliness and compassion? What makes a mother sacrifice her own interest for the welfare of her children? What keeps the humblest man faithful in the performance of some simple duty? What is it that speaks to Man through the voice of conscience? From whence come the inspirations of genius, music and art? Why does the poet picture to man's mind the Millenium, the ideal state where love, beauty and harmony reign "somewhere"—"on distant shores to mortal feet forbidden"; and why does man in his heart respond to these ideas and in his turn dream of and long for that ideal state? What is it that makes man always restless and dissatisfied with earthly achievements, always in search of something else, he knows not what? Is it a memory of some forgotten higher state, a golden age, "a paradise" that somehow was lost and that now haunts him and tries to attract his attention?

In answer to all these questions the Ancient Wisdom tells us that this upward urge, these impulses to higher things come to man from the Divine source within his own nature, his Inner God, the ray in man from the One Spiritual Sun. It is in this part of his nature that man feels his one-ness with all life. The promptings that come to him from this side of his nature are always toward harmony and good will, always tending toward unity and Brotherhood.

In his present stage of development man often fails to respond to these impulses from above and then the outer man, the "Image," the "Reflection of the Inner God" becomes warped and distorted, but when he does respond in some measure, he grows ever nearer to the ideal within. As evolution proceeds, more and more of Man's Inner God will become manifest in his outward life.

---

*ISHWARA, an individualized Ray of the cosmic spirit in every human being.

Before proceeding with our studies regarding the principles in Man's constitution below the Human Ego let us first recapitulate what we have studied so far. Beginning this time "at the top" and placing each element in its proper order, we have first a Ray from the Universal Consciousness expressing itself through various vehicles on the different planes of Nature, the highest being Man's Inner God. Next on the scale comes the Ego with its different aspects as the Higher or Reincarnating Ego, then the Human Ego or ordinary self-consciousness with its higher and lower aspects, the former being the truly Human Ego, the latter being the Personal Ego.

Next we shall study the principles or vehicles used by the Ego in its contact with the mental, intermediate and physical planes of existence.

THE MIND

When the Ego is active on the mental plane it is like one who observes a film of thought-pictures being reeled off before his inner vision. This mental activity begins when the Ego first returns to the body after its absence during sleep, and it continues until the Ego leaves the body at night.

Many people do not make any distinction between the thought pictures and the Ego, which observes them. The spectator is so interested in the pictures he sees that he identifies himself with them. When we are so wrapped up in these pictures that we fail to recognize the distinction between them and ourselves, we become the slaves of the mind. Our thoughts run hither and yon, one giving rise to the next, and we are dragged along wherever these thoughts take us. We are not aware of this slavery at the time, however, for we have erroneously identified ourselves with our thoughts.

At other times we realize our power to control the mind, for we can take it off one subject and place it on another. The mind may be obstinate, however, and revert to the first subject. It seems to run in grooves and to have a will of its own, which is often opposed to our will, but we do know that if we use sufficient will power we can overcome the obstinacy of the mind and make it obey our will.

This brings out two important facts: First we are not identical with our minds, but separate and distinct from them. It is because of this separation that we are able to turn the mind from some subject that we deem undesirable and place it on something constructive. Second, the fact that we can control the mind at times shows that we need not be the slaves of that mind, but may extend this control by practice and perseverance until we obtain full mastery over it.

The relationship between man and his mind is similar to that between a rider and his horse. The horse has desires and a will of his own and if allowed to follow his own inclinations, will roam aimlessly from place to place, perhaps bringing his master into difficulties. But a rider who knows his business will control the horse and direct him to some useful purpose which in the end will benefit both horse and rider. The horse is a good servant, but a poor master.

The mind, like the horse, is a poor master, but can be a wonderful servant when it is brought under control and properly trained. We know that with sufficient will power we can concentrate the mind on a single point, thus solving problems that could never have been worked out had the mind been allowed to wander idly and without control. The mind then, is an instrument that the Ego uses, and the brain is the tool of the mind. In ancient Hindu scriptures the mind is referred to as "the organ of thought."

The mind is dual in its nature. The higher part of it is in touch with our spiritual nature, and the lower part is dependent on the brain and the physical senses, and gravitates toward the material side of our nature.

When the Ego centers its attention in the Higher Mind, it realizes its oneness with all life. It then thinks and feels in unison with its fellows. It seeks expression in thoughts and deeds of altruism and compassion. It recognizes the better side in others and by its trust and faith helps to strengthen this better side.

The lower mind is the result of the Ray of Consciousness working through the human constitution and is so closely associated

with the brain and the desires of the body that it identifies itself
with them. It receives impulses from the organs in the body, which
demand satisfaction of their various wants. It is concerned with
personal comforts and pleasures and the little problems of everyday life. It observes that its own vehicle is distinct and separate
from other vehicles, and therefore feels that its interests conflict
with those of others. Thus it becomes interested in itself to the
exclusion of others and often plans and schemes to gain advantage
over its fellow men, for it does not recognize its oneness with them.
When not engaged in a specific task, it drifts aimlessly from one
thought to another, or is stimulated into activity by external events.

There is no distinct line of demarcation between the Higher
and the lower Mind; one merges imperceptibly into the other.
The Ego can center its attention in only one part of the mind at
a time and only that part of the mind is active for the time being.

By constant use of the Higher Mind in altruistic, constructive
thought and a lofty idealism, the spiritual side of our natures grows
stronger. When, after many incarnations, we shall have trans-
ferred our consciousness to this part of our constitution, we shall
pass *in full consciousness* through death's door into a spiritual
state of being.

MOODS, FEELINGS, EMOTIONS

Another side of our nature includes such attributes as moods,
feelings and emotions. We feel by turns serene or irritable, gloomy
or cheerful, happy or depressed. We are at times sympathetic
toward our fellows and at other times indifferent. One time we
are swayed by hate and revenge, and again by love, generosity
and good will. We do not often experience these feelings in their
extremes, but we are aware of their influence on us. As in the case
of our thoughts, we can also stand apart and watch the ebb and
flow of our emotions. Certain of these feelings we approve of;
others we deem undesirable.

In describing our moods we sometimes use the expression that
we are in a certain "frame of mind." This seems to be an ac-
curate description, for then the Ego views everything from only

one fixed angle, to the exclusion of other viewpoints. If we are happy, everything looks rosy; we cannot understand how we could have felt so miserable before. If we feel gloomy, everything looks blue and we doubt that we will ever be happy again.

Our feelings and moods can have a strong grip on us. We know from experience that moods are not permanent but are subject to change. The change may come slowly and a mood wear off as a result of the routine duties of everyday life. Or we may suddenly be jerked out of one frame of mind by some external event, as when the telephone rings or a friend calls with some important news that demands quick action on our part. However, we need not wait for outward circumstances to jar us out of an undesirable frame of mind. We can accomplish the same result if we resolutely take up some useful or constructive work that requires our entire attention. We also know that we can change our moods by the use of sheer will power, and the method is to deliberately substitute a desirable mood for an undesirable one. We can refuse to be miserable and downcast, and instead, cultivate an attitude of cheerfulness. We can refuse to give way to irritation and critical attitude, substituting for them calmness and friendliness.*

Like thoughts, our emotions also seem to have a will of their own, and it is often difficult to control them. But as we have controlled them at times, we know that it can be done, and our power over them increases with practice.

Therefore, since it is possible for us to stand apart, and watch the ebb and flow of our emotions and pass judgment on them, and since we have the power to direct the current by our will, it is evident that we are no more identical with our moods and feelings than we are with our thoughts.

---

*A very helpful article on this subject is W. Q. Judge's "Cyclic Impression and Return and our Evolution," available from United Lodge of Theosophists, 245 W. 3rd St., Los Angeles, CA 90007.

THE MODEL BODY

Medical science has accumulated a vast amount of knowledge regarding the human body, including the relation of the brain, the nervous system, the muscles and the various organs. It can also explain how light that strikes the eye, and sound waves that enter the ear, are transmitted through various intermediate mechanisms until they reach the brain through the nerves.

There is still, however, a gap in our knowledge of how a thought can result in an act; how a mental impulse, an act of will, can be transmitted from the consciousness to the brain and thus eventually cause the matter in a muscle to obey an order from the will. There is also a gap in our knowledge of how sense-impressions from the outer physical world, such as sound and light, after they have reached the brain as nerve-impulses, are transmitted from the brain to the indwelling consciousness.

The Ancient Wisdom tells us that Consciousness and Mind cannot act directly on gross, physical matter, but that there exists in Nature matter that is more ethereal and refined than the gross matter that we know. There are other forms of energy, intermediate between our mental energies and the ethereal matter referred to. It is by means of these as yet unknown energies that mental impulses are "stepped down" or transformed until they reach the brain. From there the impulses are relayed as nerve impulses that eventually affect the muscles and finally result in actions on the physical plane.

The Ancient Wisdom tells us further that man has an inner, invisible body, built on this ethereal invisible matter, and that our gross, physical body is an exact duplicate in physical matter of this ethereal body. In fact, our physical body takes its shape, is made coherent and retains its relatively stable appearance by being built, as it were "brick for brick," cell for cell, on this invisible framework or model-body. The model-body, being of a more ethereal substance, is sensitive to mental impulses, and translates these into physical acts. The Ego is thus able to enforce its will on the physical body through the intermediary of the mind and the model-body.

THE PHYSICAL BODY

In our enumeration of the various parts that go to make up man's constitution, we come finally to the most material part, his physical body. This is the only part of man that is visible; all the rest is unseen.

The human body is a truly marvelous instrument with all its organs and faculties cooperating to make a living unit—the animal side of man. By means of this body with its five senses and its physical brain, the Ego is able to contact the material world, learning and evolving by experience therein.

The body is the "facade" of man's complex nature, the part that "faces the street," the part that "shows from the outside," so to speak. Behind that facade man lives an inner life in his other and unseen principles. The body is the "Town Hall" in that little community of various elements that make up the human constitution. It is the common center where all these elements meet and confront each other with their various desires and demands, aspirations and longings. If the "town meeting" which is held by these conflicting interests is presided over by an Ego that is inspired and governed by the Ray of Divinity at its core, then the various elements will cooperate, and a harmonious and useful life will result. If the Ego surrenders to the undisciplined lower elements, the result will be inharmony and suffering, though even this suffering will in time cause the Ego to choose a wiser course.

Many people identify themselves only with their bodies, and think that the body is the principal part of themselves. A little thought will show that this is not the case.

If we watch a sleeping person, we notice that the body lies there quietly, performing certain automatic functions. The heart beats, the blood circulates, the lungs breathe, etc. The eyes are closed, but the ears receive sounds from the outside, yet there is no response to these sounds. If there were a hundred sleeping bodies in front of us they would all act about the same. The body we see before us is not the friend we know so well. The qualities in him that we like and that make him unique have separated themselves from the sleeping body and left the scene for the time being, perhaps to retire into the more ethereal part of the inner constitution. We cannot contact the real part of our friend through the sleeping body, but we do know that he is in some way linked with it. He cannot contact us unless he returns to the body and takes control over it. We see from this that the body is not the man himself, but like the mind, is a tool used by the Ego for its evolution here on Earth.

That part which is absent during sleep is more essential than the sleeping body before us. If we call this absent, essential part for the time being the "soul," we realize that it would be more appropriate to say that man *is* a soul and *has* a body rather than to say he is a body and has a soul.

The body grows weaker with advancing years, but the better part of the Human Ego, the part that has centered its consciousness in the higher principles of its nature, is unaffected by the decline of the body. The true Human Ego knows that it is not of the body and feels "young in spirit" in spite of the ailing body. It is only the lowest part of the Personal Ego, the part that has identified itself with the body, that feels itself growing old.

INTERBLENDING PRINCIPLES

The various elements of man's nature—which have just been enumerated—are not separated into different "compartments" but interblend with and interpenetrate each other so that each principle partakes to some extent of the nature of all the others. Just as the prismatic colors blend and merge, and when all are present produce white light, so do man's principles blend and merge, and when all are present produce a complete man.

During our earth-life they are all, directly or indirectly, associated with the physical body. The Ego may shift its attention from one portion of its nature to another a hundred times a day, but the transition from one to another is so smooth and gradual that we often fail to notice that a change has taken place.

It may be interesting at this point to give another extract from the Upanishads, in order to show how the teachers of that period illustrated man's composite nature:

Know that the soul (the Ego) is seated in a chariot, and that the body is that chariot. Know that the mind is the charioteer, and that the will is the reins.

They say that the senses are the horses, and that the things of sense are the road. The wise declare that the migrating soul is the *self* fictitiously present in the body, senses, and common sensory.

Now if the charioteer, the mind, is unskillful, and the reins are always slack, his senses are ever unruly, like horses that will not obey the charioteer.

But if the charioteer is skillful, and at all times firmly holds the reins, his senses are always manageable, like horses that obey the charioteer.

The senses and organs of man are constantly seeking to gratify their wants, and are therefore the "horses" that furnish the motive power for man's activity. The "things of sense"are the objects in the material world that can gratify the senses; hence these make up "the road" on which the "horses" travel. The Soul, the Ego, is the passenger in the chariot. The driver, the charioteer, is the Mind, and if this is skillful and obeys the orders of its Master, the Ego, and by means of the will keeps the senses under control, all goes well. But if the Mind slackens its attention, the senses may run rampant and endanger the safety of the Ego.

There is a modern expression which shows that the practical man of today accepts a view of life not so different from that pictured in the foregoing illustration, which was borrowed from the ancients. The modern version does not go into so much detail but simply states "It is experience we get, while looking for something else." The "something else" is usually money, which simply represents our ability to gratify our desires. It is our desires that send us on a quest for the "things of sense" and make us try this venture or that in order to gain our ends. At the end of the road, more often than not, we did not get what we had hoped for. But we did get a harvest of experience, which we would not have had if we had made no effort, and it is experience we must have if we are to evolve. Thus a selfish motive defeats itself, but may through disappointing experiences lead to some advancement.

THE CHARACTER

Since the human constitution with its various principles or "tools" enumerated above is the same for all men, it would be natural to expect men to be alike in all particulars. This however, is not the case. We see on every hand great differences in characteristics among men, differences in disposition, temperament, outlook on life, etc. We also note vast differences in natural gifts, talents and aptitudes. These differences exist not only in adults, but are also apparent among children. Mothers of large families will tell us that such differences exist from the very start and become apparent as soon as the child has developed the faculties necessary for self-expression. These different qualities appear before education or environment could have had any influence. They unfold themselves from within and are not the result of implanting from without.

Thus among children of the same parents one may have a sunny, happy disposition, another a more serious, perhaps a sullen one. One may be neat and orderly, while another is careless; one may be generous, another selfish; one reckless and unreliable, while another is cautious and trustworthy.

There is often a striking difference, even among children in the same family, in their natural talents, aptitudes and "inborn gifts." The very expression "inborn" shows a recognition of the fact that such qualities are not acquired but must have existed prior to birth. Thus we note that some children find mathematics easy, but languages difficult. Some like music and art, while others are mechanically inclined; some seem to be gifted in many directions, while others have no particular aptitudes.

When such differences appear among children of different families, a difference in heredity is usually advanced as the cause, but when equally great differences occur among children in the same family, where the heredity is identical, we must look elsewhere for the cause.

A child's musical tendencies reveal themselves early in life and often before any musical training or teaching has taken place. The life-histories of our great musicians almost all bear witness that the gift of musical genius shows itself to a remarkable degree in early childhood, and often in families where there is no heredity to warrant its appearance.

It is true that innate qualities can be modified by training, education and environment. Teaching will bring out what is already within, but unless the talent is there to begin with, the result will be meager. This is apparent when we observe the vastly different effect of exactly the same training on different students in the same group.

The qualities enumerated above, such as temperament, disposition, talents and aptitudes, when taken collectively distinguish one individual from another and constitute his character. The character can be modified by education, training and environment, but since it manifests before any of these factors have had time to operate, it must be inborn rather than acquired. And since it frequently differs from that of the parents, it cannot be explained as the effect of heredity. How then are we to explain the existence of this character? The Ancient Wisdom teaches that it is an inheritance the Ego brings with it from a former existence.

CHARACTER BUILDING

The word character comes from a Greek word meaning "to stamp, engrave or inscribe." Before the days of paper it was customary to engrave letters on stone or stamp them on clay tablets. Each letter had a mark, unique to itself, which distinguished it from all the rest. Even today, when we speak of the letters of the alphabet, we refer to them as the "characters" of the alphabet, having in mind that all these letters are distinguished from one another by characteristic marks.

A man's character, therefore, is the collective peculiarities or qualities that distinguish him from other men.

We build our character by repeated thoughts, repeated emotions and feelings, and by the acts which result from these. Think a thought often and long enough and it will find expression as a spoken word or an act. Repeat an act often enough and it will become a habit. A thought is soon dismissed, an act soon forgotten, but they leave a mark, however slight, on the character. When they become habitual, they engrave themselves deeply in the invisible part of man's nature.

We also build that part of our character that embodies our innate gifts, talents and aptitudes. We build this part by repeated efforts at training in these various lines so that these "gifts" are not gifts in the sense of undeserved favors, but gifts from ourselves to ourselves. They are memories of past skills, gained by efforts in former lives and preserved for us in the invisible part of our nature.

Character, then, is not a separate principle or independent segment of man's constitution, but it is the collective habits and consequent tendencies which we have built up in all the various parts of our constitution. It is the collective habits of body, habits of emotions and feelings, thought habits and moral habits; habits of obeying the voice of conscience, or of yielding to temptation, as well as habits of training in all fields of endeavor. It is what we have made of ourselves.

The accumulated effect of all these habits gives us a tendency, a "set" in a certain direction, a predisposition, a "leaning" which makes it natural and easy for us to act along the groove that habit has scored.

It is our character or collective habits that determines how we will react to sudden impacts from outward circumstances and what makes us "ready to go" in this or that direction. It is also our character that determines what our thoughts will revert to when they are not directed by our will. It also determines what our emotions and feelings become when they are not under control, but allowed to find their own level. Whether this level be high or low, good or bad, depends on the direction and impetus we have given.

The character is the inner, invisible clothing the Ego weaves around itself by its thoughts and deeds, strand by strand, fibre by fibre, just as the larva builds its cocoon in which it must later live. During life we improve this character or we degrade and mar it. At the end of life it still remains as an accumulation of forces and energies, and as such cannot be annihilated or destroyed. What happens to this character after death?

The Ancient Teachings state that it remains unchanged and latent on inner planes of Nature until in distant ages the Ego returns to physical embodiment, when it finds its inheritance, this character, awaiting its master. It is like a traveler's check, sent in advance, waiting at the destination when the traveler arrives. It is a "Will and Testament" which our present self is making to its future self, and when the Ego returns to Earth as a newborn child, its character — which now begins to re-manifest itself — is the "capital" with which it starts its new incarnation. The newborn entity, therefore, is virtually a reproduction of the former entity that was.

Since the character—the "clothing" in which we are now enwrapped, our work-a-day self—is the accumulated effect of our own past thoughts and deeds, it may be said that we are our own handiwork, our own Karma. With this in mind we can understand Pythagoras' statement that "We are our own children." When we consider that our disposition and tendencies, our abilities and gifts are all "memories" of habits established in former existences, and that our character therefore is our collective memory of all our past lives, we can understand the meaning of Plato's expression ". . . all inquiry and all learning is recollection."

We may have things stored in the "attics and wardrobes" of our character that we are not aware of. Some people find themselves shocked at receiving sudden and unprovoked impulses to wrongdoing. At other times the impulses may be of a beneficient nature. These impulses are injections into the consciousness of thought-deposits from a long forgotten past. In the course of time all hidden deposits in our character will come to the surface, the evil ones to be remedied or sloughed off, the good ones to be expanded and reinforced.

Many are inwardly aware of having undeveloped talents, which have not expressed themselves for lack of opportunity. In due course all such gifts will find expression and can then be cultivated and improved.

The character of man is deep-seated and does not change from day to day or hour to hour as our thoughts and feelings do. We cannot shake it off as we can a mood, but we can change it by the same method we used in building it up. If a building is not what it should be and we want to remodel or rebuild, it must be done by replacing defective bricks with new and better ones, and this must be done brick by brick. It cannot be done by a single effort, but is a slow and laborious process. That is why we should be so careful of our thoughts and deeds in the first place. We should make them so that they will not have to be replaced later.

There is no shortcut to remodel character. That is why New Year's resolutions, though beneficial, so often seem ineffective. In our enthusiasm we overlook the fact that what we hope to change with a single effort, was built up by repeated thoughts and deeds during long periods in the past. In order to be effective, the effort must be constantly renewed and steadfastly continued throughout the year.

A resolution, even if not fulfilled, however, is better than no resolution at all, for no effort is lost and it is at least one brick replaced. An understanding of the magnitude of the task we are undertaking in changing old, established habits, will keep us from losing courage, if progress seems slower than we had hoped for, and will help us to keep up the effort.

MAN'S SELF-MADE DESTINY

It has already been said that our character is what we have made of ourselves as a result of all our thoughts and deeds, with their consequent habits. Our character gives us a "set" or inclination in a certain direction, and if this remains unchanged it determines our final destiny.

There is a bit of Eastern Wisdom which says that:

If you sow a thought you reap an act;
If you sow an act your reap a habit;
If you sow a habit you reap a character;
If you sow a character you reap a destiny.

If we live up to the best that is in us, our character will constantly improve and set us on the road to a bright and fruitful destiny. If we seem to be heading in the wrong direction, this can be changed, but to change it, we must first change our character.

To do this, we must change our habits, our acts and our thoughts, which of course takes time and steady effort.

The following quotation, which is taken from the *Dhammapada,* a Buddhist scripture, shows that the Ancients taught thousands of years ago that our character is built by our thoughts:

All that we are is the consequence of what we have thought. It is based on our thoughts. It is all derived from our thoughts. If a man speaks or acts with a thought of evil, suffering follows him, exactly as the wheel follows the foot of the ox that draws the cart.

All that we are is the consequence of what we have thought. It is based on our thoughts; it is derived from our thoughts. If a man speaks or acts with an innocent and pure thought, happiness follows him, exactly like a shadow that never leaves him.

"He treated me badly; he struck me; he overcame me; he robbed me"—in those who cultivate such feelings hate will never cease.

"He treated me badly; he struck me; he overcame me; he robbed me"—in those who do not cultivate such thoughts, hatred will die.

For hate never is overcome by hate at any time. Hate passes away through love. This is the ancient rule.

Our destiny, then, is ultimately destermined by our own thoughts and deeds. We are not "predestined" to anything by anyone else. As we alter our character for better or for worse, so do we ourselves thereby determine our own destiny.

Chapter V

STATES OF CONSCIOUSNESS

STATES OF CONSCIOUSNESS

INDIRECT METHOD OF STUDY

During sleep and after death when the Ray of Consciousness has withdrawn from the outer plane, it is active on inner, invisible planes of Nature, or on levels of consciousness different from that of our waking state. The Human Ego of the ordinary individual in its present stage of evolution, is not able to follow the Ray of Consciousness as this recedes to higher planes, for it is just the withdrawal of the Ray from the human vehicle that causes the Human Ego to become non-functioning and pass into a dormant state.

There are a few rare individuals in the world, who have evolved so far that their Human Ego has become one with their Higher Ego and they can even now step across the thresholds of sleep and death in full possession of their consciousness. They are the Masters of Wisdom, Compassion and Peace, who are the custodians of the Ancient Wisdom Religion, and who have given these teachings to Mankind. They were at one time ordinary human beings and it is the destiny of all men eventually to attain this high state, and then the higher planes of consciousness will be as familiar to us as the outer world is now.

Since we cannot make a study of these planes or states of consciousness by direct observation, the next best approach will be to study our waking state and what little we know of the dream state and certain abnormal states to see if we cannot thereby get at least a side-light on the subject.

THE WAKING STATE OF CONSCIOUSNESS

In our ordinary waking state of consciousness it is the Human Ego, including in this term its higher, intermediate and lower or personal aspects, that is the active center of consciousness and its field of activity is the outer physical world and an inner, unseen world of thoughts and feelings.

61

The feature that distinguishes the waking state of consciousness from other states seems to be that it consists in a simultaneous awareness of both the physical world and the mental plane. The Ego observes the outer world through the five senses and the inner world by watching the succession of thoughts and feelings that follow each other on the "screen of the mind." Our activity may be chiefly physical, but even while we are thus occupied, there is an undercurrent of thought running through the mind; or our work may be mainly mental, but even then we are still aware of our physical surroundings. We do know, however, that if we are exerting our utmost effort in either field, the activity in the other direction is at a minimum. For instance an athlete could not run a race and simultaneously concentrate on some mental problem. What little mental activity he may have must be applied to sustain his physical effort. On the other hand if we are to give our full attention to some mental problem, the best preparation is to reduce the body activities to a minimum.

The automatic functions of the body, such as circulation of the blood, breathing, digestion of food, etc., must of course go on continuously for these make up the power plant that furnishes the energy for the brain. These functions, however, play no direct part in mental work, but neither are they a hindrance unless they have been overstimulated. We know, for instance, that it would be difficult to concentrate on a deep metaphysical problem after a heavy meal.

An active body, whether overstimulated by food or physical exercise becomes a handicap to mental activity. A body so passive that we could forget its existence would be the least obstacle to mental work.

There are then three partners necessary to produce the ordinary waking state of consciousness: the Human Ego-aspect of the Ray, the mind and the body, the latter term including the model body etc. Of these the Ray vitalizes both mind and body, the mind is the connecting link between the other two and the body is the substratum for the activity of the whole. If either partner is absent, the Ray becomes unconscious of this plane. All partners must be present and cooperating harmoniously as a unit in order that the Ray may experience the ordinary waking state of consciousness.

DAY-DREAMING

A partial disconnection of the Ego from its sense-apparatus can take place during the waking state.

After living on a noisy street for some length of time we cease to notice the noises. The sound waves come to our ears just as strongly as before, but we have sub-consciously learned to prevent these sound impulses from reaching our consciousness. We have succeeded in "throwing out the clutch" between the Ego and its sense-apparatus in this particular respect.

Or we may sit in a room deeply interested in the reading of a book, or in solving some abstract problem and not hear that the clock strikes or notice that a person passes through the room. The person passed within the range of our vision, the sound waves from the striking clock reached our ears; the eyes and the ears were as perfect as ever, yet the impressions transmitted by eyes and ears to the brain did not register in our consciousness for the Ego was preoccupied on the mental plane. This time "the clutch was thrown into full gear" on the mental side with the result that the Ego ceased to be aware of the physical plane for the time being.

We say of a person in such a state of mind that he is in a "Brown Study," "he is day-dreaming," recognizing as we do, that he is in a state similar to sleep. Or we may say: "he is absent-minded,"—"he isn't all there."

When we want to arouse him we say jokingly: "Come back to Earth" and perhaps accompany this with a gentle touch. The Ego then withdraws its attention from the mental plane and again takes note of its physical surroundings.

When the Ego returns after such an excursion on the mental plane, it may appear dazed and at first not recognize its surroundings, for mentally it "has been in some other place" and now confuses that with its actual physical surroundings. But in a few seconds the situation clears up and the Ego is back in its usual "observation seat" and is again in full possession of both its mind and sense-apparatus. It has made the transit from a purely mental state to the ordinary waking state. It has "descended into matter."

It has "shifted the clutch into mid-position" where it operates the usual combination of mental and physical activity.

It was possible, then, for the Ego to recede from the physical plane and cease to exist there and yet exist on the mental plane and be active there. This shows that it is possible for the Ego to retain full mental consciousness without physical consciousness.

During this period the physical plane might as well be non-existent so far as the Ego is concerned, for it plays no useful part in the Ego's mental activity.

During its absence from the physical plane and while existing on the mental plane the Ego still retained its identity and recognized itself as the same I-Am-I as in the ordinary waking state.

The Ancient Wisdom tells us that there are other and higher planes above the mental and that just as the Ray of Consciousness can withdraw from the physical plane and still be active on the mental plane, so can it also withdraw from the mental plane and become active on one of these higher planes. As its vehicle on the mental plane was the ordinary brain-mind, so its vehicle on the next plane is a higher Mind, part of a higher vehicle, existing independent of the physical body and brain. The reason we are not aware of these experiences in our waking state, is that they do not take place in the ordinary mind and are therefore not recorded as memories in the brain.

To us, whose ordinary experiences do not extend above the mental plane, it might be difficult to imagine any activities above the mental and to picture the nature of the plane in which such activity could take place. We might therefore conclude that no such activity and no such planes could exist. But is such an attitude justified? By comparison let us see how our mental activity appears to an entity whose chief activity is centered on the physical plane, a dog for example. Suppose his master is sitting in his easy-chair completely absorbed in reading a book, while the dog is lying on the rug watching him. He sees his master, immovable like a statue staring at the pages of a book. To the dog this is utter and useless inactivity and a sheer waste of time. He is incapable of understanding that his master is intensely active on the mental plane.

May not the apparently inactive periods of sleep and the after-death states of the Ego similarly be filled with intense activity, even though we have no way of forming an opinion as to the nature of this activity?

GOING TO SLEEP

The presence of the Ray vitalizes the mind and body into activity during the day, but this activity is a drain on the resources of the body, which towards evening results in exhaustion. In this condition the body and brain are no longer serviceable tools for the use of the Ray, and the latter then withdraws from its vehicles on the physical plane. During the ensuing period of inactivity, the body energies are restored by Nature's healing and rebuilding processes.

Our program in preparing for sleep is one of reducing the body-activity to a minimum. We seek a quiet place and a comfortable bed so that noise and discomfort will not keep the consciousness chained to the body. We turn out the light and have then as far as possible disconnected ourselves from our sense-apparatus. We have "thrown the clutch out of gear" on the physical plane. Or, borrowing a phrase from the ancient Upanishads: "we have closed the avenues of the senses."

The Ray of Consciousness continues to vitalize the brain, however, with the result that the Human Ego is still aware of its existence. While waiting for sleep to come it may think of something that happened during the day or make plans for the morrow. Gradually these mind-pictures grow vague and hazy and it becomes increasingly difficult to center the consciousness on them. If it happens to be something of importance, however, the Ego may assert its authority and force the Mind back to work, perhaps several times in succession, showing, that even to the last moment before withdrawing the Ego remains unchanged. Its function is still that of commander and observer. But as there is a limit to the capacity of even a willing servant, so there comes a point beyond which the brain refuses to work, and the Ray is finally compelled to disconnect itself from its exhausted partners. It has now completely "thrown out the clutch" between itself and its physical sense apparatus and lower mind. It then loses consciousness of the physical plane for it has abandoned its only vehicles for contact with this plane.

The co-partnership that made consciousness on this plane possible has ceased to function as a unit and is for the time being broken up into its component parts. Of these the body lies in bed inert and passive. The lower mind with its brain is de-vitalized. The Ray of Consciousness has withdrawn and the Human Ego has become dormant.

These component parts have not ceased to exist, although their state of being is now entirely different from that of the complete unit. The case might be compared to that of water when this is decomposed into its elements. The water then disappears from sight as a liquid and ceases to exist as such for the time being. It still exists potentially, however, as its component parts, although the state of the latter as two invisible gases is entirely different from that of their combined product, the water.

SLEEPING—DREAMING

When the Ray of Consciousness withdraws from the physical-mental plane it retires to the higher mental plane. Here it functions through its vehicle, the Higher Mind, as the Reincarnating or Higher Ego, and this Ego now enters upon what is its real existence. While asleep our external life seems like an unreal dream to the Higher Ego just as the activity of the Higher Ego during sleep appears to the Human Ego as blank unconsciousness or occasionally a confused dream.

The reason we in our waking state do not recollect any of the real experiences of the Higher Ego during sleep, is that these experiences do not take place in the lower mind and are therefore not recorded in the brain, but occur in the Higher Mind, and only occasionally does the Ego on its return to physical existence carry with it a few fragments which may then be transmitted to the brain. In passing through the brain and lower mind, these are usually distorted, so that we cannot in our waking state form a true conception of the activities of the Higher Ego during sleep. Our dreams do however give us hints that there are modes of existence different from our waking state.

When we return to the waking state in the morning, we may have a clear recollection of some dream, in which we know we took an active part. Other times we have a feeling that we have had a dream, but are unable to recollect what we dreamt of. Occasionally we may wake up suddenly and catch the tail-end of a dream that swiftly eludes our grasp like the last few feet of a film that is just disappearing from the screen. It is as though our Higher Ego had been watching a film on another screen in some unfamiliar portion of the Mind.

Perhaps most frequently the night is a complete blackout of all consciousness and when morning comes we have no recollection of any dream experience. But this absence of recollection is not necessarily a proof that we had no such experience. After such an apparently dreamless night it sometimes happens that later in the day there suddenly flashes into the mind the recollection of a dream, which until that moment we were totally unaware of, but that now returns to us quite clearly and with many distinct details. The Ego now remembers and recognizes itself as the actor and participator in certain experiences that took place on the dream plane, showing that after all the Ego or some part of it had been conscious and active during sleep, even though the waking Ego would at first have denied this. This shows that even what we call dreamless sleep, may not be dreamless, but that here too we may have had some form of consciousness, although in this case the memory does not return to us.

There are dreams in which we realize that there is more than one Ego in us. While one portion of our consciousness is taking an active part in some dream experience, another portion seems to stand apart and watch the event, for we find ourselves thinking: "I know that this is only a dream."

Whatever the dream experience may be, we feel ourselves, or some portion of ourselves, as taking the leading part in the dream. We do not dream of someone else as the chief actor, but we recognize the identity of the dream actor with the I-AM-I of waking life. This feeling of identity between the waking Ego and the dream Ego is due to the fact that both Egos are but different manifestations of the same Ray of Consciousness.

When we go to sleep soon after we have indulged in a heavy meal or some other unwise excess, it sometimes happens that the intensified activity of the body retards the consciousness so that this is unable to free itself from its now obnoxious partner. "The clutch drags" and the result is a stupor in which the Ego is still partly conscious on the physical-mental plane. The subsequent uneasy slumber, which is often accompanied by chaotic, idle visions, is not real sleep and it does not result in the beneficial rest that would follow if the body's activity were reduced to its automatic functions only.

The dreams experienced in this state have their locus in the stupefied lower mind, and have no relation to the real experiences of the Higher Ego during deep sleep.

A person in a deep, sound sleep is totally unaware of what is going on around him. He receives no impressions from the outer world through his senses, although these are perfect. He does not know where he is, whether he is alone or in company, whether it is day or night, hot or cold. His mind has ceased to function. He can not communicate with his friends and they can not communicate with him. Except for the automatic body functions he has ceased to exist on the outer plane, for the duration of the sleep, and could not be less active there, nor less accessible to his friends if his body were actually dead. Every time we go to sleep the consciousness undergoes a process of disembodiment. It frees itself from the trammels of the material body. It "dies a daily death."

WAKING UP

During the night Nature's beneficent processes rebuild the worn-out tissues, and when morning comes the body and the brain are rested and refreshed. The Ego now returns from its nightly wanderings in unknown territory and passing through the mist of forgetfulness that separates the two states of consciousness, reenters and revitalizes its dormant vehicles on this plane.

Although the Ego has been absent on some other plane, yet we know that this absence is not equivalent to non-existence, for we may be awakened in the middle of the night and the Ego is immediately on hand in response to the call, after which it again returns to the dream-state when its attention is no longer required here.

It seems intended that the experiences of the Ego on the inner planes should be kept separate from those on the material plane, for in passing from one to the other, the new existence entered upon completely blots out the one just left behind. Our transit from one plane to another is so gradual and gentle that we are unable to watch the process, but we seem to pass through a "swivel door" that closes on one plane as it opens on another.

When re-entering this outer plane the Ego sometimes seems to hesitate on the threshold. We half wake up, and then go back to sleep again, and it may happen that before the Ego emerges fully into the waking state it shuttles back and forth several times between this and the dream state. "The clutch drags" and the Ego hovers as it were between the two planes, until it finally steps over the threshold and "throws the clutch into full gear" on the waking side of consciousness.

The process is the reverse of that followed by the Ego in going to sleep, when it returned back to the waking state after it had begun to glide into the mist of sleep.

Upon first entering its physical vehicle the Ego sometimes seems dazed and bewildered as though it finds itself in unfamiliar surroundings, as a traveler feels when he wakes up in a strange hotel, and it may take a few seconds before it realizes that it has reentered its vehicle of yesterday.

But finally the process is completed. The Ray of Consciousness has returned and re-vitalized the brain, and the lower mind begins to function, and again the Ray is conscious and active on this plane as the Human Ego. The Observer, back at his observation post, picks up the threads of thought from the memory-deposits in the brain and lower mind where he left them the night before, and again begins to watch the pictures on the screen of the mind. Once more he feels the impulses from the bodily organs and receives impressions from the outer world through his five senses. The co-partnership of yesterday is re-established and again acting as one working unit, and the human being resumes his daily round of activities on the physical-mental plane.

Just as when hydrogen and oxygen unite, they emerge from their invisible gaseous state and appear in their visible liquid state as water, so likewise, do the co-partners of the human constitution, when they are re-united, emerge from their various inactive or invisible states to appear in combination as a human entity active on this plane.

In the process of awakening, then, the Ego has returned from an unknown higher state of existence to its material vehicle. It has descended or "fallen into matter." It is "re-in-carnis" again in flesh. It has undergone its daily process of re-birth.

ABNORMAL STATES OF CONSCIOUSNESS

In certain fevers and other diseases the patient loses consciousness of the world around him and becomes delirious. He seems to be conscious "elsewhere." He sees and observes entities and events, and passes through experiences that do not take place in the physical world. Yet these happenings seem very real to the patient and produce a deep impression on him. His body may perspire and he may show signs of being terrified by his experience. He may speak as from a far distance and incoherently describe what he sees, but does not hear what is spoken to him and is not conscious on the outer plane.

After the disease is surmounted, he may not remember any of his experiences and may be disposed to deny that he ever had any. Yet the watchers at his bedside know from his state of agitation that he did have *some* kind of experience and hence *some* kind of existence on one of Nature's planes, different from the physical or ordinary mental.

A similar case is that where the patient lapses into a state of coma or prolonged unconsciousness, which in some cases may last for months. During this period the patient does not register impressions received through the senses, even though these remain perfect, nor is he mentally active. We have no indication in this case where the consciousness may be, but when health is restored, the patient may be completely unaware of the experience he has passed through. He may even be disposed to deny that he experienced a prolonged period of unconsciousness, thinking that he just woke up after a few hours' sleep.

A person who is under hypnotic influence is not aware of his surroundings. His physical senses are unimpaired, but sense-impressions do not reach his consciousness for the delicate mechanism of Man's inner constitution has been tampered with. Another entity with a stronger will has forced itself between the Ray of Consciousness and its vehicles on the outer plane. The Human Ego has become divided and the higher portion forced to withdraw where it is no longer in control of its rightful domain. The lower portion which remains is now without the illumination and aid that come from the presence of the Ray. This poor remnant of the Man is now the helpless victim of the hypnotizer and obeys the will of the latter.

In this weakened and disorganized state the lower mind mistakes ideas held in the controlling mind of the hypnotizer for physical objects, thus showing that to "the eyes of the mind" thoughts are visible objects.

While under hypnotic influence the subject may be active both physically and with some portion of the lower mind, yet when he is released by the hypnotizer, he may have no recollection of what has taken place and may, contrary to the testimony of witnesses, insist that he was inactive during the entire period.

A sleep-walker is unaware of impressions he receives through his physical senses although he walks with eyes open and hearing unimpaired. While in this state he may be very active physically, may climb up on top of buildings and walk in places where he is exposed to the greatest danger, where one false step might mean death. In the end he may return to bed, and when he wakes up be completely unaware of his activities.

It has been shown that under certain abnormal conditions, the consciousness can be separated from the body and the latter reduced to an inactive state, referred to as "suspended animation." There are on record cases of Indian fakirs, who have allowed themselves to be "buried alive" and who have remained in this condition for several weeks, even months. The body in this case has been especially prepared so as to suspend all normal physical activities, as well as being protected from external injuries. When the time for awakening comes, and friends of the fakir have given a resuscitating treatment to the body, the consciousness returns and resumes its normal activity.

Strange examples of the failure of our memory to record our experiences even on this physical plane are often reported in the press. In this abnormal state, referred to as amnesia or loss of memory, an individual may suddenly, and for some reason not yet understood, lose awareness of his identity, his name and everything about his past life. He may find himself wandering in a strange city and in some cases seems to accept his altered circumstances and may here start a new life under another name, gradually thinking of himself as another personality.

Cases are on record where such a condition has lasted twenty years and then for some reason, just as little understood, the memory of the early life period returns with all its details, then crowding out the memory of the second period as completely as the second period had blotted out the first.

There are many mysteries here that we do not understand, but two important facts become evident: 1. Our memory can be a very unreliable witness when it comes to proving what has or has not taken place even right here on the physical plane. 2. The consciousness of the first period was not annihilated or blotted out during the second period, or it could not have returned in the third period.

DEDUCTIONS REGARDING STATES OF CONSCIOUSNESS

The Ancient Teachings tell us that the Ego during sleep and after death exists in an ethereal-spiritual body independent of the physical body, and is active on inner and to us invisible planes.

Let us now examine the little store of knowledge we have regarding different states of consciousness and see how this compares with the Ancient Teachings.

Our waking consciousness consists in a simultaneous awareness of the physical and mental planes. The necessary prerequisite for our existence here—the vehicle through which we experience these planes—is the physical body, brain and lower mind.

In dreams and also in some abnormal states of consciousness we had experiences that did not take place on either the physical or ordinary mental plane. The fact that we had such experiences shows that we had an existence, which therefore must have taken place on some inner and as yet unknown planes.

If the Ego could observe the unfolding of events, as it did on these inner planes, it must have had a vehicle or instrument, a set of inner senses, in order to make these observations.

Just as the physical body and brain are prerequisites for existence on the physical-mental plane, so is a body with suitable sense-apparatus adapted to the plane where the experience occurs, a necessary prerequisite for existence on these inner planes.

In our waking state we found that if we want to attain maximum effectiveness in either mental or physical activity, one of these had to be reduced to a minimum in order to give the other greater scope. By a separation of the two activities, as far as this was possible, the best results could be attained. The same principle may hold true regarding separation between all planes of consciousness and may be the reason we are made to forget one plane of consciousness when we pass into another. When we go to sleep, for instance, we pass through a mist of forgetfulness, a period of unconsciousness before dreaming begins. When we wake up we seem to come out of this mist and in each case we have lost the memory of the plane we leave behind more or less completely.

The same is true of abnormal states of consciousness. While active in one of these, the Ego evidently is totally unaware of the physical plane, and when it returns to normal consciousness it has usually forgotten its experiences on such planes, for one blots out the other.

When the Ego withdraws from the physical plane to the dream plane or to some abnormal plane, such withdrawal has of course made no changes in the physical plane that is left behind. Yet the loss of memory is so complete that, as far as the Ego in its new environment is concerned, the physical plane is not only forgotten, it seems to have no existence at all. Similarly, to the Ego in the waking state, the dream plane seems unreal and is usually completely forgotten, and hence for the time being it has ceased to exist so far as the waking Ego is concerned.

Under these conditions it is not strange that the Ego in one state of consciousness is disposed to deny the reality of other states. We know, however, that such denial is unjustified, for experience has shown that what looks like inactivity or even non-existence when viewed from one plane, may be a state of intense activity of a different nature when seen from the plane in which the experience took place. Experience also showed that planes of consciousness may exist, of which we in another state of consciousness are entirely unaware, and which then seem to us non-existent.

Therefore, what seems to us a period of unconsciousness or non-existence in sleep and after death may very well be filled with intense activity on planes, of whose existence we are entirely unaware in our waking state.

Just as the physical plane ceases to exist in the Ego when this withdraws to other planes, so does the Ego disappear and cease to exist to those who remain conscious on the physical plane. The return of the Ego that follows in due course, shows, however, that the disappearance was not equivalent to extinction.

Some sense of identity or awareness of the thread of continuity of its existence is felt by the Ego in various states of consciousness. In day-dreaming, for instance, we know that the Ego is the same as in the waking state. In ordinary dreams and in abnormal states, when these are remembered, we also recognize ourselves, or perhaps a shadowy reflection of ourselves as the actor. We feel the link that binds the various ego-aspects of the Ray of Consciousness and that it is the same I-AM-I or some portion of it that is the observer, spectator or experiencer of events, that vary according to the theatre in which these events take place.

Let us now see what part the physical body plays in the various non-physical activities of the Ego.

The normal automatic functions of the body do not directly affect the consciousness states of the Ego.

Accelerated body-activity reduces capacity for mental work.

The best preparation for mental work is a passive state of the body.

In day-dreaming the body is inactive.

Sleep is caused by failure of the body through fatigue to supply the energy for the brain.

Enforced physical activity prevents sleep.

Sleep is an abandonment of the body by the Ego.

Overstimulation from a heavy meal interferes with sound sleep and keeps the Ego chained to the body.

The best preparation for sleep is to loosen the chains of the body and make it passive, thus making the Ego free to take off for other planes of consciousness.

The body is not an active partner in the experiences of the Ego while in a coma or delirious from fever.

The body is completely inactive, even its automatic functions reduced to almost zero in cases of artificially induced suspended animation.

Do not all these facts indicate that the body is of no use to the Ego and may even be a hindrance to its non-physical activities?

The body's functions are similar to those of a boiler that furnishes the steam for an engine. When the engine is running the boiler is active, but when the engineer shuts off the steam and goes home, the engine stops and the boiler ceases to be of any use and becomes inactive.

Similarly when the Ego is mentally active the body must furnish the energy needed by the brain, but when the Ego withdraws in sleep, the lower mind becomes inactive and the body ceases to be of any use to the Ego.

So far as the engineer is concerned in his off-the-job activities, the boiler might as well be on the junk pile, but if he is to return to his job the next day it is necessary to leave the boiler in good condition and with a banked fire so that it will be easy to get up steam in the morning. The body with its automatic functions is kept in preparedness for next day's activities but is of no more use to the Ego during sleep than the boiler is to the engineer when the engine is idle.

If, then, the body plays such a subordinate part in the Ego's most important activity (the mental) in the waking state, and if it is still less important to the Ego's normal activities in sleep and may even become a hindrance to these, then why should it be any more necessary to the Ego's existence and activities after death?

Chapter VI

DEATH — SLEEP — BIRTH

WE FEAR WHAT WE DO NOT UNDERSTAND

In all ages men have pondered over the problem of death, and asked the question: "Is this the end of our existence, or is there a life after death?"

We do not want to lose contact with our loved ones. We have interests that we would like to follow up; dreams and hopes we would like to see fulfilled; and all of us have made mistakes which we want a chance to make good. In many ways we have just learned how to live when old age and death overtake us. It is not strange, therefore, that we should seek an answer to the foregoing question. But at the same time, we are reluctant to take it up, for it evokes fear and gloom. And so we put off a consideration of it until some time in the future, with the result that it remains as a dark shadow in the background of the mind.

Man fears what he does not understand. If he could lift, even a little, the veil of mystery that surrounds the problem of death, the subject might lose much of its terror.

SLEEP AND DEATH

The Ancient Teachings have much of an illuminating and hopeful nature to tell us on this subject, the keynote being found in the ancient Greek proverb, "Sleep and Death are Brothers." The same succession of events that takes place in death, also takes place in sleep. In sleep the Ray of Consciousness withdraws from the outer plane to inner and invisible planes of existence. In death it also withdraws to inner planes, but the withdrawal is complete and long-lasting.

When we go to sleep it often happens that the Ego becomes unconscious, only to return to consciousness again, a process that may repeat itself several times before sleep is definitely entered into. Often death also follows this pattern. The Ego has periods of consciousness on this plane, alternated with periods of consciousness elsewhere. Usually the latter periods are passed in silence, but sometimes the person may talk to himself of his experiences in scarcely audible tones.

Sleep begins with a period of unconsciousness which later is followed by dreams. Death also begins with consciousness followed by a dream state, deeper and more real than that of sleep. After sleep we return to the same body. After the rest-period that follows death, we return to earth in an infant's body, which we then build up for a new life on the material plane. Sleep is a miniature rehearsal of what takes place in death. Every time we lie down to sleep we "die an incomplete death." Every time we wake up we experience a rebirth into matter.

There is no difference in what happens to the indwelling consciousness, except in degree, but there is a difference in what happens to the vehicle, the body. In sleep the body lies dormant and inactive, but it retains its capacity for recuperation. In death the body breaks up and disintegrates.

The reason we have become accustomed to look upon death with horror is that we have fixed our attention on the rapid destruction of the body that takes place after death, and this, coupled with the erroneous assumption that man is identical with his body, has misled us to think that the destruction of the body meant the destruction of the indwelling consciousness.

The great mistake made in studying this subject in the Occident, is that too much attention has been paid to the body or vehicle side of man's nature, and not enough to the real man, the indwelling consciousness.

Man is a composite entity, and the death of the body is only the discarding of the outermost garment used by the consciousness in the material world. The discarding of this vehicle causes a change in the state of our consciousness, since the Ray of Consciousness now transfers its center of activity to higher vehicles of its inner constitution, but our essential self is not annihilated or destroyed by this change.

When we realize that every time we go to sleep we have a preview of what will happen to us in death, the thought of death will lose its terror. And when we reflect on the feeling of relief with which we drop the cares of the day and welcome the peace and rest of the night, we can visualize the still greater sense of release that will come to us when we abandon the worn-out body completely.

The Sufi poet Jalal-ud-din describes the relation between the consciousness and the body during sleep in the following beautiful poem:

> Nightly the souls of men thou lettest fly
> From out the trap wherein they captive lie
> Nightly from out its cage each soul doth wing
> Its upward way, no longer slave or king.
>
> Yet for a while each night the Spirit's steed
> Is from the harness of the body freed:
> "Sleep is Death's brother": come, this riddle read.
> But lest at daybreak they should lag behind,
> Each soul He doth with a long tether bind,
> That from these groves and plains He may revoke
> Those errant spirits to their daily yoke.

The same life which is lived piece-meal and in snatches during sleep is lived uninterruptedly after death.

THE RAY OF CONSCIOUSNESS WITHDRAWS

The higher principles of man's constitution exert a constant upward attraction on the Human Ego during its entire life. In youth and maturity, however, these attractions are crowded into the background by the interests and demands of physical existence. But when old age approaches, the worldly attractions lose their force and the spiritual attractions begin to dominate.

As these attractions become ever stronger, the Ray of Consciousness begins a gradual withdrawal from man's compound constitution which manifests on the outer plane by a more and more enfeebled condition of the physical body. This keeps increasing until finally the heart stops like a run-down clock. The primary cause of death is the withdrawal of the Ray of Consciousness, but the resulting decline of the body in its turn has the secondary effect of speeding the withdrawal of the Ray.

In the case of a normal old age after a life well-lived, death comes as a longed-for rest and a welcome relief. In case of sickness the breakdown of the vehicle may force the withdrawal of the consciousness before its regular time. The same is true of death caused by accident, violence, or suicide.*

In all these cases the course of events that follows after death differs in the earlier stages from death following old age, but even in these cases the Ego will at a later stage pick up the thread of events and meet with the same experiences it would have met had death followed a normal course.

THE PARTNERSHIP DISSOLVES

Reviewing briefly what has been stated regarding man's constitution: his central core is a Ray of Consciousness, a spark of the Universal Life. The highest foci of this ray, which collectively we called "Man's Inner God," are not directly active in the waking state of the ordinary human being, but rather illumine his consciousness as a light that shines overhead. Although not directly active as yet, we must not lose sight of these higher principles, for without them the lower principles would be non-existent.

The active partners that together produce the waking state of consciousness are the Human Ego aspect of the Ray, or the I-AM-I; the lower mind with its brain-vehicle; and the body. During the waking state these principles merge and blend into an active partnership.

Death and sleep both consist in a dissolution of this partnership. In sleep the dissolution is incomplete and temporary; in death it is complete and permanent. The separated partners are

---

*For a very illuminating treatment of these special cases, as well as the entire subject of death, the reader is referred to Chapters XXVII and XXVIII of *The Esoteric Tradition* by G. de Purucker, as well as other of his works, which are the source of most of the information given here.

not annihilated in the process, but their mode of existence is entirely different from that of the united partnership, just as the elements of a chemical compound differ in appearance and characteristics from their combined product.

What happens to the various principles of the human being when they separate after death?

The highest principles return instantly to their spiritual home, the "Father in Heaven." The lowest part, the physical body with its lower energies and model body, no longer vitalized by the controlling consciousness, begins to disintegrate.* The lower mind ceases to function, in death as it does in sleep, when the Ray of Consciousness withdraws its vitalizing force from the brain.

This explains what happens to the higher and the lower principles of man's constitution, but still leaves the intermediate part, the Human Ego with its various aspects, to be accounted for.

The withdrawal of the Ray of Consciousness from the brain is not instantaneous, and long after the last heartbeat and the last breath, when the body to all outward appearances is lifeless, the process of dying continues on inner planes. During this first post-mortem period—which may last many hours, perhaps longer—the brain automatically dislodges from its innermost recesses every memory that was stored in it during the life just ended.

The Ego then sees passing in review before its inner vision every detail of its past life, beginning with its first conscious experience in early childhood and ending with its last moment of self-consciousness before death. The memory of these experiences is then stored as a permanent record in the imperishable part of man's inner nature. By this panoramic vision the Ego is enabled to see the justice of all that has happened to it and to realize what the effect of this life will be on its future incarnations.

It is not uncommon in cases of near-drowning, when the victim was rescued at the last moment, that he will relate having had just a panoramic vision of his past life. The writer has a first-hand account of such an experience from an old friend, who as

---

*This process can be hastened and the liberation of the Human Ego from its lower partners greatly aided by cremation.

a boy nearly lost his life by drowning; and who related how the memory of every event of his life, "every mean little thing I had done" (and presumably also the good ones) came back to him in the greatest detail and with extreme vividness and lucidity.

This post-mortem review of the life just ended may be compared to the retrospective view the Ego takes when just before losing consciousness in sleep, it reviews the events of the day just ended and realizes the effect that these events will have on the future.

There is this important difference, however, that the pre-sleep experience takes place in the lower mind, while the panoramic vision occurs in the higher mind. The use of the higher mind is made possible because the Human Ego at death is temporarily raised into union with the Higher Ego, and thus enabled to condense a whole life's experiences into a relatively brief period of time.

Referring to the period following upon the apparent death of the body, one of the Masters who was instrumental in forming the Theosophical Society writes:

Speak in whispers, ye, who assist at a death-bed and find yourselves in the solemn presence of Death . . . . . Speak in whispers, I say, lest you disturb the quiet ripple of thought, and hinder the busy work of the Past casting its reflection upon the Veil of the Future.

The Mahatma Letters, p. 171

After the panoramic vision, the Human Ego finds itself unable to maintain its union with the Higher Ego, unless during earth life it has accustomed itself to live in this part of its nature. The change of focus of the consciousness from the familiar brain-mind to the unfamiliar higher mind is too sudden and too great for the Human Ego to remain in this high state, and so it lapses at first into a state of unconsciousness.

We have a similar experience in daily life when we fail to keep ourselves mentally and otherwise on the higher levels that we attain occasionally, and where we would like to remain always.

A PROCESS OF SEGREGATION

The Human Ego that sinks into the dormant or unconscious state at the end of the panoramic vision, is a combination of high aspirations and ideals — originating in the Higher Ego — and worldly interests and earthly desires, originating in the lower mind. The better part of the Human Ego, the truly human part, must now free itself from all the dross by which it is weighted down, before it can rise into union with the higher Ego. It therefore has to pass through a process of segregation, during which it has to face not its creator, but its own creation, that accumulation of effects it has built up during life by its thoughts and deeds, feelings and uncontrolled appetites.

The ease or difficulty with which the Ego disentangles itself from the lower qualities of its nature depends on the kind of life it has led while embodied, and therefore differs for different individuals. The average decent man passes through the sloughing-off process with relative ease, and in a dreamlike or scarcely conscious condition. A very spiritual man is hardly aware he is undergoing a purification, and passes through this state very quickly.

A man who has lived a grossly material life and habitually indulged in passions, selfishness or evildoing, is, on the other hand, deeply entangled in the webs of his lower nature and will naturally require a much longer period of liberation before he can free himself from all the base elements of his nature. It is a serious and sobering thought, this, to realize that one day after we have left this material plane we shall have to face the labor of freeing ourselves from the bonds we ourselves so thoughtlessly and perhaps recklessly forged while embodied.

No one is entirely free from taint, and no one is so evil but that there is something good in him to be liberated. Therefore all must pass through the segregation process. The conditions met in this after-death state vary as much as the experiences met within material life. The time spent also differs greatly, all according to the life lived on earth, but long or short, difficult or easy, there is an end to the separation period. In every case there comes a time when all the base materials have been cast aside and the higher part of the Human Ego is free to join its "Father in Heaven." This final casting off by the Human Ego of its last impediments is what the Ancients called "the second death."

THE RAY ABSORBS ITS PROJECTION

During the waking state the Ray of Consciousness is active through its projection—the Human Ego.

When we go to sleep the Ray of Consciousness withdraws this projection and thus temporarily absorbs the Human Ego back into itself. The Ray of Consciousness then begins to act on the next higher plane through the Higher Mind, as the Higher or Reimbodying Ego. The Human Ego being unable to rise to this high level of existence and being dislocated from its daytime habitation, the brain-mind, loses consciousness and is unaware that it has been reabsorbed by the Higher Ego.

It sometimes happens that due to the condition of the body, the Ray is unable to withdraw its projection completely from the brain, with the result that some small portion of consciousness is still active there. This fractional remnant of the Ray then rummages around among the various memory-deposits in the brain and produces the confused and incoherent dreams that we know so well. In this case the withdrawal of the Ray was incomplete, and the Human Ego was not fully absorbed into the Higher Ego, with the result that the sleep was restless and not as beneficial as it would have been if the absorption had been complete.

If, on the other hand, the withdrawal is complete, the Human Ego is fully absorbed into the Higher Ego and a restful and beneficial sleep is the result, with no memories of any dreams. A complete withdrawal, then, is the prerequisite for the most beneficial sleep.

After death the same withdrawal of the Ray occurs, and here too the withdrawal in its initial stages is incomplete. For although the higher part of the Ray of Consciousness frees itself immediately, yet its projection, the Human Ego, is still entangled in its lower qualities.

While it is struggling to free itself from these, it exists in a confused, chaotic dream-state comparable to an ordinary, confused night dream. But after the second death, when it has freed itself completely from the lower qualities, the Human Ego is re-absorbed into the Higher Ego, and by slow degrees awakens to a partial consciousness in the Higher Mind. It is the higher, truly human part of the Human Ego that has this awakening; the cast-off lower personal part remains dormant.

The case, then, is similar to that of sleep except that in sleep the Ego is still encumbered by its lower qualities, and therefore not pure enough to experience an awakening in the Higher Mind. Also the period is too brief to allow time for the necessary segregation. For these reasons the period of absorption during sleep seems to be one of unconsciousness and is not recollected by the Human Ego after awakening.

REST-PERIOD BETWEEN EARTH-LIVES

After the second death, when the Ego slowly awakens to consciousness in the Higher Mind, there begins for it a new state of consciousness. This resembles a dream state during which the Ego lives over again all its happy experiences of earthlife, unalloyed by any sad or discordant memories. The body and all the lower qualities have been cast aside and the limiting and retarding effect of these on man's spiritual aspirations and nobler feelings is removed. The Ego is now free, and in its consciousness carries to fulfillment all the good resolutions of its former earthlife; brings to completion the lofty plans it had built in imagination while embodied, but could not then realize.

The function of the Ego during this phase of its existence is not one of producing new causes, but is rather a period of rest during which the Ego assimilates and permanently incorporates into its own nature all that was good during its past earthlife. It weaves all these experiences into its character, which is ennobled thereby, and when the Ego, reinvigorated and refreshed after its long rest, returns to earth again, the better side of its character has thus been strengthened and recrystallized into a new and improved mold for the life that is about to begin.

The duration of the rest-period between incarnations varies greatly for different individuals and depends on the nature and direction of their interests and longings during earthlife.

Those whose lives have been filled with spiritual longings and idealistic endeavors have much material for contemplation and assimilation, and their rest-period is of long duration. Those whose interests have been chiefly with material concerns, with few thoughts of self-forgetfulness, love, or yearnings of a lofty character, have a small harvest of a spiritual nature to occupy their attention. Those who have lived base and ignoble lives have a very meager harvest, and their stay in the rest-period is relatively short, and the greater part of it is spent in almost complete unconsciousness.

The appropriate average time between incarnations for the whole human race is said to be about 1500 mortal years. So vivid are the experiences of the Ego in its blissful contemplation, however, that it does not notice the passage of time, which in this state is not divided into hours, days and years as it is on earth. Centuries and even thousands of years may go by without the Ego being aware of their passage. It is the same as in ordinary sleep: if we wake up while it is dark we cannot tell whether we have slept a few minutes or several hours.

CHARACTER SEEDS

The foregoing accounts for what happens to the higher part of the Human Ego after it has separated itself from the lower qualities at the second death. But what happens in the meantime to the lower elements, discarded by the Ego during the segregation period?

Each such vehicle or garment disintegrates on the plane to which it belongs, but in each case it leaves behind a residue, a kind of "seed," that retains in a latent state the nature and characteristics of the discarded element or garment.

These "seeds" lie dormant on their respective inner planes of Nature, and thus preserve in germ-state the characteristics of the perishable part of the former entity. The higher principles of the entity, including the higher part of the Human Ego, do not disintegrate. These, together with the "seeds" of the lower elements, then, are the repositories for the entire character of the human being, so that in future ages, when the Ego returns to earth life, it will again be clothed in the same basic character it had at the end of its former existence, but now made better by former efforts at self-improvement.

THE RAY RE-ENTERS MATTER

After ages spent by the Human Ego in its blissful rest following the second death, there comes at last a time when the Ego has carried to its ultimate completion every hitherto unfulfilled aspiration and made it a part of its character. The material for its dreams has gradually been exhausted and the Ego begins to long for a more active existence. Vague memories of former earth lives now begin to haunt the imagination. The Ego longs to revisit old familiar scenes and to test again its strength in the activities of earthlife. Just as, prior to death, the spiritual aspirations exerted their "upward" pull, so now do the longings for earthlife grow ever stronger, until finally the Ego starts on its earthward journey.

During its descent to the material plane, the Ego follows the same pathway it used in the ascent, but now travels in the opposite direction. Slowly it loses consciousness of the plane of spiritual aspirations, and gradually passes into a state of complete unconsciousness. As it descends through the intermediate and lower planes of Nature, it passes on each one of these planes the "seeds" it left behind on its ascent. These seeds now feel the stimulating and vitalizing effect of the presence of their Master, and just as iron filings are drawn to a magnet, so do these "seeds" now attach themselves to the returning Ego, and in due course rebuild the garments that formerly enshrouded it. Therefore, when the Ego is ready to re-enter the material plane, it is equipped with all the essentials required to rebuild its former vehicles just as they were before.

It is said that just before the Ego re-enters earthlife it has a brief period of vivid consciousness, during which it sees again the same panoramic vision of its former earthlife that it saw at the end of that life, starting as before with the earliest memory of childhood, showing the entire life with all its details and ending with its last conscious moment before death.

The Ego recognizes its responsibility for all its acts and sees the consequences that must follow from these acts. Then, we are told, it sees a preview of the new earth life that is about to begin, and sees the justice of all the experiences that will come to it.

It is psycho-magnetically attracted to those parents that can furnish the heredity and circumstances of life most closely corresponding to its deserts. Love is the strongest bond that brings parents and children together, but hate can also be a factor in those unfortunate cases where problems of dislike and disharmony were left unsolved in the past. Such Egos are again brought together until they learn to understand each other and come to realize that "hatred ceases not by hatred; hatred ceases only by love," as all great religious teachers have taught.

As the Ego in the distant past left this plane through the door of Death, so does it now re-enter it through the door of Birth. The little infant body is of course a very weak and imperfect instrument, and this must now be strengthened and built up. This task Nature tackles with vigor, for the infant spends almost its entire time eating and sleeping, the first prerequisite for growth. Only occasionally and for brief periods do we see the consciousness beginning to assert itself. It seems to come and go. It tries to use its little instrument, but the latter is too weak and feeble and undeveloped. The view it gets of this world through the "windows of the senses" is blurred and misty. The consciousness gives up the effort and returns temporarily to its more familiar dream plane, only to return again and again.

As weeks and months pass by and the body develops, the consciousness can remain for longer and longer periods before the little body is overstrained by its presence, and sleep with unconsciousness of this plane again becomes necessary.

It is a slow "awakening" of the Ego to consciousness on this material plane, a process that extends over months and years before the Ego has developed self-consciousness. It repeats on a larger time scale what happens when we half-wake up in the morning only to fall asleep again, an act that may recur several times before the Ego finally becomes fully conscious on this plane.

During its waking periods the Ego seems to realize that it must now become acquainted with the new world it has just entered, for we notice that whenever the consciousness is active on this plane, it is observing and studying its surroundings. The baby watches its fingers move, feels the bedclothing, handles some little toy and puts it in his mouth. He watches the light in the ceiling and reaches for it, only to find to his surprise that distance or space is one of the characteristics of this new, strange world.

Parents often complain that the baby so soon "tires of his nice new toys" and always wants something else, but quickly tires of that also. When the baby gets hold of a new object he looks at it, feels it and usually also puts it in his mouth. To the baby this toy is not an object with which to pass away idle time. It is an object of serious research, a bit of the new world to get acquainted with. But after the baby has handled it a sufficient number of times and knows its characteristics, the object has served its purpose and holds no further interest; baby wants some new object to study.

We see that whenever the consciousness is present, its activity is that of observer, learner, experiencer, in the little limited world in which it exists.

But the years pass and gradually the soil becomes suitable for the germination of the character seeds that had been lying dormant since the end of the former earthlife, and slowly the character of the incoming Ego begins to manifest itself. This is the "inheritance" the Ego willed to itself by its own thoughts and deeds during its former existence, and that now shows itself in disposition, temperament, talents and aptitudes, or the lack of these. As the Personal Ego draws on its stock of day-to-day memories stored in the brain, so does the higher part of the Human Ego draw on the deeper and more lasting memories in the permanent storehouse of the character.

Finally, after more years have come and gone, the individual has passed through adolescence to maturity. The Higher Ego has again projected its Ray into the human constitution where it now functions as the Human Ego working through the Personal Ego. The co-partnership of the former life is again assembled, the body is full grown and functioning. The brain and lower mind are re-vitalized and active and the Human Ego is back at its observation post. The Ray of Consciousness has again "fallen into matter" and is ready to continue its evolution, using its rebuilt vehicle which is virtually a duplicate of the one used in its former existence on earth.

Thus as the Ego at night goes to sleep and after a period of rest awakens in the same body, so does the Ego after death have its period of rest, after which it slowly "awakens" in a new— and if it has so deserved—better body. As the individual is rested and refreshed after a night's sleep and is ready to tackle the duties of a new day, so is the Ego reinvigorated and filled with youthful enthusiasm, ready and eager to tackle the duties of a new life.

PHYSICAL BODY USEFUL FOR
PHYSICAL EXISTENCE ONLY

Going to sleep is a process of disimbodiment, after which the Ego loses consciousness of this plane and passes beyond the reach of those who remain conscious here. Death is also a process of disimbodiment, followed by the same sequence of events.

The two events, then, are identical, except that in the case of sleep the disimbodiment is temporary while in death it is permanent. Since the consciousness frees itself from the body in both cases, the relative value or usefulness of the body to the consciousness is also the same in both cases. Inasmuch as the body was of no use in sleep and may even be a hindrance, it should be reasonable to conclude that the body is equally unnecessary to the Ego's existence after death. Since it is possible for the consciousness to exist and be active during sleep without the use of the body, it should also be possible for it to exist and be active after death without the use of the body, and the destruction of the latter does not mean the destruction of the indwelling consciousness.

OUR ENTRANCE INDICATES PRE-EXISTENCE

When the consciousness withdraws from the body in sleep and death, those who remain conscious on this plane are unable to follow it further. At this point the thread of the story is lost in an impenetrable mist, and further investigation in this direction is blocked.

Since we are unable to follow the consciousness as it departs from this plane, our next best approach would seem to be a study of our entrance here, for an understanding of this may throw some light on our future.

Taking a retrospective view of life from the present time— going back to youth and early childhood, even to the first event that we are able to recollect—we know that we were one and the same Ego that passed through all the experiences of life, and we are positive of our existence that far back. Is the fact that we can remember nothing earlier than this event a proof that the Ego did not exist before this, its first memory?

Let us go back in imagination to the day in early childhood when something unusual happened that made a deep impression on us and that later turned out to be our earliest conscious memory. Let us think of ourselves as we were then. We know that on this day we would remember what happened to us on the previous day. We would probably remember much farther back than that, perhaps a month, perhaps several months. In each case let us go back in imagination to that earlier date which we could then recollect, and continue the process of retracing our conscious existence as far back as possible. Finally we would reach a point where the picture would be too hazy, but in each and every case as we went farther and farther back in our imaginary journey toward infancy, we would recognize ourselves on that day as the same Ego, the same I-AM-I as on the "yesterday" before it. We know by this that the Ego did not come into existence with its first conscious memory, but that it existed, was active, and observing events much earlier, and that it had a day-to-day recollection of other and earlier events which it later forgot. We can confirm all this, for it becomes very evident, if we watch a two or three-year-old child, that the Ego is present, active and observing, much earlier than the child will be able to recollect later in life.

Our interests and our fields of experience vary greatly during the different periods of our life. In maturity they may extend over a wide range, while in infancy they are limited to the four walls of the nursery. But no matter whether the field is great or small, the nature and essential function of the Ego is to observe and learn from life, and this is characteristic of the infant just as much as it is of the full grown man. Right from the start and all through life the occupation of the Ego is that of spectator and experiencer of life.

When we took the retrospective view, trying to determine if the Ego came into existence with its earliest memory, we arrived at a point where the Ego was probably unable to recollect any event in its earlier existence because the picture was too hazy. Does this mean that the Ego had no existence prior to its first faint recollections?

If we watch an infant in its earliest months, even shortly after birth, we notice that during its relatively brief waking periods, part of the time there is an observing consciousness present, for we can see the eyes following the mother as she moves around the room. But at other times the eyes, as if exhausted, stare vacantly into space, and though the body is not asleep, the consciousness has absented itself, much as it does when an adult is "day-dreaming." After awhile sleep returns and the consciousness is completely absent. This appearance and disappearance of the consciousness keeps repeating itself with gradually shortening sleep periods and lengthening periods of conscious existence. In this we see a duplication of what often happens to an adult when he awakens only to fall asleep again, and we see a "repetition in reverse" of what so often occurs at death when the consciousness withdraws, only to return again, perhaps several times before final withdrawal.

What happens to the infant's consciousness during its absent periods? There seem to be two possible alternatives: 1. The consciousness passes out of this plane onto some other plane of consciousness where it dwells until it returns to this plane, or 2. The consciousness is annihilated each time it goes, and a new consciousness comes into existence each time the infant wakes up. If the second alternative were true we would have a new consciousness coming into existence with each waking-sleeping cycle. That would make a whole string of different consciousnesses coming into being, only to be snuffed right out again, and each time the baby woke up there would be one more to add to the list. The idea does not appeal to the reason.

The first alternative is supported by the fact that as soon as memory begins to operate we have proof that it is the same consciousness that comes and goes, for the infant in one conscious period will remember events from a former, even though the two periods were separated by intervals of unconsciousness. The fact that the memory was non-operative in the earliest stages should not produce a change in the status of the consciousness itself. And if it is the same consciousness unit coming and going *after* memory is developed, it should be reasonable to conclude that is the same consciousness unit, the same Ego, that has been present ever since birth.

If then, during its absence from this plane, the consciousness has retreated to some other plane, it must have had some kind of vehicle for existence on this, to us, invisible plane. If it can exist in this vehicle and on this inner plane during the periods of its absence from the body and the material plane, it can just as well exist in this same vehicle on this same inner plane before its first visit to the body, or before the body existed. So it seems that there is nothing in our knowledge regarding the first appearance of consciousness in the body contradicting the ancient teaching that this consciousness existed before the birth of the body.

A circumstance that also points to an existence of the consciousness before its entry into the body is the early appearance in children of definite gifts, aptitudes and talents. These gradually come to the surface without being in any way prompted or inculcated by the parents. For instance, there may be two children in the same family, one of which has distinct artistic ability that the other completely lacks. The first one will produce with a few lines scrawled on a piece of paper the picture of a natural and even good-looking face, while the other child, even with help and instruction, can produce only a crude caricature—a "goblin-face."

The artistic child did not acquire his ability in this life; neither did prodigies in music, mathematics and other fields learn these subjects in this one life. When and where could these arts have been mastered then, except in former existences?

Does not the growth from infancy through childhood and youth show every sign of an incoming soul overshadowing, vitalizing and gradually taking possession of a material body furnished it by Nature? It is the soul that left a dying body sometime in the far distant past that is now "waking up" in a new body, gradually displaying the heritage it brought with it.

OUR EXIT INDICATES CONTINUITY OF EXISTENCE

It might be said that a man's house is in one sense a part of himself, for it is a necessary adjunct to his life here. Every time he passes out through the door he finds himself in open space where the conditions are vastly different from those inside the four walls of the house. Perhaps his work keeps him out-of-doors all day, but in the evening he returns and re-enters his home where he again finds the old familiar surroundings. But a house will in time get out of repair; perhaps the foundation settles, and one evening when he comes home the door jams, and he finds himself locked out.

The passing of the man from indoors to out-of-doors did not change the man except that it enlarged his view and perhaps put him in a different frame of mind. The fact that he could not return through the jammed door did not in any way change his condition in the out-of-doors.

Man's consciousness lives in a body, a "house" of flesh. Every twenty-four hours it passes out of this house through the door of unconsciousness into sleep, and then finds itself in some sort of "out-of-doors" of consciousness, with conditions of existence very different from those inside the "house." When morning comes, the same consciousness, the same I-AM-I returns to the body, so that whatever its condition had been during sleep, this in no way changed its identity or interfered with the continuity of its existence.

Preceding death the consciousness also passes out of its "house" through the door of unconsciousness and may remain absent for long periods, only to return and repeat this coming and going many times before final withdrawal. During each of these absent intervals the consciousness has some sort of an existence in some "out-of-doors" of consciousness, which for all we know to the contrary is the same or similar to that experienced in sleep.

Each time when the consciousness returns after one of these pre-death absences, it is the same Ego, the same I-AM-I as before, so that in this case also the out-of-the-body existence did not change the identity of the Ego and did not interfere with its continuity of existence.

Now let us suppose for the sake of illustration, that the Ego passes into unconsciousness six times, and six times returns to consciousness, but the next time it loses consciousness it does not return. Does the number of times it returns have any influence on the out-of-the-body existence of the Ego? Suppose it had come back a seventh time; would it not still have been the same essential Ego as the one that came back the fifth, fourth or third time? And suppose it came back many more times; would it not still be the same Ego as before? Does not this indicate that the Ego had a continuous existence whether in or out of the body? And may it not be possible that even when the Ego failed to return, it had tried to re-enter the body this time also, but found it too far disintegrated? The Ego was locked out as the man who could not re-enter his house, because of the jammed door, but the Ego had not ceased to exist any more than the man who was locked out.

And why should we think, when the consciousness failed to return after its last disappearance, that its condition in the "out-of-doors" on the other side of death was any different from what it would have been if the door had not jammed and the consciousness had returned this time also?

Is there not a remarkable similarity, operating in reverse, between the consciousness slowly, gradually and intermittently taking possession of the body after birth, and that same consciousness slowly and alternately interrupted by briefer and briefer return visits, gradually withdrawing from the body at death?

Death then, is the opposite to Birth, not the opposite to Life. Life is continuous. Consciousness comes into this material plane through the door of birth from some "out-of-doors" of consciousness. It sojourns on this plane for a period of years and then leaves through the door of death to re-enter the "out-of-doors" of consciousness from which it came.

CHANGING SCENERY DOES NOT CHANGE
THE TRAVELER

But what happens to the consciousness after it has left this material plane and entered the great "out-of-doors" on the other side of the portal of death?

Here as also in sleep the ordinary human consciousness is unable to follow. The friends who watch at a deathbed are like those who gather on the seashore to bid farewell to a departing friend whose boat is slowly passing out to sea. At first it is within hailing distance but gradually it passes farther and farther out of reach and approaches closer and closer to the horizon. Finally it seems to pass the line where it drops out of sight behind the horizon, and to those on shore it seems that a sudden and complete change has taken place. But to the man in the boat there was no sudden change, for it all came gradually and naturally. He is gone from the sight of his friends on shore, but to him there are opened other horizons, new vistas, new experiences in other states of consciousness—other mansions of life.

But the traveler does not remain permanently in any one place. He continues his journey farther and farther, like a ship that keeps sailing always in the same direction, to the West, let us say. When, after months or years, this ship finally returns to its starting point, it comes not from the West where it disappeared, but from the East, where it seems to come out of nowhere. While out of sight to those who stayed at home, it has still existed and been busily engaged in circumnavigating the globe.

This may be considered a figurative representation of what happens after death, for during the long absence of the consciousness between earth lives, when it is completely out of touch with this world, it journeys through many mansions in the house of life, and when it returns to earth life, it makes its entry at the opposite side of the stage from where it left. It enters at birth.

TRUST NATURE

When we go to sleep we do so in the full conviction that we shall awake the next morning. We know that we shall become unconscious, but that does not frighten us in the least, for we know that in the morning our consciousness will return to its familiar setting, pick up the threads from yesterday and continue life where it left off.

We know so well the complete cycle of activity and rest which we experience every twenty-four hours, that we hardly give it a thought. It feels so good to lay down the tired body after a day's hard work and forget it all, especially as during the night Nature will renew the worn out tissues and in the morning we shall awaken rested and refreshed. All in all then, sleep is both a happy experience and a beneficial one.

We should feel the same way with regard to the longer sleep of death, says the Ancient Wisdom, for sleep and death are both rest-periods for the Human consciousness. And as sleep is followed by an awakening in the same body, so is death in due course followed by an awakening in the body of a newborn child.

It should be with a feeling of relief that we lay aside the aged, worn-out instrument, in the knowledge that we shall again start out in life with a new instrument that should be—and if we have lived right will be—stronger and better than the old.

Even when we grow old we should not center our attention on death, for it is only death to the body. It is only one step in the universal process of repetition that we see everywhere in Nature. It is the consciousness disappearing from one plane in order to appear on another. It is the end of one cycle and the beginning of a new, and even if we do not understand the details of the process, we should have confidence that Nature has the same ability to lead us gently out of this existence that she had in leading us into this life.

OLD AGE

Old age need not and should not be a period of retrogression or decrease in man's spiritual and intellectual faculties. At this period of life the body vitality is reduced and this gives greater freedom for the expression of man's spiritual and intellectual faculties. These can and should be active and expanding until even a few hours before death.

The body, of course, grows feeble with advancing years, but it is not uncommon to hear aging people, who have not lived chiefly in the material side of their natures, say: "I don't feel a bit older than when I was twenty. Perhaps in some ways I feel even younger."

There will still be much that we can do and much that we can learn, remembering that no effort is wasted and that even if we cannot in this life make use of these late experiences, it will be that much gained for our next incarnation.

We should have our inner vision directed forward, not backward, even to the last, remembering with Victor Hugo that "Death is not a blind alley; it is a thoroughfare. It closes on the twilight; it opens on the Dawn."

Chapter VII

REINCARNATION

DISIMBODIMENT AND REIMBODIMENT

As stated in previous chapters the evolution of all Monads or life-units, is accomplished through experience gained during repeated embodiments in the various forms of nature.

To comprehend the doctrine of reincarnation, as man's reimbodiments are called, it is necessary to have an understanding of man's complex nature and what happens to its component parts when these have separated after death. We will therefore review briefly what has been said earlier on this subject.

It will be recalled that the core of man's being and the origin of his existence is a Ray of Divinity, a part of the Universal Consciousness. The different principles of man's nature are but different aspects of this Ray acting through different vehicles on various planes of Nature.

When the Ray is active on the outer plane it functions through a human, mental-physical vehicle, a human body with its brain and mind.

This vehicle acts as a "lens" that focuses a certain portion or aspect of the Ray and the combination of vehicle and Ray produce a sense of I-AM-I-ness or egoic consciousness which we call the Human Ego.

When the body dies, the Human Ego loses consciousness of the mental-physical plane, for the lens that focused it here is broken. It then enters on a series of experiences as related in Chapter VI—on "Death—Sleep—Birth" to which the following details are added.

After the second death the Human Ego is dependent on its mental-spiritual vehicle or spiritual body for *conscious* existence on the mental-spiritual plane. Without this vehicle there would be no lens to focus the consciousness on this plane, and the Human Ego would remain unconscious. While still embodied on the outer or mental-physical plane, the Ego lived in, and made use of, its spiritual body during its periods of aspiration and while

103

engaged in unselfish work. It is therefore already somewhat acquainted with this vehicle and its new life on the spiritual plane is a continuation of all that was high and noble in its former life. Since the mental-spiritual vehicle used before death is the same as that used after death, the Ego still retains its sense of identity and thinks of itself as the same I-AM-I as that of its earthly existence.

The blissful state into which the higher part of the Human Ego enters after the second death resembles that of a "day-dream," but it is much more vivid and absorbing than an ordinary experience of this kind.

During this time it lives over again all the happy experiences of its former life and carries to completion all the high aspirations, which remained unfulfilled during earth-life.

When, after ages, the store of spiritual energies which was built up during the Ego's former earth-life, has been exhausted and the last happy memory faded away, there is no longer any material left, pertaining to the former Human Ego on which the Ray may focus its attention. The Ray then withdraws to its focus on the next higher plane and the Human Ego loses consciousness of the mental-spiritual plane as it earlier lost consciousness of the mental-physical plane, when the Ray withdrew from the physical body.

When the Human Ego loses consciousness of the mental-spiritual plane, its essence passes into a latent state and remains dormant, like the life-germ of a seed, within the Ray as this withdraws to higher planes.

All the experiences and lessons learned during the past life of the Human Ego have been shared by the Ray and these are now added to other experiences gained in former existences. This is the sublimated essence of that human life and constitutes the permanent harvest gained by the Ray through its human vehicle.

The whole human being now exists "in plan" on the several planes of Nature, to which the various principles belong. Its highest aspect is a projection of the Ray and this is preserved in the Ray itself to which it has returned. The intermediate and lower parts exist "in plan" as "seeds," each on its own plane. Each such seed with its life-germ contains potentially all the tendencies and peculiarities of character, good or bad, impressed on it by the entity during its previous existence.

During the period between incarnations the highest portion of the Ray is active on its own plane, but when it has finished its cycle of activity there, it is ready to continue its evolution on the material plane. It then starts the Ego on its earthward journey down through the various intermediate planes, where the dormant "seeds" are awaiting the return of the vitalizing and unifying Ray. This journey has already been outlined in Chapter VI under the heading: "The Ray Re-enters Matter."

The Ray must now build a new mental-physical vehicle before it can re-establish contact with the material plane. It therefore projects the sleeping life-germ of the former human ego, a portion of the Ray itself, into material existence and this life-germ, animated by the Ray, is the vitalizing force of the human embryo as it begins to form according to the "plan" carried over from its previous existence.

The entity now coming into being is therefore in reality a portion or projection of the Ray itself and this projection of the Ray is the permanent part of the Human Ego. It is the same projection that produced the Human Ego of our last life and of all our former lives. It will be the same in our next life and in all our future ones, but as the ages pass it will be an ever greater portion of the Ray that will manifest through the gradually improving human constitution.

The mental-physical vehicle with the purely personal consciousness, the "lens" in other words, is new, but since it is produced by the same Ray and built around the same character, according to the "plan" carried over from the last incarnation, it is virtually an exact copy of its former self.

A human entity is therefore in its higher part a continuation, and in its lower part a reproduction of its former self.

EXISTENCE OF EGO CONTINUOUS
SELF-CONSCIOUSNESS OF EGO INTERMITTENT

The Higher or Reincarnating Ego exists continuously, and is continuously conscious on its own plane — the mental-spiritual.

The higher part of the Human Ego, which is a projection from the Reincarnating Ego, exists continuously, but is not self-conscious continuously. It is self-conscious on the outer plane when it functions through its mental-physical vehicle. In sleep it is unconscious of the outer plane, and it may be either completely unconscious or it may be partly conscious on the mental-spiritual plane.

After death it is first completely unconscious. After the second death it gradually awakens to a partial consciousness on the mental-spiritual plane, where it experiences the happy, post-mortem dream state previously referred to. In the case of a very gross or material nature, the Human Ego may remain completely unconscious between incarnations.

During the period of its blissful post-mortem dreams, the Human Ego still identifies itself with the human entity of its last incarnation. At the end of the dream-period it passes into complete unconsciousnes and loses all memory of its former identity. When the Human Ego loses consciousness of the mental-spiritual plane, it becomes completely inactive and remains dormant until, provided with a new physical body, it again becomes self-conscious on the outer plane.

The lower aspect of the Human Ego, or the Personal Ego, which during physical existence identified itself with the body, loses consciousness and fades out when its vehicle, the body. disintegrates.

The higher aspect of the Human Ego, then, exists continuously, part of the time self-conscious and active on the outer plane through a human vehicle; part of the time dormant, either unconscious or partly conscious on inner planes.

Between two incarnations there has been a break in the continuity of the vehicle and therefore, a break in the continuity of the Ego's self-consciousness, but no break in the continuity of it existence. The Ego bridges over the gap between two incarnations, by receding to inner planes, just as the life in the foliage of the perennial plant recedes into the root between two active growing-seasons.

In sleep there is also a break in the continuity of the lens, a temporary paralysis of the body, a "little death," and therefore a break in the continuity of the Ego's self-consciousness.

In the case of sleep we have definite proof that a break in the continuity of our consciousness does not mean a break in the continuity of our existence, for in the morning our consciousness re-establishes itself just as it was before we went to sleep. It recognizes its identity with its former self, for the brain retains the store of memories of its former experiences.

In sleep as in death, the Ego bridges over the gap between two conscious periods by receding to inner, invisible planes. No ordinary Human being has a clear understanding of what takes place during sleep, even though he passes through this experience every twenty-four hours.

If, in the case of sleep, when the body is still present and intact, we are unable to carry with us a complete picture of our experiences, during our absence from the physical plane, it should not surprise us that we are unable to recall our experiences in the period between incarnations, when we have no physical body to help us to regain consciousness on this plane and to re-establish our identity with our former self.

The ordinary human being can not cross the thresholds of sleep and death and retain his self-consciousness, because he has not yet learned to live in his mental-spiritual vehicle, which is necessary for this purpose. There are exceptions to the general rule, however, for there have always been and still are on earth, human beings, whose evolution has advanced far beyond that of the ordinary individual. These beings are the "Elder Brothers" of the human race, the Masters of Wisdom, sometimes referred to as Adepts or Mahatmas, a Sanskrit term which means "great soul."

The Adepts live, even while physically embodied, in their mental-spiritual vehicle, which exists independent of the physical body, and are therefore able to retain full self-consciousness even when the physical body is paralyzed in sleep or after it has disintegrated in death. It is this ability that has enabled them to enter the invisible planes of existence and bring back to their less evolved brothers a description of the experiences the Human Ego meets in these to us unknown states of consciousness.

The power possessed by the Adepts is the result of self-directed efforts continued through many lives. They have, even while embodied, lived more and more in their mental-spiritual vehicle, so that in their case the Human Ego has in reality been raised to and become one with the Higher Ego. They started out as ordinary human beings, but have by their continuous efforts hastened their evolution and accomplished in relatively few lives what it will take the average human being ages upon ages to accomplish.

Since the Adept can pass unhindered from plane to plane and return while retaining full self-consciousness, he recognizes the continuity of his existence and the identity of his Ego throughout all of these changes. Being fully conscious in the permanent part of his nature, where all his past lives are recorded, he is able to remember not only his last incarnation, but all his former existences.

Until we ourselves have raised our Human Ego into becoming one with the Higher Ego we shall be unable to retain our self-consciousness in crossing the thresholds of sleep and death and will therefore be unable to remember our past lives.

Every member of the whole human race, who does not deliberately choose evil, is destined in time, however, to evolve to the point where he too will have become one with his Higher Ego, and will then be able to recognize the continuity of his existence through all phases of life.

As *we* have definite proof that the interruption of self-consciousness in sleep is not a break in the continuity of our existence, which proof is furnished by our human consciousness when this re-establishes itself in its waiting body, so do *the Adepts* have definite proof that death of the physical body causes no break in the continuity of their existence, for they are continuously established in their mental-spiritual vehicle, which is unaffected by death.

Whether the ability to remember our past lives in our present stage of development would be a help or a hindrance in our evolution is a subject that will be discussed in connection with "Reincarnation and the Loss of Memory."

DUALITY—INDIVIDUALITY—PERSONALITY

Opposing Attractions.

By observing and examining the changing thoughts, feelings and interests within ourselves, as we know them from daily experience, we can differentiate between those belonging to the enduring and those belonging to the perishable side of our nature. Such analysis will show a duality of interests and tendencies within ourselves, and it will therefore be convenient to place these into two groups and for the time being consider man's nature as dual.

There is a side in our nature that recognizes its relationship with something greater than itself. It knows itself to be a member of a family, a community, a nation, and feels a strong attachment to these greater life-aggregates. It is the oneness of all life that produces this feeling within us and that forms the invisible, but unbreakable link between us and our fellow beings. It is through this side of our nature that we can understand and sympathize with other members of the human race, and it is this that arouses us to action when fellow beings are in distress.

But there is also another side in our nature that feels its separateness from others. It closes itself within its own shell and thus blinds itself to the sufferings and needs of others.

We feel intuitively that life should be harmonious and happy. We have visions of a better world, free from suffering and want and feel an urge to try to make it so. But there is another side in us that cares little how others have it, if we can only make ourselves happy.

There is something within that speaks to us as the Voice of Conscience, something that urges faithfulness in the performance of duties, even when these are unpleasant or monotonous. It is the tie that links us with others that makes us realize our duty towards them. But there is also a part in us that wants to evade its obligations when these are unpleasant or irksome.

There is a side in our nature with interests far beyond its own immediate sphere—something that wants to study the beauties of nature and the wonders of the stars, that ponders over the problems of life and the purpose of existence. And there is another side that identifies itself with the body and is chiefly concerned with its pleasures and comforts.

When we seek to determine what is characteristic of these two divergent currents within us, we note that in one case these are directed to our relations with our fellow men—to Nature and the Universe, while in the other case they are directed to the personal self and its little sphere of interests.

Between these two poles of its being, and constantly affected by their opposing attractions, stands the Human Ego, unconsciously yielding to, or consciously choosing one or the other.

The Individuality—A Higher Source Within Ourselves.

When we contemplate the stars and our mind is filled with the grandeur of the Universe and then think of our own little Personality, we realize the insignificance and impermanence of this, and we can see what an unimportant part it plays in the Universe.

That part of our nature which is thus able to stand aside and realize the impermanency of its vehicle is not a part of this vehicle. It belongs to the permanent side of our nature.

We are aware of our own existence as the I-AM-I or Human Ego, whose identity has remained unchanged during our entire life. We know that even in our waking state this Ego is something different from body, brain-mind, memory and feelings, for it can stand apart, observe, direct and dominate all these. It must therefore even now have an existence independent of all these shifting currents within, and if it does now, while embodied, it can also have this same independent existence after these changing aspects have disappeared in death.

When we feel the ties that bind us to our fellow men, it is because there is something of our fellow men within ourselves.

When we marvel at the wonders of the Universe and reach out, however feebly, towards the Infinite trying to form some conception of it, it is because there is something of the Universe and Infinitude within ourselves.

Thoughts cannot rise higher than their source any more than water can rise to a level higher than the reservoir from which it flows. Thoughts and intuitions that deal with interests far beyond our personal self cannot have their origin in that self. They must come from a source within us, which is akin to the subjects with which they deal, and that source is the Ray of Universal Consciousness acting in the Higher or Spiritual Mind. This higher side of our nature with its vehicles exists on planes above the mental-physical, independent of the physical body.

This higher source already exists within us and does not need to be "developed." It is the Human Ego that has to evolve to a higher state of consciousness so that it may rise into conscious union with its higher source.

This raising and refining of the Human Ego is accomplished by translating into deeds and words, here and now, while embodied, the higher impulses that reach us from within. Just as we became accustomed to, and learned to use our physical body by living in it and exercising its various functions, so must we become acquainted with and learn to use our mental-spiritual vehicle by thinking such thoughts and practicing such deeds as are akin to our Higher Nature and the plane on which it exists.

The characteristic of this higher plane is its greater proximity to the One Universal Life and hence existence on this plane results in a greater realization of the unity of all life and therefore in understanding, sympathy and love for all that lives.

On the spiritual plane our fellow men are in reality other aspects of the same Universal Life of which we are parts. Actions pertaining to this plane therefore always take into account the interests and welfare of others. When we sacrifice some personal interest or advantage in order to render a service to the common good; when we want to give rather than take; when we try to spread happiness and sunshine rather than seek happiness for ourselves alone, we, the human part of us, are for the time being, living in and making use of the more universal part of ourselves—our mental-spiritual vehicle. We are then true to our "other selves"—our fellow men, true to all—altruistic. We have entered the path that will lead to conscious union with our Higher Ego and conscious use of our mental-spiritual vehicle.

Since this is the vehicle in which our consciousness shall have to live after death, we can understand the importance of becoming accustomed to live in it while we are still embodied. We can also see why ethical teachings have always been so strongly emphasized by all great religious teachers. Such teachings have more than one purpose. They not only help us to live in harmony with our fellow men, but they also raise the individual into closer union with his Higher Ego and gradually prepare him to live consciously in his mental-spiritual vehicle.

That part of the Human Ego that responds to the higher of the two currents within, and takes an interest in the welfare of others and in matters greater than itself, is in reality an aspect of the Higher Ego. This, together with the higher foci of the Ray of Divinity, exists on planes higher than the mental-physical and is therefore unaffected by the death of the body. They constitute the altruistic pole of our nature and since they are not divided by death, they may be referred to collectively as the *Individuality* of the man.

Separateness Breeds Selfishness.

Just as there are people who live in the higher part of their nature and radiate friendliness and good will to all whom they contact, so there are others who seldom look beyond the interests of their personal self and take little or no interest in the welfare of others. They are aware of their existence as the Personal Ego only, and live and act in this capacity alone. They too have the altruistic pole in their nature, but seldom live in it. In their case the Personal Ego regards itself as the apex of the whole human constitution. It has become so absorbed in its own concerns that it turns away from its higher pole and even fails to recognize the existence of this side of its nature. The Personal Ego then makes the mistake of considering itself the one-and-only Ego, the whole of the Ego, when in reality it is only a minor part, a projection, of the Higher Ego captivated by the personal apparatus.

The mental-physical vehicle of an individual is of course separate from that of other individuals, and when the consciousness persistently turns in the direction of this vehicle, the Personal

Ego also acquires a sense of separateness; this Ego then becomes the dominating element of the human entity. There has been a reversal of polarity and the projection of the Ray of Consciousness has been deflected from its true course by the gross materiality of its focusing lens. It has been turned away from its altruistic pole with its ever expanding consciousness, in the opposite direction to a consciousness limited by its own personal self.

As long as the consciousnss is focused in the mental-physical vehicle, this sense of separateness will persist and the Personal Ego will fail to recognize its oneness with its Higher Ego and hence its oneness with its fellow men.

When we promote our own interests to the detriment of others, when we seek advantages at their expense, it is evident that we do not feel the tie that binds us to them.

When we are uncharitable or critical of others; when we feel arrogance and pride and seek in some way to establish our superiority over them, we are evidently not realizing our oneness with them. If we were, we would not push ourselves ahead at their expense; we would rather share with them any advantage that we might possess.

When we are indifferent to the hardships and sufferings of others, and are content as long as we ourselves are comfortable, it is because we feel separate from them and have failed mentally to put ourselves in their place.

If we have no interests beyond ourselves it is because we have shut ourselves off within the shell of our lower selfhood, the mental-physical vehicle.

Selfishness in all its forms can be traced directly back to this sense of separateness that exists in the Personal Ego-consciousness. It is this sense of separateness that makes so many turn their life's effort in the wrong direction by seeking to promote the interests of the personal self, while in so doing they lose the opportunity of becoming at home in their Higher Nature.

It is as though we were living in a cave that expands towards the light, but grows ever narrower towards the rear. When our attention is centered on our own interests alone, we are looking towards the rear of the cave and turn our back on the opening.

We stand in our own light and see only the small fraction of light that filters into the rear. If we turned in the opposite direction we would face the opening of the cave and a view that would keep expanding the farther we advance in this direction.

The Personality—A Temporary Vehicle.

The self-centered pole of our being includes the physical body, the model body, our self-centered desires, emotions and thoughts as well as the Personal Ego with its brain-mind and its day-to-day memories of current events stored in the brain. This group of qualities, taken collectively, constitute the self-centered pole of our nature and will in the following be referred to as the *Personality*.

The Personality came into active existence at birth or later. It remains as a unit during life, but breaks up into its component elements at death.

The material for the body comes from nature and returns to nature. Medical science tells us that every day millions of cells leave our bodies, while millions of new ones take their places. This change goes on constantly so that after a number of years— generally set at seven—we have a completely new body. A person who reaches the age of seventy years has therefore used and abandoned ten different physical bodies in his lifetime.

This fact is the basis for the Hindu metaphor that "Man stands in a flowing stream of matter." "Man" here refers to the Individuality, the permanent part, that remains unchanged, in spite of the constant change that takes place in his body.

The reason that the body retains its outward appearance **relatively** unchanged, except for such modifications as naturally accompany an advance in years, is that the model-body, on whose framework the physical cells arrange themselves, itself remains relatively unchanged. The model-body changes only as the character slowly changes. After death the model-body disintegrates just as the physical body does.

On account of the temporary nature of the Personality, it becomes evident that it would be very short-sighted to concentrate one's chief efforts on satisfying purely personal interests and concerns. The fruit of all such efforts will have to be left behind, while altruistic efforts will help us to gain and preserve consciousness in our mental-spiritual vehicle, which is unaffected by death.

The use of the term "Personality" to designate the vehicular part of man's nature is very appropriate, when we consider the origin of this word. It comes from the Latin word "persona," which means "mask." Persona in its turn is made up of two words, *per,* meaning "through" and *sona* "to sound, to speak." It was customary in dramatic performances of ancient times for the actors to wear masks during the entire play and copies of such masks were commonly used as motifs for decorations in theaters, until quite recent times, when they were replaced by modernistic decorations. The masks had openings for eyes and mouth through which the actor could see and speak, and thus constituted a sort of tool or mouthpiece by means of which the real actor, himself unseen, could play his part and make himself heard. It is in this sense that the Personality is both an instrument used by the Individuality for contact with the material plane, and a mask behind which the Individuality is hidden.

The Individuality Endures Continually.
The Personality a Recurring Manifestation.

If we consider the subject of Reincarnation without reference to details, it is the Individuality that is the real, the immortal part of man and it is this that incarnates, from life to life. The Individuality is the "cause", the Personality is the "effect." There would be no Personality if there were no Individuality to produce it. For each incarnation the Individuality builds for itself a new Personality, which then becomes the instrument through which the Individuality works on the material plane.

The character, the accumulated effect of all our past thoughts, deeds and experiences, is the governing factor in shaping, equipping and endowing the new Personality. We can alter our character while embodied, but since this character remains unchanged between incarnations, the new Personality will in all essentials be a reproduction of the Personality as it was at the end of our last incarnation.

The Personality is the "reflection in matter" of the Individuality; it is "Man, made in the image of God." But this image, this personal self, lives a life of its own during the waking state. It has free will and can choose between the prompting of its Higher Self and the impulses from the lower, animal self. When it chooses the latter course the "image" becomes disfigured as the reflection of the sun on the ruffled surface of a pond.

The Thread-Self—In Eastern Philosophy the Individuality is referred to as the "Thread-Self," to which the various Personalities are added as beads are threaded on a string. The Personalities differ, but the string that supports them, the Individuality, is the same through life after life.

The Actor and his Parts—There is another illustration that is often used to describe the relation between the Individuality and the Personality. An actor plays many different parts on the stage during his lifetime. One evening he may represent Hamlet, another time King Lear, or again, perhaps Othello. The audience sees these characters on the stage, but may not even know the off-stage name of the actor. The stage characters are temporary and unreal. King Lear does not know of Hamlet, who appeared the night before nor of Othello, who will appear tomorrow, but the real actor knows these parts and many more.

The various stage parts are "masks", put on for a day and then discarded, while the actor is the real entity behind the mask, just as the Personality, lasting but a lifetime, is the "mask" through which the Individuality expresses itself.

Just as the actor continues to exist after he has removed his stage-clothing, and disappeared from the theater, so does the Individuality continue to exist after it has dropped its "mask", the Personality and disappeared from this plane as it does both in sleep and death.

And as the actor after leaving the theater enters upon his normal off-stage life, so does the Individuality, after it is freed from the hampering limitations of the Personality, recede to inner, higher planes of consciousness where it now enters upon its real existence.

REINCARNATION AND THE LOSS OF MEMORY

Reincarnation—Part of Nature's Plan.

As will be seen from the foregoing the doctrine of Reincarnation in its broad outline is not difficult to understand. But there are naturally many questions that will arise in the mind of an inquirer to whom the subject is new. Since these have occurred to many others in the past they can be anticipated and the most common ones will be discussed below.

In seeking the answer to these questions we should bear in mind:

1) That there is a purpose in life:—the advancement of the soul towards ever higher states of being.
2) That there is a plan in Nature to accomplish this purpose: i.e. evolution by means of repeated experiences on the material plane.
3) That the time required for these experiences is provided for by an almost endless chain of embodiments in human form.
4) That Man is a part of Nature and therefore subject to the same laws that govern the rest of Nature. In experiencing repeated embodiments Man is simply following the law of periodicity or cyclic activity that we see operating everywhere in Nature.

Reincarnation, therefore, is not just a theory, but is an explanation of how one of Nature's most fundamental processes operates when it applies to Man. It should not be studied as an isolated event, but should be seen in its relation to other doctrines of the universal plan.

If we have lived before, why don't we remember it?

The question implies that since we do not remember, we could not have lived before; in other words it is based on the assumption that what we cannot remember, we could not have experienced.

A little thought will show that this assumption is not well founded, for we know of many experiences that we must have passed through and that we still do not remember.

For example the first few years of our lives are completely forgotten. Many, perhaps most, events of common occurrence are forgotten. In old age memory frequently fails the indvidual completely. Victims of amnesia may have whole years of their lives blotted out from their memory as already noted under the heading "Abnormal States of Consciousness."

In all these cases the fact that we have no memory of events, or even of whole years of our lives, does not prove that we did not live during these forgotten periods. If a human being, while living in the same physical body and using the same physical brain can forget whole years of its life it should not be surprising that a former existence, lived in another body and using another brain, is forgotten. But this brings us to another question:

Is an existence and experience that is forgotten of any value to the Individual?

We have forgotten the tumbles we took and the bruises we got when we took our first steps, but we have not forgotten how to walk. We have forgotten when we learned the alphabet but we have not forgotten how to read. Those who daily use mathematics in their work have usually forgotten the detailed steps they had to take in order to acquire this knowledge. But if later in life they have to teach mathematics to others they will find that they will have to go back over much forgotten ground and repeat the steps they had formerly taken. The steps had been forgotten, but the fruit of those steps had been used unwittingly in practical application of the knowledge. Is it not plain, then, that experiences, although forgotten, can have taught us valuable and permanent lessons?

More than one kind of Memory exists.

Memory includes two functions, storing up and bringing back or re-collecting. Inability to recollect does not necessarily mean that the memory is not there. Have we not often to our embarrassment been unable to recollect the name of an individual that we meet on the street, although we are positive that his name is known to us?

An event experienced in youth may be completely forgotten. A similar experience in later life may bring back memory of the earlier experience with vivid details. The memory was there, recorded, all the time but we were completely unaware of it.

When we speak of memory in general, we usually have in mind a record of events and details of every-day life. This record is stored in the brain, and no part of it can extend farther back than the early years of childhood, neither can it last beyond the life of the brain. But this is not the only kind of memory we have. Every event we have experienced, every act we have performed, every thought we have harbored, down to the smallest detail, is permanently recorded in the interior structure of the Higher or Reincarnating Ego. It is a memory stored in the Higher or superconscious Mind. This record is not accessible to the Human Ego during normal conditions of its earth life, however.

Our memory is like the filing system of a business concern. The memories stored in the brain are like the active records kept in the office files where they are handy for ready reference. But copies of all records are simultaneously stored in the vault, where they are kept under lock and key. There is one vault for each incarnation, but the Human Ego has lost the key to all except the office file.

Sometimes under abnormal conditions, a door to one of these memory-vaults may spring open, and knowledge, unknown to the individual in his normal state now becomes available to him.

An instance of this nature that has aroused much attention in California medical circles, is that of Pat Marquis, a Los Angeles boy, twelve years of age at the time referred to.* When in a semi-trance this boy reveals a remarkable knowledge of subjects of which he is totally ignorant in his ordinary state.

His super-normal powers were demonstrated one time before 150 physicians at the Hollywood Hospital and another time before 200 physicians at a meeting of the County Medical Association. He has also appeared before professors at the California Institute of Technology at Pasadena, etc.

When he enters the semi-trance state, he seems to become a different personality—an ancient Persian physician who calls himself "Napeji", a Parsi who lived in the Himalayas in the eleventh century A.D. Though normally he does not know a word of Persian, he writes in that language in reply to questions from

---

*The case is reviewed in the Theosophical Forum of October, 1936.

one of the investigating scientists Dr. Ameen Fareed, a Persian himself and a physician. Pat Marquis in the character of "Napeji," can also write in Persian when Dr. Fareed is not present. He sometimes uses an archaic form of that language. He correctly describes Persian customs, and his manners are those of a very dignified personage, not at all those of a lively youngster of twelve. When asked technical questions about the seat of consciousness in the brain, "Napeji" replied in the language of a trained anatomist. Dr. C. Reynolds, F.R.C.S., who presented Pat Marquis to the Hollywood committee of physicians, said, "How he could know anatomy and modern medical terms is beyond me. Certainly *the boy* knows nothing of them."

On another occasion, after being completely blindfolded, and in the trance required, the boy, now being in the personality of "Napeji," took up the foils in a fencing-bout with Mr. F. Cavens, an expert fencer. Pat Marquis knowns nothing of fencing, but apparently "Napeji" is a master of the art, for Mr. Cavens said, "I know of no master of fencing in the world who could do it. The fact that he can see my point coming and parry, and not be deceived in his parry with the point menacing him, and make the correct retreat is remarkable. I defy any great expert to do it. It would be utterly impossible for me." Sixty seconds after the fencing-bout "Napeji" had disappeared and the laughing, healthy schoolboy had resumed his normal personality.

Other instances dealing with such memory-storage of hidden knowledge could be cited. A most remarkable one is that of Edgar Cayce, whose life-story is told in a book called "There is a River," by Thomas Sugrue.* Although completely ignorant of medicine and anatomy in his normal state, Mr. Cayce, when in a self-imposed trance, was able to diagnose many ailments correctly and prescribe suitable remedies. Hundreds of complete case reports containing affidavits of the patients and reports by physicians exist.

Since it is impossible in a brief summary to do justice to the vast mount of material contained in this book it will be necessary to refer the interested reader to the book itself for details.

---

*Henry Holt and Co. N.Y., 1943.

Do not such facts as those related above show that there is a "reservoir" of memory, which is not ordinarily accessible, but can under certain conditions be "tapped" and then reveal a store of unsuspected knowledge?

But there is still another kind of memory, a sort of general or collective memory which is summarized in our character. It is an intuitive awareness of the memories held by the Reincarnating Ego, but with all details left out. It is the harvest of permanent value that we have retained from numberless experiences and lessons long since forgotten, just as the ability to walk and to read is the fruit of lessons from a forgotten past.

Although rooted in the past and lacking in details as to how it was acquired, this character-memory is so vital and dynamic that it strongly affects our life, our thoughts and acts here and now.

All the lessons and experiences of the past, although never recorded in our present brain as memories, are thus found to influence us every day of our lives.

If we have lived before, why are we unable to identify ourselves with specific individuals of former existences?

Because in each incarnation we have a new brain that had no part in the experiences of our former lives and therefore is a blank in regard to these. The Ray of Consciousness projected into this life and the Individuality is the same as in our former existences, but since the vehicle is new, the egoic consciousness resulting from this new partnership naturally identifies itself with its new vehicle, and since there is no tangible connection between the old and the new vehicles, the Human Ego is unable to identify its present self with that of its former incarnation. It therefore thinks of itself as a new "creation" whereas in reality it is a re-creation of its former self.

Is a future life, in which we are unable to identify ourselves with our present self, worth accepting as personal immortality?

The doctrine of Reincarnation does not teach personal immortality or a continuity of personal consciousness from one incarnation to the next. It teaches the continuity of Individuality and a periodic reproduction of the Personality. This reproduced Personality is in all particulars the Personality of the former incarnation with a new name. Why should not this teaching satisfy Man's hope for immortality or a continuity of existence? Let us go back in imagination to our last existence here on earth and since we are now what we were then, we must then have speculated on life and "our future existence". Suppose we had been told then that after a long period of rest we would again return to this earth and that we, in "that future time" (i.e. now), would be the same Personality as in that former incarnation, but that we should forget the details of that life and our former name. Suppose further that we had known then what we know now about our present existence—had known that the I-AM-I or Human Ego, that we identify ourselves with, would again be here continuing its existence where it had left off before and that this cycle would be repeated again and again until we reach some higher state of being—suppose we had known all this *then,* would it not have satisfied our hope for immortality and given us assurance of continuity of our existence? And if it had satisfied our hopes *then,* should not the same knowledge *now* give us assurance and hope for the future?

Suppose we did remember.

Suppose we were unable to blot out the memories of our former lives. We would then remember the details of not only our last life, but also of numberless other existences, and we would remember them in detail just as we do with this one.

Have we not enough to control the thoughts and memories of this one life? How could we manage if we had the memories of hundreds of incarnations streaming in on us? Instead of a single station on the radio, it would be as though we turned on all at once. Would not such a flood of memories, many perhaps of a sad or terrifying nature, overpower us and prevent us from attending to the duties of this life and the all-important present moment? Do we not waste enough time now in useless thought about unimportant details of this present life?

Our memories would, of course, not all be unhappy. There would be many happy ones and we would enjoy recalling these, but it should not be forgotten, that if our happy memories returned to us, the sad ones would also come back, and how would we know that the happy memories would outweigh the sad ones?

As we look back on history we see civilizations rise, reach a climax and then decay, often wiped out by hordes of barbarians and followed by periods of ignorance and spiritual and intellectual darkness. We lived during all these periods and took part in all those events. If we look upon some of the more primitive races of humanity today and note their way of life and then realize that we too in some distant past were members of just such races and lived and acted as they now do, then it must occur to us, that our own record must contain many discreditable episodes, that we too must have taken part in many tragic events, must have had many harrowing experiences. Is it not a fact that people who have experienced some tragic event often receive therefrom such a shock, such a lasting impression, that they are unable to shake it off, for the remainder of their lives, and that the memory of the tragedy henceforth exerts a paralyzing effect on all their activities? How could we attend to present day duties if we were haunted by not one, but many such memories from numberless incarnations in the past?

Let us hope that all such scores have been balanced during many intervening incarnations. But suppose that there still remained some unsettled score, that was bound to return to us, perhaps in the form of some accident. Would not the anticipation of this event have such a depressing psychological effect that both our mental and physical activities would be seriously retarded thereby?

Does it not appear, then, on deeper thought, as a merciful arrangement that the memories of the past are shut off from our view, and that we are given a new brain, and, unhampered by the "ghosts" of the past, can start this life with a clean slate?

Suppose we could identify our former personalities.

Seen from another angle the notion that we should remember our past lives takes on an aspect that borders on the ridiculous.

If we remembered our past lives, as we do this, we should be able to identify ourselves with our former Personalities. We would also remember our friends and enemies of those days and they would remember us. This would be true not only of our last life, but also of countless preceding ones. We would of course have many friends to meet, but we would also have many enemies, and many old scores to be settled. Every time we met a person we would be asking ourselves: "How much do I owe this man— what is he going to dun me for?" We would be running down side streets trying to dodge creditors only to run into other ones, for all our financial transactions and transgressions would of course also be remembered.

If we carry the picture a little farther in imagination, we can see, that if all our memories were preserved, this would be a very uncomfortable world to live in.

Have we not got along very nicely so far without this knowledge and is not life made easier by its absence, for, without it, we are free to look upon every person we meet as a former friend or a potential friend? If it is an old friend we will soon be drawn towards each other, for "the friends I seek are seeking me" as Walt Whitman puts it.

If, on the other hand, it happens to be an old enemy, the sooner we make him into a friend, the better for both of us, and the less we know about former disagreements, the easier the transformation can be made.

What could be gained by knowing who we were in former incarnations?

If it happened to be one of the great characters of history of course it would be pleasing to our vanity, and those who profess to remember their past incarnations generally claim to have been some great ruler or military leader, princess or other famous individual of the past. There is hardly a mental institution that does not have at least one Napoleon, sometimes several, and there are not a few Joan of Arcs floating around. Occasionally some- one modestly announces that he is an incarnation of Jesus.

The only difficulty with these claims is that no ordinary hu- man being can remember his past lives in detail until he has reached union with his Higher Ego and then he is no longer an ordinary human being. We are told that the Masters of Wisdom, who have attained this union, do remember their past lives, but that those who do, never lay claim to this power publicly. Individuals who make such claims are subject to self-deception, which may be entertained honestly, but it is nevertheless deception or delusion.

Could we gain anything by knowing who we were in a past incarnation, something that would outweigh the disadvantages of this knowledge?

Would our present life have taken a different direction if we had known? We would still have had the same character, the same collective memory of all our past lives, and if we had the same character, would we not eventually have ended up in about the same place whether we did or did not recognize our past personalities?

Evolution and loss of Memory.

The purpose of life is advancement towards higher states of being and the means to this end is experience gained during repeated existences. To get the greatest benefit from our existence here it is necessary that our whole nature should be untrammeled and free to concentrate its full attention on its duties here, and this would be impossible if our minds were littered with all kinds of memory-debris from former existences. The only way we can take full advantage of the opportunities offered by a new life is to start it with a mind free from such mental debris and this is just what Nature provides for by giving us a new body and a new brain.

The Personality is our vehicle for the time being, but when it has served its purpose it is cast aside as an empty shell. The kernel is in the character and in the permanent part of the Human Ego.

The ancient Greeks, who still retained some of the Wisdom Teachings, realized that before the Soul returned to earth for another incarnation, all memories of former existences had to be blotted out. They presented the idea symbolically by teaching that the Soul, in its descent from higher spheres, and before entering material existence had to cross Lethe, "the river of forgetfulness" and drink of its waters. This blotted out memory of not only past incarnations but also of the blissful dream-state between incarnations and the Soul's knowledge of its divine origin. Unless such forgetfulness intervened the detailed memories of past existences would retard our progress, and a constant longing for the peace and bliss that are experienced in higher states of being, might make us impractical day-dreamers, instead of active individuals engaged in bringing that peace and bliss into practical life right here on earth.

Record kept in Higher Ego.

While detailed memories are blotted out from the consciousness of the Human Ego, a perfect record of these is preserved in the permanent part of the Higher Ego. It is by looking into this record that the Human Ego, under the special conditions that prevail at death and just before birth, is able to get the "panoramic vision" of its past and future life.

It is because of this record that the Higher Ego sees that the future is but the outcome of the past, and recognizes the justice of all that is to come to its agent, the Human Ego, in its next incarnation, and it is because the Human Ego intuitively senses this super-conscious knowledge, that the average human being accepts the often lowly station in life that has been assigned to him by what looks like "Blind Fate."

For is it not a remarkable fact that the vast majority of men take up the burden of life and carry it patiently to its end, in spite of the *apparent* injustice under which most of them suffer?

A Solemn Ordeal.

Sometime in the future when the Human Ego has become one with the Higher Ego, the complete record of all its former lives will be unrolled before its inner vision. The Masters of Wisdom who have passed through this experience tell us that in almost every case this retrospective view is taken with a feeling of extreme sadness and regret. An ordinary human being could not stand the shock—it might bring insanity or death, but it is a necessary step in our evolution and must sooner or later be taken by all.

No one who has passed through this solemn ordeal would talk flippantly about remembering past incarnations, but once the vision had been seen, would be glad to shut the door on the past and turn instead to the future.

The fact that we do not remember our past lives, then, is no proof that we did not live those lives, and it is a most merciful arrangement and best suited for our unhampered growth and evolution.

Why does the population of the Earth vary?

How can the variation in the Earth's population be explained when the Ancient Wisdom teaches that it is the same souls that incarnate over and over again and no new souls are "created" and no old ones annihilated? Under these conditions, should not the population of the Earth remain constant?

The number of human souls that have their "home" on this Earth is constant, but out of this vast number only a small fraction is incarnated in physical bodies at any one time. The far greater portion exists on inner, spiritual planes of being.

The idea might be explained by the following illustration: Let us assume that a city with fixed limits has a large hall in its center for the transaction of business. The population inside the city limits is fixed and constant, but the number of visitors in the hall varies from time to time; a greater number in the hall means a smaller number outside and vice versa. Similarly an increase or decrease in the Earth's population means a corresponding decrease or increase in the number of ex-carnate entities, but no change in the sum-total of entities that belong to the Earth.

Why should the Ego return to this Earth? Why not to some other planet?

Because the Universe is a "School of Experience" and this Earth is the "class-room" that corresponds most closely to our stage of development. It is therefore the place most suited for us and the place where we can learn most quickly and easily.

We must pass through all experiences, learn all lessons on our march towards perfection, and even if we could escape to another planet or state of consciousness, we still would have to learn the lessons that we failed to learn here and then under possibly less favorable circumstances.

A little boy upon his return after his first day at school was asked how he had made out, to which he answered: "Not very well. I have to go back again tomorrow." Before we realize the magnitude of the task ahead of us, we too may think that we should graduate in one day, but as mother the next day takes Junior back to the same school, where he is beginning to get acquainted, so also does Mother Nature take us back to the school that we are most acquainted with until we are ready to graduate.

But there is still another reason why we should return just to *this* Earth instead of going elsewhere. It is that this Earth is the field in which we sowed our seeds of thoughts and acts in former lives and just as a farmer reaps his harvest in the field where he planted it, so we too must come back here and reap our harvest where we did our planting.

How shall we find our friends and loved ones in another life?

The same way that we found them this time. We came into a family circle that brought us loving parents and perhaps brothers and sisters, and in our next life we will again be associated with them, perhaps not in exactly the same relationship, but as close as our mutual attraction will draw us.

Our friends outside the family circle we will meet in diverse ways, just as we did this time. We sometimes hear a person say, after meeting a stranger: "It seems to me as if I had known that person all my life." The stranger may turn out to be someone with whom we have many interests in common and perhaps form a life-long friendship. It is an old friend with whom we have renewed a tie.

Others we meet seem antagonistic to us and a similar feeling wells up within ourselves towards them. It is an old antagonist we face again, someone that we perhaps have wronged, or that may have wronged us. All scores must be settled; balance and harmony must be restored wherever they have been disturbed says the Ancient Wisdom. Ill feeling must be replaced by good will for "hatred ceases not with hatred; hatred ceases with love." We must try to understand this individual and see the good in him, for it is there, and the sooner we begin the task the better, for he will cross our path again and again until we have learned to understand each other.

Alternating cycles of activity and rest promote Man's evolution.

If our evolution requires so much time, would it not be better if we remained alive continuously, rather than die and be re-born?

We spend one third of every twenty-four hours in sleep and we do not consider this a waste of time, for we recognize the benefits that come to us from this interruption in our physical activities. What seems to us an insurmountable task, when we are exhausted after a day's labor, may be easily accomplished after a night's refreshing sleep. A problem that we could not solve with a tired, dull brain may easily yield to a fresh attack the next morning. If we tried to keep active twenty-four hours day after day we would gradually accomplish less and less and eventually have a physical and nervous collapse.

On the greater time-scale, too, the body wears out and the consciousness grows weary. It must rest and refresh itself and, just as Nature, with her wise arrangement of day and night, practically compels us, for our own benefit and protection, to take a daily rest, so also, and for the same reason, does she compel man to take the longer rest of death, during which he renews his vitality by an existence on inner, spiritual planes.

And there are other benefits made possible through these cyclic interruptions and resumptions of our physical existence.

We cannot wear the same suit of clothes from infancy to old age; if it did not wear out, it would be outgrown. The suit that fits a child would be a misfit on an adult and would hamper his actions. The adult must have a new suit that fits his size and is better adapted for his enlarged activities.

Likewise an individual may outgrow his environment and Nature's method of "giving him a new suit" or placing him in a new set of circumstances, is by the method of re-incarnation.

A continuous existence, with small gradual changes would not give the same chance for improvement as a complete change. When a house is outmoded a few alterations here and there will not produce a modern dwelling — this requires the tearing down of the old structure, and, using some of the old material and some new, rebuilding to a new and better plan.

Nature constantly repeats her processes. The trees and plants have their seasonal activity in spring and summer and their rest-period in fall and winter. This break of continuity is a benefit, not only to the trees and plants, but also to the farmer, who may have neglected to control the weeds in his fields. When the winter frost comes the weeds are killed, and when spring follows, the farmer has a new chance to watch his crop and uproot the weeds, while they are still young and tender.

We human beings are parts of Nature and subject to its laws. We too know how hard it is to uproot or overcome a habit or a fault that has been allowed to grow during a lifetime, and what an advantage it is if this work of forming good habits and molding noble characters can be started in childhood or in early youth.

Nature offers us this chance of making a new start with each new birth into physical existence.

DISPROPORTIONATE PERIODS OF TIME

Why is the period between incarnations so long as compared to incarnated existence? We human beings are parts of something far greater than our human selves, and during the interval between earthlives, while the Human Ego is experiencing its blissful post-mortem dreams, or rests unconscious waiting for its next incarnation, this higher side of our nature is pursuing its own evolution in spheres far above that where the Human Ego dwells. The time-periods required for these experiences are proportionately as much greater than those of incarnated existence as the higher principles within us are greater than our human consciousness.

The time of our incarnated existence is therefore only a fraction of a greater time-cycle, a recurring interlude between two much longer periods, during which the Ray is active on spiritual planes.

As "daytime to the body is night-time to the soul," so is the inner God deprived of its freedom of action during incarnated existence. But death breaks the bond with the lower part of the human constitution, and this leaves the higher principles free to return to their respective planes of origin. As "the night time of the body is the daytime of the soul," so the higher principles now become fully active on their own planes and begin what is to them their real existence. It is these activities that require such immense time periods, that the duration of incarnated existence seems insignificant in comparison.

WHY DOES THE INNER GOD EVER DESCEND TO LOWER PLANES OF BEING?

If man's Inner God has its real existence on spiritual planes far above the physical, why does it ever have any connection with this material plane?

Because Nature, visible and invisible, is one vast organism of interdependent entities in which all life-units mutually aid each other in their evolution. The more highly evolved aid those less evolved, while at the same time this experience promotes their own evolution. Thus man's Inner God, his Father in Heaven, is constantly seeking to help and raise its "child," the human being, by radiating its spiritualizing influence into man's consciousness.

During incarnated life the Inner God voluntarily limits its own freedom and "steps down" its rate of activity to the plane where the Human Ego functions. It is like a bit of slow-motion in the middle of a rapidly moving film, which the less evolved Human Ego is able to profit by. It is during this time that the Human Ego has its opportunity for advancement.

But at the same time that the Human Ego is benefited the Inner God also gains experiences which it could not obtain any other way. It is like the relationship between parents and children. The child benefits from the aid it receives, but, unknown to itself, it also teaches lessons to its parents, which the parents can learn in no other way. They have to give up much of their freedom and in a sense sacrifice themselves for the protection and welfare of the child, but this in turn brings out sympathy, understanding, compassion, thus promoting the evolution of the spiritual side of their nature.

Plotinus (205-270 A.D.), the great philosopher of the Neo-Platonic school, in a wonderful word-picture gives us the reason for the soul's descent into matter and the benefits it receives therefrom, and shows that the soul must experience material life, the better to appreciate its spiritual existence.

Plotinus' statement is quoted below. Within the brackets is the writer's interpretation of certain terms used.

The soul, though of divine origin, and proceeding from the region on high, becomes merged in the dark receptacle of the body, and being naturally a posterior god [a god in the making], it descends hither through certain voluntary inclination, for the sake of power and of adorning inferior concerns [to add meaning and dignity to material life]. By this means it receives a knowledge of its latent powers, and exhibits a variety of operations peculiar to its nature, which by perpetually abiding in an incorporeal habit, [a disimbodied state], and never proceeding into energy [active use of latent powers], would have been bestowed in vain . . . . Through an abundance of desire the soul becomes profoundly merged into matter, and no longer totally abides with the universal soul. Yet our souls are able alternately to rise from hence, carrying back with them an experience of what they have known and suffered in their fallen [embodied] state; and whence they will learn how blessed it is to abide in the intelligible [spiritual] world, and by a comparison, as it were, of contraries will more plainly perceive the excellence of a superior state. For the experience of evil produces a clearer knowledge of good. This is accomplished in our souls according to the circulations of time [cyclic incarnations], in which a conversion takes place from subordinate to more exalted natures [the human evolves into the divine].

THE SYMBOLISM OF THE CRUCIFIXION

The period of incarnation, while the Inner God is linked with and illumines the intermediate and lower parts of the human being, is in a sense a "crucifixion" of the Inner God on the "cross of matter" and it is this that has given rise to the story of the crucifixion of Christ.

In this story, which should be taken symbolically rather than literally, the human body and the Personal Ego is "the cross of matter," the "burden," which the Inner God has voluntarily taken upon itself to carry, and to which it is "nailed" during the period of incarnation.

In the symbolism of the robbers crucified with Christ, the repentant one to whom Christ is quoted as saying: "Today shalt thou be with me in paradise," (*St. Luke* XXIII, 43), represents that part of the Human Ego that during life has aspired upwards. This is the higher aspect of the Human Ego, which, after the second death, enters the blissful post-mortem dream-state. The un-regenerate tendencies of Man's lower nature are represented by the other robber.

SPECIAL CASES

An Actual Memory of a Former Life.

An ordinary individual can not under normal conditions re-member his past lives for reasons that have already been explained. Genuine exceptions to this rule are few, but once in a while we hear of someone who remembers a former life with details that are subject to verification.

One such case was reported in the "American Weekly" section of the San Francisco *Examiner* of Dec. 1, 1937. This report, which is accompanied by photographs, and covers more than two pages, newspaper size, is submitted by a committee of three prominent citizens of Delhi, India, who investigated the case. The head of the committee was the managing director of the leading newspaper of Delhi. With him served a leader of the National Congress party of India and a close associate of Mohandas Gandhi, also one of the leading attorneys of Delhi (names given).

The committee took all possible care to check all data that came to their attention. From this report, which is very complete, and gives names, addresses and dates, we learn that a little girl in

Delhi, 11 years old at the time of the report, began talking at the age of four to her parents about things she remembered from her former life, which she said was spent in Muttra, a city 90 miles from Delhi.

When she grew older she said that she had been married in Muttra, gave the name of her husband and said that he was a cloth merchant. She said her former body died at the age of 23 years, one year before she, the present child of eleven, was born. In the former life she had a daughter and a son. She gave the address of the former store, described details of the house as well as a temple in the neighborhood and streets and roads leading to her former home. She said that there was a well in one corner of the yard, and that in one room she had hidden some money under the floor.

The former husband in Muttra was reached by correspondence and he verified the information given as substantially correct. Later the husband with a son — the child of the deceased woman whose soul is now embodied in the eleven year old girl — traveled to Delhi to meet the girl, who immediately recognized her former husband. Questions that only his former wife could answer were put to her by the husband and were answered correctly. The husband became fully convinced that it was the same soul as of his first wife.

A man, whom she had not seen before, came to visit her and asked her if she knew him. She answered correctly that he was the younger cousin of her former husband.

The committee then took the girl by train to the city of Muttra, her former hometown.

Getting off the train she recognized an older brother of her former husband in a small crowd on the station platform.

Leaving the railroad station she was placed in the front seat of a carriage and told to direct the driver to her old house. She showed the way without difficulty, commenting that the road was not tarred before, recognizing buildings along the road and correctly answering questions regarding these, pointed out new buildings and finally directed the carriage to stop at a lane on which the old house was located. The color of the house had been changed, but she located it without much difficulty. She pointed out the room where she used to live and showed that she was very familiar with every nook and corner of the house.

She asked to be taken to her other house (for she had lived in two places). She alone led the party there and later recognized her second house also without any difficulty. It was here that she had hidden the money and where the well was supposed to be located.

This was the place she said, where she had spent the major portion of her former life and she entered the house as if she were still its mistress.

Asked to point out the well she used to tell about in Delhi, she ran to the small courtyard in the house and was very much perturbed not to find any well there, but pointing to a certain corner said confidently: "the well was here." The removal of a stone exposed the well, which had been closed some years earlier.

When asked about her so-called treasure she led the company to her former room, and, pointing to one spot in a corner, said that the money was hidden under that spot. The floor was opened and a receptacle used for keeping valuables under ground was found, but there was no money. The girl insisted that the money must be there, but it could not be found. Later it was learned that the money had been taken out by her former husband after the death of his former wife.

While she was in Delhi she had very little recollection of her parents, in her previous life, but when she was taken to her "parents'" house in a neighboring street in Muttra she not only recognized it, but was also able to identify her old "father" and "mother" in a crowd of more than fifty persons.

The son born to her in her former life whose birth was the indirect cause of her death, was now twelve years old, a year older than herself, yet she felt a mother's affection for him. She felt closer ties of relationship with this son and her former husband, than she did with members of her new family, and was heartbroken when she had to leave the old setting and return to Delhi.

The report ends with a sworn statement by the cousin of the former husband, recording a series of questions asked by him and answers given by the girl. As a result of this interview the cousin became convinced that the girl was his own relative "now personating in another body."

Here, then, is a case, as well authenticated as any reasonable investigator could expect, telling of a soul, an Ego, that remembers its former life and gives proof of doing so. The case is abnormal, for reincarnation took place almost immediately after death. If it had been normal there would have been an interval of hundreds or thousands of years between incarnations, and we would never have heard of it, for no detailed memories could have bridged such a gap. It is due to its abnormality that this case can serve as an outward visible demonstration that reincarnation is a reality.

What caused this abnormality?

Why it happened to just to this soul may be easier to understand after studying Ch. VIII "Karma."

How it happened is difficult to explain. Possibly an unusually strong attachment to her loved ones together with the fact that her lifespan was broken off prematurely, was sufficient to overcome the natural tendency to glide into the normal post-mortem states and draw her back to incarnation. There might be some material for explanation of the transfer of memory in the fact that the model body and psychologic energies of the personal nature, did not have time to scatter completely. One can only speculate. It would require the insight and wisdom of a Master to give a full explanation.

It is a sad case and very unfortunate for the soul that has to experience it, for it finds itself placed between conflicting interests and duties that exert their pull in different directions. It shows the complications that might arise and perplex us if we all were to remember our past lives, and it shows how fortunate it is for us that we are not able to do so.

The Adepts know by experience.

To those who have succeeded in raising their Human Ego into conscious union with their Higher Ego, reincarnation is not only a working hypothesis, it is a demonstrated fact, for they have undergone this experience in full possession of their egoic consciousness.

It is their teaching on this subject that H. P. Blavatsky and her successors have made available to us in various Theosophical works.

The inquirer, who wishes to pursue the study of this subject further, is referred especially to *The Esoteric Tradition* by G. de Purucker, chapters on "Reimbodiment as Taught through the Ages" and "How Man is Born and Reborn."

TRANSMIGRATION
MISUNDERSTOOD AND TRUE

Popular Misinformation on the Subject.

One reason why the doctrine of reincarnation has met with so much opposition is the fact that the uninformed have taken it to mean the re-birth of the human soul into an animal body.

This popular misconception, which has existed for ages, is very general and has resulted in much unwarranted criticism and much ridicule being directed against the true teaching. Thus it is not uncommon, when the word reincarnation is mentioned, to hear someone burst into a roar of laughter and exclaim: "I don't want to come back a cat." The joke that seems so amusing is based on the ignorance of the critic and has no application to teachings of the Ancient Wisdom on this subject. Those definitely state that once the Monad has evolved to the human stage it can not embody itself in anything sub-human. The lesser can not contain the greater and an animal brain and mentality is as incapable of accommodating a human consciousness as a pint measure is incapable of holding a gallon of liquid. Furthermore the march of evolution is forward and upward and there would be no inducement for the Monad to step down to a lower stage, even if it could do so.

Another factor that has contributed to the misunderstanding of this subject is the confusion that exists in regard to the terms used to denote the re-birth of the human soul.

There are, says Dr. G. de Purucker in his *Esoteric Tradition*

(p. 594), different aspects of the general doctrine of Reimbodiment designated by the following terms:

>Pre-existence
>Rebirth
>Palingenesis
>Transmigration
>Metempsychosis
>Reincarnation
>Metensomatosis

Each of these has a specific meaning, but encyclopedias and dictionaries treat them more or less as synonyms and generally associate them all with the idea of rebirth into animal bodies.

Of these terms reincarnation is relatively new, being popularized largely through the writings of H. P. Blavatsky and her followers in the last century. The common terms in earlier literature are pre-existence, metempsychosis or transmigration.

As already explained the term reincarnation refers to embodiments in vehicles of flesh. The term therefore applies properly to reimbodiments of Human Egos in human bodies, but should never be interpreted to mean the rebirth of Human Egos in animal bodies.

Exoteric and Esoteric Teachings.

At this point the question naturally arises: How could this erroneous idea arise and become so widespread if it is contrary to the Ancient Wisdom teaching on the subject?

There are many factors that have combined to produce this result. Perhaps the most important is the dual method of teaching used by the ancients and outlined below.

The Ancient Wisdom contains many teachings regarding the hidden forces of Nature, which, if used selfishly could produce incalculable harm. For this reason it would have been dangerous to give out all the teachings openly and to anyone. The inner, deeper teachings were therefore given only to those who after years of training and many severe tests had been found trustworthy, and who had the necessary background to understand them. Those who received these teachings had to pledge themselves to secrecy and it is therefore small wonder that only fragments of these teachings have survived to our day.

But the masses, who were unable or unwilling to pass the required tests, or who were incapable of grasping the deeper teachings, also needed enlightenment and something to guide their actions by. For their benefit the inner teachings were hinted at in fables or parables or presented in a veiled form as dramatic performances in which ideas were represented by persons and qualities in human nature symbolized by various animals.

This dual method of teaching was general among the ancients. It was used in the temples and Mystery Schools, by Pythagoras, Plato and all great masters. That Jesus used it we know for he is quoted as saying to his disciples: "Unto you it is given to know the mysteries of the kingdom of God: but to others in parables; that seeing they might not see, and hearing they might not understand." —*Luke* VIII, 10.

The Qabbalah or Kabala is the secret doctrine of the Jews. In its main book, the "Zohar," we find a statement to the effect that the man who understands the Hebrew Bible in its literal meaning is a fool. (quoted in *The Esoteric Tradition,* p. 62).

Maimonides, one of the greatest Jewish Rabbis of the Middle Ages writes: "We should never take literally what is written in the book of the creation . . . . Taken literally that work contains the most absurd and far fetched ideas of the Divine." (quoted in *The Esoteric Tradition,* p. 62).

Origen, the Alexandrian scholar and church father, who lived during the second and third centuries, A.D. writes:

> In Egypt, the philosophers have a most noble and secret Wisdom concerning the nature of the Divine, which Wisdom is disclosed to the people only under the garment of allegories and fables . . . . All the Eastern nations—The Persians, the Indians, the Syrians — conceal secret mysteries under the cover of religious fables and allegories; the truly wise [the initiated] of all nations understand the meaning of these; but the uninstructed multitudes see the symbols only and the covering garment.—(Origen: *Contra Celsum,* Bk. I Chap. xii, quoted in *The Esoteric Tradition,* p. 61-2).

Fabre d'Olivet, (1768-1825) the French scholar and author of *Examinations of the Golden Verses of Pythagoras* writes (p. 275):

It is well known that all of the eminent men, as many among the ancients as among the moderns, all the savants commendable for their labours or their learning, are agreed in regarding the precepts of Pythagoras as symbolical, that is, as containing figuratively, a very different meaning from that which they would seem to offer literally. It was the custom of the Egyptian priests from whom he had imbibed them, to conceal their doctrine beneath an outer covering of parables and allegories.

d'Olivet gives many references to substantiate this statement.

It is this dual method of teaching together with the fact that the hidden inner meaning has been lost, while the outer garment, the symbols and fables have remained, that has given rise to the widespread popular misunderstanding of transmigration, metempsychosis and reincarnation.

The highest authorities reject transmigration into animals.

We do have evidence, however, that those who knew the true teachings, rejected the erroneous notion that the human soul ever transmigrates through the lower kingdoms of Nature, as will be seen by the following extracts from the writings of some of the greatest leaders of thought of antiquity.

One such leader of thought was Pythagoras. He had travelled in Egypt, Chaldea, Persia and India, and was initiated in the Temples and Mystery Schools of these countries. He was a reformer of Orphism, an earlier Greek cult.

He founded a School at Krotona in Italy, where he gave his secret teachings to specially trained and pledged candidates. Plato was a student in this school and gives credit to Pythagoras for the best of his doctrines. The Gnostic, the Stoic and the Neo-Platonic systems of thought were all influenced by the teachings of Pythagoras and his follower Plato.

The Neo-Platonists, according to G. de Purucker,[*] taught more

---

[*]*Fundamentals of the Esoteric Philosophy*, p. 56.

or less openly what had been the secret teachings of Pythagoras and Plato. One of the Neo-Platonists, Hierocles (410-476 A.D.), who enjoyed such a high reputation for character and learning that he was called a second Plato, is the author of a Commentary on "The Golden Verses of Pythagoras" which has been preserved to our day.

In his closing remarks of this Commentary Hierocles says:

> This is the Commentary we have thought fit to make on these Golden Verses; and that may be called a Summary, neither too prolix nor too succinct, of the Doctrine of Pythagoras.*

This commentary is the source of most of our knowledge regarding the Pythagorean philosophy.

In commenting on verses LII and LIII, and referring to the experiences of the soul after death, including the idea of transmigration into animals, Hierocles writes:

> . . . If through shameful ignorance of the immortality pertaining to our soul, a man should persuade himself that his soul dies with his body, he expects . . . what can never happen; in like manner he who expects that after his death he shall put on the body of a beast, and become an animal without reason, because of his vices, or a plant because of his dullness and stupidity — such a man, I say, acting quite contrary to those who transform the essence of man into one of the superior beings, and precipitating it into one of the inferior substances, is infinitely deceived, and absolutely ignorant of the essential form of our soul, which can never change, for being and continuing always man, it is only said to become God or beast by virtue or vice, though by its nature it cannot be either the one or the other, but only by its resemblance to the one or the other.**

---

*Quoted from *The Commentaries of Hierocles on the Golden Verses of Pythagoras in Dacier's Life of Pythagoras, with his Symbols and Golden Verses, together with the Life of Hierocles and his Commentaries upon the Verses* p. 388 (London, 1707).

**Ibid. pp. 334f.

Does not this say first that the soul survives death and then that transmigration into animals would be a reversal of the current of evolution sending the soul backwards into something inferior instead of forward to something superior and therefore contrary to the true teaching? Does it not say that when man is called "a god" or "a beast" it is a figurative expression which only the ignorant would take in a literal sense?

If we turn to the teachings of ancient Egypt we find that they also reject the popular misconception of transmigration into animals.

In Chapter X, of *The Pymander*, one of the Hermetic books, Hermes informs his disciple of the punishment that befalls the impious soul after death. Speaking of the complaints and lamentations of the soul over its sufferings, Hermes says:

> These are the voices of the soul being punished, not as the many suppose . . . that a soul going forth from the body becomes a wild beast, which is a very great error.*

In another paragraph of the same chapter, Hermes tells his disciple that:

> . . . the impious soul remains in its own proper essence, being self-punished through its efforts to effect entrance in another earthly—that is, human—body. For no other kind of body can be the dwelling-place of a human soul, which can never descend into the frame of an irrational animal. Divine law preserves the human soul from such a wrong.**

In India we find the same popular misconception regarding transmigration as elsewhere. That this is not accepted literally by those who know, is seen by a statement made by a Brahman to

---

* Quoted from *The Theological and Philosophical works of Hermes Trismegistus* Part I *Poemandres* (*Pymander* Ch. X, 20) by John David Chambers, of Oriel College, Oxford, Edinburgh, MDCCCLXXXII (1882) page 65.

**Louis Ménard, *Hermès Trismégiste* I, x, quoted in Walker's *Reincarnation* p. 333. (The same quotation is found in *The Pymander* by J. D. Chambers, p. 63).

E. D. Walker, author of *Reincarnation, a Study of Forgotten Truth.* The Brahman says (p. 270):

> The whole question of rebirths rests upon the right understanding of what it is that is born again . . . . The essential characteristic of humanity cannot possibly exist in an animal form, for otherwise it cannot be essential to humanity . . . . It must be insisted that the true human ego in no sense migrates from a human body to an animal body, although those principles which lie below the plane of self-consciousness may do so. And in this sense alone is transmigration accepted by Esoteric Science.

Origen, the great third century Christian Father, accepted the doctrine of reincarnation, but rejected that of transmigration into animals. In his work *On First Principles* Bk. I, Ch. VIII, Sec. 4, he writes:

> We think that those views are by no means to be admitted, which some are wont unnecessarily to advance and maintain, viz. that souls descend to such a pitch of abasement that they forget their rational nature and dignity, and sink into the condition of irrational animals, either large or small . . . . All of which assertions we not only do not receive, but, as being contrary to our belief, we refute and reject.*

Here we have statements by the highest authorities, all of them rejecting the idea that the human soul migrates through the lower Kingdoms of Nature.

Other Misleading Factors.

In addition to the dual method of teaching, other factors may have contributed to the misunderstanding regarding transmigration. One such is the fact that the human *body* is an animal body — more highly evolved than other animal bodies, but animal nevertheless. In this sense it is true to say that when we are re-born, we enter animal bodies. It would be more correct to say that we enter *human*-animal bodies, but if the prefix *human* is left

---

*Quoted from *The Esoteric Tradition*, II, p. 629.

out it is easy to see how someone, who is only superficially acquainted with the subject might misinterpret the rebirth of man into a human-animal body to mean a re-birth into the body of some lower animal. Add to this the fact that when a man leads a sensuous life and yields to gluttony or other base appetites, it may be truly said that he lives in the animal part of his nature; he becomes for the time being an animal, his own animal, and we find that here is ample material for misunderstanding of the true teaching. This is what Hierocles refers to in the latter part of the quotation given above.

The Symbolism of the Sphinx.

Records of ancient Egyptian teachings that have come down to us seem to indicate that the Egyptians believed in the transmigration of the soul into animals.* Yet these same Egyptians, evidently anticipating the misunderstandings that might arise on this point in the future, left us a record, written in stone, of just what they did mean by "animal transmigration." Their initiates and philosophers, artists and sculptors gave to posterity the Sphinx, an immense statue with a human head carried on the body of a recumbent lion. On its face is a most wonderful expression of serenity and calm, and its eyes seem directed to some distant scene as though their owner were engaged in contemplation of something far beyond this earth.

Could there be a more striking way of illustrating the idea that man is a composite being — consciousness and intelligence temporarily housed in an animal body, which for the time being is the vehicle of the consciousness during its sojourn in the material world?

A statue with a human head on a human body would have taught no lesson, but a human head on a lion's body called attention to the duality of man's nature, and by showing the body in repose they symbolized that when man's body with its feelings and appetites is under control and at rest, then the consciousness, even while

---

*See the quotation from Herodotus in H. P. Blavatsky's *Theosophical Glossary*, s.v. "Pre-Existence."

in this world, is free to rise in contemplation to other and higher planes of being.

The idea of illustrating the duality of man's nature by the symbol of a human head superimposed on an animal body was not unique to Egypt. The ancient Assyrians used exactly the same method of teaching, but utilized the body of a bull instead of that of a lion. The Assyrians added an extra feature, making the bull winged, to emphasize still further that the human consciousness is not earth-bound, but may rise to higher planes of consciousness even while embodied.

The ancients did not need to safeguard against their contemporaries mistaking the symbolism, for these were intelligent enough to know that no such creatures as the Sphinx or the winged bull existed. Should not we likewise know that when the ancients speak of men as incarnating in animal bodies, they mean in human bodies with animal propensities?

Kindergarten Teachings for Kindergarten Minds.

Another factor that may have contributed to the general misunderstanding on this subject is that due to the undeveloped mentality of the masses it was impossible to explain to them the intricate workings of the Law of Cause and Effect, whereby the causes sown in one life produce their effect in a future incarnation. Yet these masses needed some teaching that would instill respect for virtue and promote self-control. Also something was needed to arouse sympathy and compassion towards the lower forms of life. The teaching that the human soul after an evil life might inhabit the body of some animal was a convenient simplification that could be used for this purpose and this makes it understandable why those who knew better used this as a threat to keep others "in line" who could not be reached through the undeveloped higher faculties of their immature natures. It was used as a "kindergarten teaching" for "kindergarten minds."

Do not we use a similar method ourselves when we try to teach three or four year olds the dangers of playing with matches? It is impossible to do this by speaking to the child about dangers that the child has not experienced and so we conjure up some frightening picture, and perhaps tell it that "the goblins will get you" or something similar that might make an impression on the child's mind. It is a temporary expedient, used for the child's protection, but should be followed by a true explanation as soon as the child is able to understand. It is a truth taught in the form of a fable. The danger is real, but the description of it is symbolical.

Is not the doctrine of Heaven and Hell a similar case? This was accepted literally at one time and perhaps still is in some quarters, but this conception is gradually being replaced by an understanding that it is a symbolic presentation of actual facts, namely that clean and virtuous living will bring health and happiness and that the reverse will bring suffering and unhappiness. It is a convenient abbreviation with all the details left out.

The danger in using such methods of teaching lies in the fact that when the mind has developed sufficiently to see that the literal interpretation is not true, it may not recognize the truth behind the symbology, and then conclude that there is no basis for the teaching.

It is at this critical point that further teaching must be given to explain the hidden truth and it is to furnish this hitherto lacking information that the Ancient Wisdom has been re-stated for the benefit of mankind.

We too use Symbolic Expressions.

Before we ridicule the ancients for their symbolic statements, which seem so foolish to us because we take them literally, it might be well to remember that we too use symbolic statements, which are liable to misinterpretation by future generations.

Our Christian Bible is full of such figurative expressions. There we find men compared to sheep and goats and Jesus, the Son of God and the Savior referred to as a lamb. Jesus also speaks of himself as a vine and his disciples as the branches of this vine. The symbology of this is well understood today, but suppose that our civilization is destroyed and that after some 10,000 years only a few incomplete records, such as those referred to above, remain, and that someone tries to reconstruct our ideas on religion from these incomplete fragments. Would this individual be justified in drawing the conclusion that the "men" of the 20th century really used sheep and goat bodies, and that the world was actually saved by a grapevine?

If we could speak across the interval of a hundred centuries would we not address our 120th century descendant in perhaps not too polite language, and ask how he could possibly take literally something that is so clearly a symbolical presentation intended to convey an idea and make it understandable to the man in the street? And would we not tell him that even the most simple-minded individual of our time, the 20th century, would understand that such expressions are symbolical?

And suppose the ancients who accepted Reincarnation could see the misconceptions that have arisen in regard to it in the twentieth century, is it not probable that they in their turn would express surprise at our failure to understand their symbology?

Pre-Human Transmigrations.

As explained in Chapter I (Involution and Evolution) and Chapter II (The Schoolhouse of Nature), the evolving life-unit or Monad begins its evolutionary journey by embodying in the lowest forms of Nature after which it gradually and after immense time-periods embodies in successively higher Kingdoms of Nature. All this evolution takes place *before* the Monad has reached the human stage and is an orderly upward march, not a helter-skelter, back-and-forth process.

This process can be compared to a "migration of Monads" through the various Kingdoms of Nature, "a moving across imaginary borders from one place to another" and can therefore very properly be called a Transmigration.

Every one of us has passed through such transmigrations before we reached our present stage as self-conscious human beings. During these transmigrations we only had the consciousness of minerals, plants and animals.

The pre-human phases of the Monad's evolution are referred to in an aphorism found in the Jewish Qabbalah, which states that: "a stone becomes a plant, a plant becomes a beast, a beast becomes a man and a man becomes a god." This does not mean that the bodies of one kingdom change into the bodies of the other kingdoms, but refers to the transmigrations of the Monad from one type of body to another.

The Sufi poet Jalal-ud-din refers to the same subject in the following poem —

> I died from the mineral, and became a plant;
> I died from the plant and reappeared as an animal;
> I died from the animal and became a man;
> Wherefore then should I fear?
> When did I grow less by dying?
> Next time I shall die from the man
> That I may grow the wings of angels.
> From the angel, too, must I seek advance.

Death and the post-mortem experiences of the Human Ego include a passing of the consciousness from the material plane to inner, invisible planes and eventually back again to the material. If the term "transmigration" is used at all in connection with the post-mortem experiences of the Human Ego, it should be restricted to such movements of the human consciousness from one plane or condition to another plane or condition within its own proper human sphere of activity.

Poets and writers have not always distinguished between the pre-human transmigrations of the sub-human Monads and the post-mortem transmigrations of the Human Ego or Soul, but fused the two ideas into one and this has contributed to the erroneous notion that the Human Ego transmigrates into the lower Kingdoms of Nature.

True Transmigration.

The atoms that build man's physical body scatter after death. The same happens to all that is discarded at the second death, including the more ethereal particles of the model body as well as certain other energies intermediate between the Human Ego and the model body. All these parts of the former human constitution now return to Nature, each one to its own appropriate plane. Here they are free to enter as building blocks in the vehicles of other entities, to which they are attracted.

In their association with the human entity, whose vehicle they helped to build, they received certain impressions, high or low as the case might have been and it is these impressions that now determine the direction of their travels. They may enter the Plant Kingdom or be drawn into the bodies of various animals or perhaps enter other human bodies.

The atoms of the entire lower part of the human constitution are thus migrating through Nature and transmigrating from one Kingdom to another and then perhaps back again.

It is this fact that the ancients referred to when they said that Man transmigrates through the lower forms of Nature, which statement is correct, if by "Man" is meant the elements of his constitution below the Human Ego, but incorrect if it is applied to the Human Ego or the higher principles above this Ego.

For further elucidation of this subject the reader is referred to *The Esoteric Tradition* by G. de Purucker, chapters on "Reimbodiment" and "How Man is Born and Reborn."

REINCARNATION THROUGH THE AGES

An Ancient and Widespread Doctrine.

A study of the religions and philosophies of mankind from the remotest antiquity down through the ages will show that reincarnation is one of the oldest and most widely distributed doctrines in the world.

Earlier references to reincarnation lack the details that are found in Theosophical literature for such information was not given out publicly in the past.

In some cases only portions of the doctrine have been presented, while other parts have been omitted. Thus, for instance, some writers dwell almost exclusively on pre-existence without touching on the post-mortem phases of the teaching. The doctrine may not always appear in its true form, but under one form or another it has been known all over the world and will be found in many lands even today.

Reincarnation in the Hindu Religions.

Brahmanism and Buddhism, with hundreds of millions of adherents in Asia, both teach the rebirth of the human soul.

In one of the *Upanishads* called *The Bhagavad Gîtâ*, which is India's most widely read and best beloved book of devotion, we find man's Inner God, represented by the divinity Krishna, speaking to the Human Soul in these words:

> I myself never was not, nor thou, nor all the princes of the earth; nor shall we ever hereafter cease to be. As the lord of this mortal frame experiences therein infancy, youth, and old age, so in future incarnations will it meet the same. One who is confirmed in this belief is not disturbed by anything that may come to pass.

> . . . .

> These finite bodies which envelope the souls inhabitating them, are said to belong to Him, the eternal, the indestructible, unprovable spirit, who is in the body . . . . This spirit neither kills nor is it killed . . . . It is not slain when this its mortal frame is destroyed.

> . . . .

> As a man throws away old garments and puts on new, even so the dweller in the body, having quitted its old mortal frames, enters into others that are new . . . . Death is certain to all things which are born, and rebirth to all mortals.

> . . . .

> Both I and thou have passed through many births . . . . Mine are known unto me, but thou knowest not of thine.

> The man whose devotion has been broken off by death goes to the region of the righteous, [the blissful dream-state between incarnations] where he dwells for an immensity of years and is then born again on earth in a pure and fortunate family.

> . . . .

> It is even a portion of myself which, having assumed life in this world of conditioned existence, draws together the five senses and the mind in order that it may obtain a body and may

leave it again. And those are carried by the sovereign Lord to and from whatever body he enters or quits, even as the breeze bears the fragrance from the flower.

Reincarnation in the Bible.

Reincarnation is not presented in the Bible as a specific teaching, but we find a number of statements pertaining to pre-existence and the rebirth of individuals, which demonstrate that their authors accepted the doctrine. Some of these follow:

In *Proverbs* VIII, 22-31, Solomon says that he existed even before the creation of the Earth, and that his delights were with the sons of men, and in the habitable parts of the Earth; in other words, he must have been born as a human being in that early period, and since he is now, at the time of writing his *Proverbs* speaking as Solomon, he is again in human form. This is re-incarnation. It does not point to future repeated births, but it does not exclude this idea.

In *Jeremiah* I, 5, the Lord, speaking to the prophet says: "Before I formed thee in the belly I knew thee; and before thou camest forth out of the womb I sanctified thee, and I ordained thee a prophet unto the nations."

This implies the pre-existence of Jeremiah.

In *Jeremiah* XXX, 9; *Ezekiel* XXXIV, 23 and XXXVII, 24, there are statements that David shall be "raised up" and again become king or shepherd to his people. David had been dead a long time: being "raised up" evidently means that the same soul was to be born again, just as it had been born into the body called "David" in the previous incarnation.

We find the following in *Malachi* IV, 5:

"Behold, I will send you Elijah the prophet before the coming of the great and dreadful day of the Lord."

This is a clear reference to pre-existence and re-birth; Elijah, a prophet known to have existed in the past, is to return in the future. Nothing is said in regard to repeated returns, but it is evident, that if Elijah lived in the past and was reborn here on earth, lived his life, and in due course died, there is no reason why he could not again return from his new post-mortem condition, and repeat the process indefinitely.

In *John* IX, 1, 2, we find the following references to pre-existence —

"And as Jesus passed by, he saw a man which was blind from his birth. And his disciples asked him, saying, Master, who did sin, this man or his parents, that he was born blind?"

The form of the question demonstrates that pre-existence is taken for granted by the disciples and Jesus shows by not repudiating the idea in his answer that it was acceptable to him.

Jesus asked his disciples: "Whom say the people that I am?"

They, answering said, "John the Baptist; but some say Elias; and others say, that one of the old prophets is risen again."

—*Luke* IX, 18, 19

An individual now existing, is here said to be an incarnation of someone known to have existed in the past. The answer to the question is in itself an acceptance of pre-existence, followed by reincarnation and since it does not shock or surprise Jesus the idea must have seemed acceptable to him, in fact the offhand manner in which the idea is treated shows that it must have seemed axiomatic to both Jesus and his disciples.

Incidentally, the quotation shows that "risen again," or "raised again," expressions also used elsewhere in the Bible in similar cases, means the reincarnation of the individual.

There was a belief among the Jews, based on ancient prophesies, that the appearance of their Messiah was to be preceded by the *return* of the prophet Elijah, and what does "return" mean if not re-birth into a human body?

Referring to ancient prophesies and speaking of John the Baptist, Jesus says:

For this is he, of whom it is written, Behold, I send my messenger before thy face, which shall prepare the way before thee.

Verily I say unto you, Among them that are born of women there hath not risen a greater than John the Baptist . . . .

And if ye will receive it, this is Elias, which was for to come. —*Matt.* XI, 10-14

And how did Elias "come"? He came by being re-born.

After John the Baptist had been beheaded, and when the disciples had failed to recognize in him Elias, who was to precede the coming of Christ, they ask Jesus:

> Why then say the scribes that Elias must first come?
> And Jesus answered and said unto them, Elias truly shall first come, and restore all things.
> But I say unto you, that Elias is come already, and they knew him not, but have done unto him whatsoever they listed . . . .
> Then the disciples understood that he spake unto them of John the Baptist.
> —*Matt.* XVII, 10-13

In this quotation and the preceding one, we have Jesus himself stating in unmistakable terms that the soul of John the Baptist was the same as that of Elias. This statement is in full accord with the doctrine of reincarnation. Jesus calls attention to an event that could never have taken place unless reincarnation were a fact. He does not teach the complete doctrine, for that is not his object; he only shows how it applies in one specific case.

The fact that in the Bible reincarnation is taken for granted, rather than taught as a specific doctrine, should not be surprising when it is remembered that for ages before the life of Christ this teaching was well known and generally accepted by the peoples around the Mediterranean.

Various religious sects and schools of philosophy in these countries were based on, or influenced by, the Mystery Schools. These, in their turn were based on Orphic and Pythagorean teachings, which included the doctrine of reincarnation.

Among the Jews the largest and most influential sect, the Pharisees, believed in reincarnation. The Jewish general Flavius Josephus (37-98 A.D.), who was also a priestly official and historian of his people, was himself a Pharisee. In one of his works, *The Antiquities of the Jews* Bk. XVIII, Ch. I, par. 3, 4, he writes:

> They [the Pharisees] believe, that souls have an immortal power in them, and that there will be under the earth rewards or punishments, according as men have lived virtuously or

viciously in this life; and the latter souls are to be detained in an everlasting prison, but the former will have power to live again. On account of these doctrines they have very great influence with the people, and whatever they do about divine worship, or prayers, or sacrifices, they perform according to their direction. Such great testimony do the cities bear them on account of their constant practice of virtue, both in the actions of their lives, and in their conversation.

In another of his works called *The Jewish War* Bk. III, Ch. VIII, par. 5, he writes:

. . . Do not you know that those who depart out of this life according to the law of nature . . . enjoy eternal fame; . . . their souls are pure and obedient, and obtain a most holy place in heaven, from whence, in the revolution of ages, they are again sent into pure bodies . . . .

Another Jewish sect, The Essenes, also believed in reincarnation.

We do not go into detailed explanation of something that is well known or considered self-evident such as the rotation of the earth producing days and nights, if this subject is mentioned, and when a doctrine is so well known and so generally accepted as that of rebirth was at the time of Jesus, we should not expect him to go into detail in regard to it. The off-hand, matter-of-fact way in which the subject is treated implies that it was taken for granted, rather than that there was any doubt about it.

Reincarnation in the Early Christian Era.

During the first few centuries of the Christian era, there was little established church organization, but the teachings were preserved and elaborated on by the followers of the Apostles. The leaders among these, the most learned and most highly respected, were the so-called "Church Fathers." Among the best known of these are Clement of Alexandria, Origen and Synesius. According to H. P. Blavatsky's *Secret Doctrine* (Vol. I, p. xliv) these men had all been initiated into the Mysteries and must therefore have been well acquainted with the doctrines of pre-existence and re-incarnation, a fact apparent from their writings.

Clement (about 150-220 A.D.) who was duly canonized a saint of the Christian Church shows that he believed in pre-existence when he writes in Chapter I of his *Exhortation to the Heathen*: "But before the foundation of the world were we, who, because destined to be in him, pre-existed in the eye of god . . . ."

Origen (186-254 A.D.), a disciple of St. Clement and of Ammonius Saccas, the founder of the Neo-Platonic School, is considered one of the greatest Christian scholars and thinkers. One quotation from his writings, showing that he rejected the idea of transmigration into animals, has already been given. Other quotations showing that he accepted the doctrines of pre-existence and reincarnation, follow:

> [T]hose who maintain that everything in the world is under the administration of divine providence (as is also our own belief), can, as it appears to me, give no other answer, so as to show that no shadow of injustice rests upon the divine government, than by holding that there were certain causes of prior existence, in consequence of which the souls, before their birth in the body, contracted a certain amount of guilt in their sensitive nature, or in their movements, on account of which they have been judged worthy by Divine Providence of being placed in this condition. (Origen's *On First Principles* Bk. III, Ch. III (Sec. 5)

In this quotation Origen deals with the age-old problem of injustice and points out that the doctrine of pre-existence is the only explanation that can remove the stigma of injustice from the divine government.

In Bk. IV, Ch. I. Sec. 23 of the same work Origen writes:

> Everyone, accordingly, of those who descend to the earth is, according to his deserts, or agreeably to the position which he occupied there, ordained to be born in this world, in a different country, or among a different nation, or in a different mode of life, or surrounded by infirmities of a different kind, or to be descended from religious parents, or parents who are

not religious; so that it may sometimes happen that an Israelite descends among the Scythians, and a poor Egyptian is brought down to Judaea.

Although these statements put emphasis on pre-existence it is easy to see that they include reincarnation, even if this is not specifically referred to. If an "Egyptian is born in Judaea" it means that the Egyptian died and the soul was later incarnated in the body of a Judaean. And how did the Egyptian come into being? Was he not an incarnation of some earlier individual, perhaps a member of some other nation? And was not this earlier individual the incarnation of someone still earlier and so forth? And if this chain extends indefinitely backwards does not this imply that it must also extend indefinitely into the future? Why should it be assumed that the "Judaean" was the end of the chain? When he dies, must not his soul seek new embodiment?

Synesius, the Christian bishop, who lived in the fourth and fifth centuries was a Neo-Platonist, and the Neo-Platonists taught reincarnation.

E. D. Walker in his *Reincarnation* (p. 214) says that it is known of Synesius "that when the citizens of Ptolemais invited him to their bishopric, he declined that dignity for the reason that he cherished certain opinions which they might not approve, as after mature reflection they had struck deep roots in his mind. Foremost among these he mentioned the doctrine of pre-existence."

We find then that up to the fifth century A.D. the doctrines of pre-existence and reincarnation were known to, accepted by and openly taught by the highest church authorities, and if these church leaders accepted these doctrines it must be assumed that their followers also accepted them.

Reincarnation condemned as heretical.

The question now arises: If these doctrines were so generally accepted in the early centuries of the Christian era, what caused their later disappearance?

It is possible that the church leaders found the doctrine of re-incarnation too difficult to explain to the multitude. It is also possible that the popular misconception of transmigration into animals, which was so generally associated with reincarnation, did its part to discredit the true doctrine, and that for these reasons the later church leaders introduced the doctrine of a new soul being created for each individual at his birth.

As this idea became more generally adopted, the older teaching was gradually pushed into the background and was taught more and more secretly, if at all.

Even after it had been dropped as an official church doctrine, however, the old idea still lingered on and retained a large number of adherents. For a long period the two doctrines existed simultaneously, but since they were mutually contradictory something had to be done to stamp out the older teaching, which was now looked upon as heretical.

A council of church leaders was consequently summoned to pass judgment on this doctrine as taught by Origen, together with some of his other teachings, which were also considered heretical. This meeting, or Home-Synod as it was called, was convened in Constantinople, about the year 538 under the Patriarch Mennas. Fifteen specific teachings of Origen's were taken up for discussion and all of these were, after much heated debate, formally condemned and anathemized. Those referring to pre-existence are listed below.

Origen's teachings were to the effect*

#1) That the soul pre-exists before its present earth-life; and is ultimately restored to its original spiritual nature and condition.

#4) That man now has a material or physical body as a retributive or punitive result of wrong-doing, following upon the soul's sinking into matter.

#5) That even as these spiritual beings formerly fell into matter, so may and will they ultimately rise again to their former spiritual status.

#13) That the soul of Christ pre-existed like the souls of all men; and that Christ is similar in type to all men in power and substance.

---

*From a summary by G. de Purucker in *The Esoteric Tradition* pp. 42, 43.

After the condemnation of these Origenistic doctrines by the church authorities, pre-existence and reincarnation could no longer be taught or tolerated as part of the church teachings. This being the case, does it not seem likely that the literature of the Church would be subjected to a reexamination and any references to them eradicated? May it not therefore be possible that the earlier writings such as the gospels might have contained more direct references to pre-existence and reincarnation, than they do now?

The Greek original of Origen's great work *On First Principles,* in which are found most of his references to reincarnation, is no longer available, but a Latin translation of it exists. In the Prologue to this translation, made by the Latin theologian Tyrannius Rufinus (345-410), the translator refers to earlier translators of Origenistic writings and their practice of making changes from the Greek original, where the latter disagreed with the then prevailing Christian beliefs. Rufinus then states that he has adopted the same method, according to which the translator, if he found any so called "stumbling blocks" in the original Greek, "so smoothed and corrected them in his translations that a Latin reader would come upon nothing discordant with our Christian belief." (Quoted in *The Esoteric Tradition* II, 624f)

Bearing in mind that in Rufinus' time the Church authorities began to look with disfavor on the doctrines of pre-existence and reincarnation, is it not likely that these doctrines would have been singled out as just such "stumbling blocks" as Rufinus refers to and that they therefore were subjected to Rufinus' method of "smoothing and correcting?"

Even the Latin translation as it is leaves no doubt of Origen's belief in rebirth, but Rufinus' own admission arouses the suspicion that if the Greek original were available, we might find in it still more explicit and stronger references to the subject.

Referring to the anathemas of the Home-Synod, is not the whole procedure of a group of students, supposedly followers of Jesus, taking upon itself to condemn a doctrine, definitely affirmed by him, open to question and criticism?

In *Matt.* XI, 10-14 and XVII, 10-13, referred to above, Jesus himself makes use of the doctrines of pre-existence and rebirth to explain to his disciples the identity of John the Baptist with

Elijah. Jesus shows that he knows these doctrines; instead of condemning them as erroneous, he shows by using them, that he approves of them.

Added to this we have the testimony of the earliest Church Fathers showing that these doctrines were still retained by the Church in the early centuries of our era.

Then, 500 years after the death of their Teacher, we find a group of his supposed followers condemning doctrines, which their Teacher had endorsed.

Here is a direct conflict of ideas. If Jesus was right, the Home-Synod was wrong, and vice versa. Who was in the best position to know, Jesus or the later Church authorities?

If Jesus' utterances are accepted by his followers as coming from the Son of God, how can these same followers pick out one of these utterances and condemn it as being wrong? Is not this a case of the pupils correcting their Teacher?

The Church authorities might have protested against the false notion of transmigration into animals, which was so widespread among the uneducated, for this was a doctrine which Jesus never endorsed and one which does not appear in the Bible. If this was the case, they should be highly commended for removing a gross popular misconception. But when they went so far as to reject the true doctrine with the false, they threw away the kernel with the shell.

Are we justified in accepting parts of Jesus' teachings and rejecting other parts? And if we accept all his teachings, we must also accept reincarnation, for it is one of them.

Other Believers in Reincarnation.

Among other religions, philosophies, sects and racial groups, who have taught reincarnation or accepted it in some form or other, are the following:

Taoism in China.
The Mysteries taught in the temples of Egypt.
The Hermetic Philosophy.
Zoroastrianism or the Mazdean religion.
The Orphic religion.

The Pythagorean philosophy.
The Mystery Schools of Greece and Asia Minor.
Platonism.
The Jewish Kabala.
The Talmud.
The Pharisees and Essenes.
The early Christian Church.
Neo-Platonism.
The American Indians and the Eskimos.
West African natives.
Autralian aborigenes.

Besides the founders or heads of the various groups referred to, who of course believed in reincarnation, there are a number of individuals, who show by their writings that they approve of the idea. Among these we find the following names:

Patañjali	Carlyle
Ovid	Longfellow
Lucretius	Andre Pezzani
Flavius Josephus	Victor Hugo
Hierocles	Prof. Francis Bowen
Dr. Henry More	James R. Lowell
Lessing	Walt Whitman
Fichte	William R. Alger
Kapila	Thomas Bailey Aldrich
Cicero	Jack London
Vergil	Rudyard Kipling
Philo Judaeus	John Masefield
Plotinus	Wordsworth
Rabbi Manasseh	Jean Reynaud
David Hume	Bulwer Lytton
Herder	Emerson
Napoleon	Rosetti
Goethe	Richard Wagner
Shelley	James Freeman Clarke
Honoré de Balzac	Prof. Frederick H. Hedge
Schopenhauer	Tennyson
Jean B. F. Obry	Whittier

Sir Edwin Arnold   Sir H. Rider Haggard
William Sharp   George Russell (AE)
Prof. William Knight   Henry Ford
Ella Wheeler Wilcox   Sir Humphrey Davy

More names could be added to this list, but what is given should be sufficient to show the antiquity and widespread prevalence of the doctrine as well as its appeal to philosophers, writers and poets up to the present time.

The fact that a certain group or certain individuals accept a doctrine is in itself no proof that this doctrine is true. Neither is the fact that another group or other individuals reject the same doctrine a proof that it is false. But if in one of these groups we find some of the greatest philosophers and religious teachers that the world has known as well as many lesser, but well known thinkers, should not this indicate to us that here is a subject that should not be passed over lightly? We accept their ideas on other matters, for which they are famous; why should we ignore their opinion on reincarnation?

Quotations giving the opinions on reincarnation held by the groups and individuals listed, are available. To present all of these a small volume would be needed, and therefore only a few such quotations will be given for the present. Much of the following is quoted from E. D. Walker's *Reincarnation,* 1923 Edition.

Rabbi Manasseh Ben Israel (1604-1657) Jewish theologian and Kabalist, Chief rabbi at synagogue at Amsterdam writes in *Nismath Hayem*:

> The belief or the doctrine of the transmigration of souls [i.e. reincarnation] is a *firm* and *infallible dogma* accepted by the whole assemblage of our church with one accord, so that there is none to be found who would dare to deny it . . . . Indeed, there are a great number of sages in Israel who hold firm to this doctrine so that they made it a dogma, a fundamental point of our religion. We are therefore in duty bound to obey and to accept this dogma with acclamation . . . . as the truth of it has been incontestably demonstrated by the Zohar and all the books of the Kabalists.

The German philosopher Schopenhauer (1788-1860) writes in his *The World as Will and Idea*:

> What sleep is for the individual, death is for the will [Ego]. It would not endure to continue the same actions and sufferings throughout an eternity, without true gain, if memory and individuality remained to it. It flings them off, and this is Lethe [the river of forgetfulness]; and through this sleep of death it reappears refreshed and fitted out with another intellect, as a new being . . . .

. . . .

> These constant new births, then, constitute the succession of the life dreams of a will [Ego] which in itself is indestructible . . . .

Speaking for himself and quoting J. B. F. Obry, a French authority on Hinduism, Schopenhauer says:

> The deep conviction of the indestructibleness of our nature through death, which every one carries at the bottom of his heart, depends altogether upon the consciousness of the original and eternal nature of our being.

> We find the doctrine of Metempsychosis [i.e. reincarnation], springing from the earliest and noblest ages of the human race, always spread abroad in the earth as the belief of the great majority of mankind; nay, really as the teaching of all religions, with the exception of that of the Jews and the two which have proceeded from it: in the most subtle form, however, and coming nearest to the truth in Buddhism.

> With reference to the universality of the belief in Metempsychosis, Obry says rightly in his excellent book, *Du Nirvana Indien*, p. 13, "This old belief has been held all round the world, and was spread in the remote antiquity to such an extent that a learned English churchman has declared it to be fatherless, motherless, and without genealogy." Taught already in the "Vedas," as in all the sacred books of India, metempsychosis is well known to be the kernel of Brahmanism and Buddhism. It accordingly prevails at the present day in the whole of non-Mohammedan Asia, thus among more than half

the whole human race, as the firmest conviction, and with an incredibly strong practical influence. It was also the belief of the Egyptians, from whom it was received with enthusiasm by Orpheus, Pythagoras, and Plato. The Pythagoreans, however, specially retained it. That it was also taught in the mysteries of the Greeks undeniably follows from the ninth book of Plato's *Laws*. The *Edda* also, especially in the *Voluspa*, teaches metempsychosis. Not less was it the foundation of the religion of the Druids. Even a Mohammedan sect in Hindustan, the Bohrahs, of which Colebrooke gives a full account in the *Asiatic Researches*, believes in metempsychosis, and accordingly refrains from all animal food. Also among American Indians and Negro tribes, nay, even among the natives of Australia, traces of this belief are found . . . .

Ralph Waldo Emerson (1803-1882), the American philosopher and essayist, writes in *Representative Men*:

The soul having been often born, or, as the Hindus say, "traveling the path of existence through thousands of births," having beheld the things which are here, those which are in heaven and those which are beneath, there is nothing of which she has not gained the knowledge; no wonder that she is able to recollect, . . . what formerly she knew . . . . For inquiry and learning is reminiscence all.

In his essay *The Oversoul* he says: "The child is born full grown, assuming a past developing through previous existences" and in *Experience* he says: "We wake and find ourselves on a stair. There are stairs below us, which we seem to have ascended; there are stairs above us, many a one, which go upward and out of sight."

Emerson also says in *Immortality*: "We must infer our destiny from the preparation. We are driven by instinct to have innumerable experiences which are of no visible value, and we may revolve through many lives before we shall assimilate or exhaust them."

In the journal of Charles Emerson is found the following from his brother Ralph Waldo:

The reason why Homer is to me like a dewy morning is because I too lived while Troy was, and sailed in the hollow ships of the Grecians . . . . my soul animated the frame of some nameless Argive . . . We forget that we have been drugged by the sleepy bowl of the present.

In *Ways of the Spirit, and other Essays,* by the Unitarian clergyman and author Frederick Henry Hedge (1805-1890), the twelfth chapter, upon "The Human Soul" argues strongly for reincarnation.

We reach back with our recollection and find no beginning of existence. Who of us knows anything except by report of the first two years of earthly life? No one remembers the time when he first said "I," or thought "I." We began to exist for others before we began to exist for ourselves. Our experience is not co-extensive with our being, and memory does not comprehend it. We bear not the root, but the root us.

What is the root? We call it soul. *Our* soul, we call it; properly speaking, it is not ours, but we are its. It is not a part of us, but we are a part of it. It is not one article in an inventory of articles which together make up our individuality, but the root of that individuality. It is larger than we are and other than we are—that is, than our conscious self. The conscious self does not begin until some time after the birth of the individual. It is not aboriginal, but a product,—as it were, the blossoming of an individuality. We may suppose countless souls which never bear this product, which never blossom into self. And the soul which does so blossom exists before that blossom unfolds.

How long before, it is impossible to say; whether the birth, for example, of a human individual is the soul's beginning to be; whether a new soul is furnished to each new body, or the body given to a pre-existing soul. It is a question on which theology throws no light, and which psychology but faintly illustrates. But so far as that faint illustration reaches it favors the supposition of pre-existence. That supposition seems best to match the supposed continued existence of the soul hereafter. Whatever had a beginning in time, it should seem must end in time. The eternal destination which faith ascribes to the soul presupposes an eternal origin. On the other hand, if the pre-existence of the soul were assured it would carry the assurance of immortality.

. . . .

The birth of the soul into the present was the death of the old—"a sleep and a forgetting." The soul went to sleep in one body, it woke in a new. The sleep is a gulf of oblivion between the two.

. . . .

It is commonly conceded that there are native differences of character in men,—different propensities, tempers, not wholly explained by difference of circumstances or education. They show themselves where circumstances and education have been the same; they seem to be innate. These are sometimes ascribed to organization. But organization is not final. That, again, requires to be explained. According to my thinking, it is the soul that makes organization, not organization the soul. The supposition of a previous existence would best explain these differences as something carried over from life to life,—the harvest of seed that was sown in other states, and whose fruit remains, although the sowing is remembered no more.

In the *Princeton Review* for May, 1881, the American philosopher Professor Francis Bowen (of Harvard University) (1811-1890) published a very interesting article on "Christian Metempsychosis," in which he urges the Christian acceptance of reincarnation.

Our life upon earth is rightly held to be a discipline and a preparation for a higher and eternal life hereafter. But if limited to the duration of a single mortal body, it is so brief as to seem hardly sufficient for so grand a purpose. Threescore years and ten must surely be an inadequate preparation for eternity. But what assurance have we that the probation of the soul is confined within so narrow limits? Why may it not be continued, or repeated, through a long series of successive generations, the same personality [individuality] animating one after another an indefinite number of tenements of flesh, and carrying forward into each the training it has received, the character it has formed, the temper and dispositions it has indulged, in the stage of existence immediately preceding?

.   .   .   .

Why should it be thought incredible that the same soul should inhabit in succession an indefinite number of mortal bodies, and thus prolong its experience and its probation till it has become in every sense ripe for heaven or the final judgment? Even during this one life our bodies are perpetually changing, though by a process of decay and restoration which is so gradual that it escapes our notice. Every human being thus dwells successively in many bodies, even during one short life.

.   .   .   .

If every birth were an act of absolute creation, the introduction to life of an entirely new creature, we might reasonably ask why different souls are so variously constituted at the outset. We do not all start fair in the race that is set before us, and therefore all cannot be expected, at the close of one brief mortal pilgrimage, to reach the same goal, and to be equally well fitted for the blessings or the penalties of a fixed state hereafter. The commonest observation assures us that one child is born with limited capacities and perhaps a wayward disposition, strong passions, and a sullen temper; that he has tendencies to evil which are almost sure to be soon developed. Another, on the contrary, seems happily endowed from the start; he is not only amiable, tractable, and kind, but quick-witted and precocious, a child of many hopes. The one seems a perverse goblin, while the other has the early promise of a Cowley or a Pascal. The differences of external condition also are so vast and obvious that they seem to detract much from the merit of a well-spent life and from the guilt of vice and crime. One is so happily nurtured in a Christian home, and under so many protecting influences, that the path of virtue lies straight and open before him—so plain, indeed, that even the blind could safely walk therein; while another seems born to a heritage of misery, exposure and crime. The birthplace of one is in central Africa, and of another in the heart of civilized and Christian Europe. Where lingers eternal justice then? How can such frightful inequalities be made to appear consistent with the infinite wisdom and goodness of God?

If metempsychosis [reincarnation] is included in the scheme of the divine government of the world, this difficulty disappears altogether. Considered from this point of view, every one is born into the state which he has fairly earned by his own previous history. He carries with him from one stage of existence to another the habits or tendencies which he has formed, the dispositions which he has indulged, the passions which he has not chastised, but has voluntarily allowed to lead him into vice and crime.

. . . .

Nothing prevents us, however, from believing that the probation of any one soul extends continuously through a long series of successive existences upon earth, each successive act in the whole life-history being retributive for what went before. For this is the universal law of being, whether of matter or mind; everything changes, nothing dies in the sense of being annihilated. What we call death is only the resolution of a complex body into its constituent parts, nothing that is truly one and indivisible being lost or destroyed in the process . . . . The human soul, which, as we know from consciousness, is absolutely one and indivisible, only passes on after the dissolution of what was once its home to animate another body . . . . We can easily imagine and believe that every person now living is a *re*presentation of some one who lived perhaps centuries ago under another name, in another country, it may be not with the same line of ancestry, and yet one and the same with him in his inmost being and essential character. His surroundings are changed; the old house of flesh has been torn down and rebuilt; but the tenant is still the same. He has come down from some former generation, bringing with him what may be either a help or a hindrance; namely, the character and tendencies which he there formed and nurtured. And herein is retribution; he has entered upon a new stage of probation, and in it he has now to learn what the character which he there formed naturally leads to when tried upon a new and perhaps broader theater. If this be not so, tell me why men are born with characters so unlike and with tendencies so depraved . . . . They bring with them no recollection of the incidents of their former life, as such memory would unfit them for the new part which they have to play. But they are still the same in the principles and modes of conduct, in the inmost springs of action, which the forgotten incidents of their former life have developed and strengthened. They are the same in all the essential points which made them formerly a blessing or a curse to all with whom they came immediately in contact and through which they will again become sources of weal or woe to their environment. Of course, these inborn tendencies may be either exaggerated or chastised by the lessons of a new experience, by the exercise of reflection, and by habitually heeding or neglecting the monitions of conscience. But they still exist as original tendencies, and as such they must make either the upward or the downward path more easy, more natural, and more likely to reach a goal so remote that it would otherwise be unattainable.

.   .   .   .

An eternity either of reward or punishment would seem to be inadequately earned by one brief period of probation. It is far more reasonable to believe that the future life which we are taught to expect will be similar to the present one, and will be spent in this world, though we shall carry forward to it the burden or the blessing entailed upon us by our past career. Besides the spiritual meaning of the doctrine of regeneration, besides the new birth which is "of water and of the Spirit," there may be a literal meaning in the solemn words of the Savior, "Except a man be born again, he cannot see the kingdom of God."

Rev. William R. Alger (1822-1905), a Unitarian minister and author, devoted half his lifetime to the production of a large volume on immortality entitled *A Critical History of the Doctrine of a Future Life* a book considered a standard authority on that topic. In the first edition, published 1860, the writer characterizes reincarnation as a plausible delusion, unworthy of credence. For fifteen years more he continued studying the subject, and the last edition (1878) gave the final result of his ripest investigations in heartily endorsing and advocating reincarnation:

> [O]f all the thoughtful and refined forms of the belief in a future life none has had so extensive and prolonged a prevalence as this [reincarnation]. It has the vote of the majority, having for ages on ages been held by half the human race with an intensity of conviction almost without a parallel. Indeed the most striking fact, at first sight, about the doctrine of the repeated incarnations of the soul, its form and experience in each successive embodiment being determined by its merits in the preceding ones, is the constant reappearance of the faith in all parts of the world, and its permanent hold on certain great nations . . . .

> . . . .

> The thoughts embodied in it [reincarnation] are so wonderful, the method of it so rational, the region of contemplation into which it lifts the mind is so grand, the prospects it opens are of such universal reach and import, that the study of it brings us into full sympathy with the sublime scope of the idea of immortality and of a cosmopolitan vindication of Providence uncovered to every eye. It takes us out of the littleness of petty themes and selfish affairs, and makes it easier for us to believe in the vastest hopes mankind has ever known.

The late industrialist and automobile manufacturer, Henry Ford, in an interview with Geo. Sylvester Viereck (*The San Francisco Examiner*, August 26, 1928), gives his views on reincarnation.

> I adopted the theory of reincarnation when I was twenty-six . . . .
> Religion offered nothing to the point—at least, I was unable to discover it. Even work could not give me complete satisfaction. Work is futile if we cannot utilize the experience we collect in one life in the next.

When I discovered reincarnation it was as if I had found a universal plan. I realized that there was a chance to work out my ideas. Time was no longer limited. I was no longer a slave to the hands of the clock. There was time enough to plan and to create.

The discovery of reincarnation put my mind at ease. I was settled. I felt that order and progress were present in the mystery of life. I no longer looked elsewhere for a solution to the riddle of life.

If you preserve a record of this conversation, write it so that it puts men's minds at ease. I would like to communicate to others the calmness that the long view of life gives to us.

We all retain, however faintly, memories of past lives. We frequently feel that we have witnessed a scene or lived through a moment in some previous existence. But that is not essential; it is the essence, the gist, the results of experience, that are valuable and remain with us.

John Masefield (1875-1967), playwright and Poet Laureate of England, expresses his views on Reincarnation in a beautiful poem called "A Creed."

> I hold that when a person dies
>   His soul returns again to earth;
> Arrayed in some new flesh-disguise
>   Another mother gives him birth.
> With sturdier limbs and brighter brain
> The old soul takes the road again.
>
> Such is my own belief and trust;
>   This hand, this hand that holds the pen,
> Has many a hundred times been dust
>   And turned, as dust, to dust again;
> These eyes of mine have blinked and shone
> In Thebes, in Troy, in Babylon.
>
> All that I rightly think or do,
>   Or make, or spoil, or bless, or blast,

Is curse or blessing justly due
  For sloth or effort in the past.
My life's a statement of the sum
Of vice indulged, or overcome.

I know that in my lives to be
My sorry heart will ache and burn,
And worship, unavailingly,
  The woman whom I used to spurn,
And shake to see another have
The love I spurned, the love she gave.

And I shall know, in angry words,
  In gibes, and mocks, and many a tear,
A carrion flock of homing-birds,
  The gibes and scorns I uttered here.
The brave word that I failed to speak
Will brand me dastard on the cheek.

And as I wander on the roads
  I shall be helped and healed and blessed;
Dear words shall cheer and be as goads
  To urge to heights before unguessed
My road shall be the road I made;
All that I gave shall be repaid.

So shall I fight, so shall I tread,
  In this long war beneath the stars;
So shall a glory wreathe my head,
  So shall I faint and show the scars,
Until this case, this clogging mould,
Be smithied all to kingly gold.

Chapter VIII

KARMA: THE LAW OF CONSEQUENCES

LAWS INHERENT IN NATURE

There is an inherent tendency in Nature to restore balance and harmony wherever these have been disturbed.

If the branch of a tree is bent out of position it reacts with an equal and opposite force which will return the branch to its original position when released. If a stone is thrown up into the air it returns to earth with a velocity equal to that with which it was thrown. If a weight is suspended by a rope it produces a tension in the rope equal to the weight, but pulling in the opposite direction.

These are examples on the material plane of an automatic tendency in Nature, which in Mechanics is expressed by the formula: "to every action there is an equal and opposite reaction." We see other examples of a tendency in Nature to restore balance in such common phenomena as water resuming its level after it has been disturbed; the air of the atmosphere moving from high pressure areas to those of a lower pressure or a swinging pendulum returning eventually to its position of rest.

The ancient teachings tell us that the same tendency operates throughout the Universe on all its planes, unseen as well as seen. We human beings are also governed by the same law, since we too are parts of Nature. In our innermost essence we are one with the Universal Life. Through this inner source we are united with one another as are the leaves of one tree or the cells and organs of the human body. The natural relationship between human beings is therefore one of harmony and cooperation for the common good. If this harmonious relationship is broken, Nature responds by setting up reactions of a similar kind. Thus if our motives, feelings, thoughts and actions are of a detrimental nature the same will return to us, and if they are of a beneficent nature the reaction will be beneficial. Thus life gives us back what we put into it.

The tendency in Nature to respond to external impulses by producing equivalent reactions is described by phrases such as "The Law of Cause and Effect," "The Law of Consequences," etc. In Hindu philosophy it is referred to by the Sanskrit term "Karma." Since there is no adequate term in Occidental languages to convey this idea, and in order to avoid cumbersome expressions, the Sanskrit term has been adopted in Theosophical literature for this purpose.

Literally translated Karma means "action," but to the Hindu this word has a more comprehensive meaning than it does to an Occidental. To the Hindu the effect is inherent in the cause. He considers that an initial act is only one half of an operation that is not complete until the reaction has taken place. The term Karma therefore includes both the cause and the effect. It is sometimes referred to as a "law," but this should not be understood in its judicial sense as an edict pronounced by some outside authority, but in the scientific sense as a quality inherent in Nature.

Karma is the fundamental law that governs all actions. It is the preserver of equilibrium, the restorer of disturbed balance. It does not punish or reward, it merely adjusts.

In *The Secret Doctrine,* Vol. I, pp. 643-4, H. P. Blavatsky writes:

> [T]he only decree of Karma—an eternal and immutable decree—is absolute Harmony in the world of matter as it is in the world of Spirit. It is not, therefore, Karma that rewards or punishes, but it is we, who reward or punish ourselves according to whether we work with, through and along with nature, abiding by the laws on which that Harmony depends, or— break them.

> .   .   .   .

> [V]erily there is not an accident in our lives, not a misshapen day, or a misfortune, that could not be traced back to our own doings in this or in another life. If one breaks the laws of Harmony, . . . one must be prepared to fall into the chaos one has oneself produced.

.   .   .   .

Karma-Nemesis is no more than the (spiritual) dynamical effect of causes produced and forces awakened into activity by our own actions.

The *Book of the Golden Precepts** says of Karma:

Learn that no efforts, not the smallest—whether in right or wrong direction—can vanish from the world of causes. Thou canst create this "day" [this life] thy chances for thy "morrow" [future lives]. In the "Great Journey" [cycle of existences] causes sown each hour bear each its harvest of effects, for rigid Justice rules the World. With mighty sweep of never-erring action, it brings to mortals lives of weal or woe, the karmic progeny of all our former thoughts and deeds.

LAW IN NATURE

If we study Nature we find that its forces, wherever we have been able to subject these to rigid tests, obey definite laws.

Thus for instance the laws governing the force of gravitation have long since been established. Many laws governing electricity, magnetism, chemical reactions, heat, light, sound and radiation-phenomena are also known. The movements of suns and planets are found to follow laws of physics. Other examples could be cited. In all these instances it has been found that Nature's reactions are consistent and that experiments conducted under the same conditions will always produce the same effects.

All scientific efforts might be said to be directed towards the discovery of new phenomena in Nature, the forces that produce these, and the laws that govern these forces. All this effort is based on the firm conviction that natural phenomena must be based on immutable laws, which, though as yet unknown, are only waiting to be discovered. Every research scientist, by his labor, demonstrates his belief that all phenomena in Nature must be governed by law.

---

*See *The Voice of the Silence* by H. P. Blavatsky which is a translation of some of these precepts.

In the world of ideas, we can also see how effect follows cause. This is strikingly demonstrated in the case of mathematics, where every successive step from the simplest arithmetic up to the highest branches of this science is based on facts previously established. A proposition in geometry is demonstrated by a rigid chain of deduction, fact following from other facts, previously demonstrated. Mathematics might be said to be the "measuring stick" by which knowledge gathered in other fields is "measured", for one of the common steps in interpreting experimental data, is to see if these can be reduced to mathematical formulas.

NATURE'S LAWS MUST BE UNIVERSAL

But what about the vast number of phenomena in Nature that we have so far been unable to subject to rigid tests? And what about the experiences of human life, that so vitally affect each one of us human beings in our individual lives, and in our relations with Nature and with our fellow men?

Shall we assume that these phenomena belong to a different class from those that we know to be governed by Nature's laws? Shall we assume that they are haphazard events of chance—or shall we recognize that these phenomena must also conform to definite laws, even though we have not as yet discovered these laws? The main obstacle to an acceptance of law in these cases, lies in the fact that we are unable to trace the workings of such laws. But is our failure to do this sufficient reason to conclude that these phenomena are the result of chance?

There are phenomena that were unknown or unexplained to our forefathers, that are known and understood by us today.

There are phenomena that are unknown and unexplained to large sections of the human race today, but these same phenomena are known and understood by other, more educated people.

If our forefathers in the past and the less educated people of today, being unable to explain these phenomena, had concluded that they were the results of chance, we know that such a conclusion would have been an error of judgment, for our scientists have proved that these phenomena are governed by laws of Nature.

If phenomena that were not understood in the past, have yielded to scientific investigation and are now understood, is it not reasonable to suppose that other phenomena, not understood by us, will similarly yield to future investigations and be found to follow definite laws? Can there be any doubt that Nature's laws are universal and that if some of her phenomena are *known* to be governed by law, all of them must be?

May it not be true that phenomena unexplained to us, are understood by others more evolved than we are? This is indeed the case according to the Masters of Wisdom, who have evolved beyond the human stage. They are able to transfer their consciousness to the unseen planes of Nature and they tell us from this vantage point, that every phenomenon in Nature is the result of the operation of some law of Nature, and that in those cases, where the chain of causation cannot be followed on the outer physical plane, it exists and can be traced on the inner planes of Nature.

The forces of Nature act automatically and with precision regardless of whether they are seen and understood or not. It is like a person working an adding machine. The mechanism is hidden under the hood and the operator may not understand the principle on which it works, but for each key pressed the corresponding number is added to the column of previous numbers. When the button is pressed that gives the sum-total, the operator knows that all figures have been included and that the sum is correctly added up.

So it is with Man in his relationship with Nature and his fellow men. The sway of Karma is complete, and it is futile for us to try to escape the consequences of our acts, for we carry the seeds of these with us in our inner nature wherever we go. In due time we shall reap what we have sowed. If it was evil, the harvest will be evil, but nothing evil will come to us that we have not sowed; only that which is justly due, no more and no less.— And if the seed was good, the harvest will be good also. It cannot be kept back; it will come to us whether we seek it or not. We do not have "to fight for our rights." Karma will do that for us. But we cannot receive any benefits that we have not earned. If we seek to do so, they shall in due time have to be returned to the one to whom they justly belong.

DELAYED EFFECTS

If a stone is thrown up into the air it will fall to the ground in a few seconds. The impetus given to it by the hand that throws it, imparts energy to the stone. While the stone moves through the air, this energy remains unexpended. When the stone hits the ground its inherent energy is expended in producing some sort of effect where it strikes.

We see then that there are three steps involved in an act:

1 The originating impulse ("the throwing of the stone"),
2) The lapse of time between cause and effect ("the stone in the air") and
3) The effect produced when the energy in the stone expends itself, ("the stone strikes the ground").

1) is "Karma in the making";
2) is unbalanced Karma "suspended" or "stored" as it were, awaiting its opportunity to be balanced;
3) is Karma in the process of being balanced.

It may avoid confusion to note that the term Karma is sometimes used in a special sense as in the expression that "someone is working off a lot of unpleasant Karma." In that case the term does not refer to the complete three-step process outlined above, but only to the accumulated and latent energy of step 2) being transmuted into the active energy of step 3).

When the stone was thrown up into the air and allowed to fall without interference, the interval of time between cause and effect lasted only a few seconds. But suppose that at the apex of its travel, the stone landed on the roof of some building. It would then be prevented from continuing its journey and its stored energy would remain latent. The stone may remain on that roof for years, possibly even centuries, before someone accidentally pushes it over the edge, but when this happens, the stone resumes its fall and when it strikes the ground, the effect will be the same as it would have been if it had fallen immediately. The length of the time period had no influence on the final effect. The same principle applies to a compressed spring. The exact amount of energy used in compressing it will be released when the spring is freed, regardless of the length of time it was under compression.

In human affairs there is also a lapse of time between action and reaction that may vary from zero to many years, perhaps a life-time or even more. It is this delay that causes so many to think that the effect may never come, just as the man who threw the stone that landed on the roof may walk off and forget the incident without realizing that sometime in the future the effect from his act must follow.

Whenever Man thinks, feels or acts, a change is made in the invisible part of his nature; a psycho-magnetic force is generated that henceforth irresistibly draws the man to those circumstances where the balancing of the act can and will take place. Thus Man himself is the link between his act and the effect that must follow. Man is a storehouse of forces and energies of his own making, each one the result of some former act, and each one awaiting its turn to be balanced. As the magnet picks out the iron filings and leaves the sand, so will each one of these unbalanced forces attract its own counterpart.

"THE NICK IN THE TYPE"

In this connection there comes to mind a principle of selection employed in a machine which the writer saw in a printing establishment some years ago, one where printing was done with individual, loose type, a separate one for each letter to be printed. After printing, all this type had to be sorted out and each one placed in its proper pocket for use the next day. This sorting was done by a "distributing machine" through which all the type had to pass. Each type had a notch or nick of a certain shape cut in its edge and located at a certain height, all different for different letters. As the type passed through the intricate system of passages of the distributing machine, they all sooner or later passed by a slot which had a projection corresponding to the nick in the type and this nick led the type to its proper destination.

When Man thinks or acts, he makes a "nick" in the invisible part of his nature, which he henceforward carries with him. As he passes through life he will face many experiences, but he will be deeply affected only by those that correspond to the "nick in the type" of his own inner nature.

The fact that the "nick in the type" is invisible should not be surprising, since the thought or feeling that led to the act is also invisible. For those who have developed their inner faculties, thoughts and feelings are visible for they have form and substance on their own planes, the Ancient Wisdom tells us.

AGENCIES USED BY KARMA

Heredity and Environment.

Karma uses many different agencies for the accomplishment of its purposes. Two such media are heredity and environment.

When a soul or Ego is ready to return to incarnated life all the old ties that linked it to other Egos in the past begin to assert themselves, and the strongest of these will attract the Ego to that family circle with which it has most in common. The incoming Ego will therefore be drawn to those parents that are more or less similar to itself, at least in some respects. The consequence of this inner similarity often reflects itself in a similarity in outward appearance. But since the inner similarity is not complete in all its details, there are also differences in outward appearance.

The characteristics of the incoming Ego are due to its own former thoughts and deeds, i.e., its Karma. It is therefore Karma that determines our family connections and with this our heredity. The sequence, therefore, is not that children are like their parents because they are born together, but that they come to their parents because they are similar to them in character. It is a case of "Birds of a feather flock together." They flock together because they are inherently alike; they do not become alike by flocking together.

Whereas love, similarity of character, common interests are the factors that usually draw the Ego to its future family, there can also be other forces at work. Souls may be drawn together in order to work out some unsolved problem; to settle some old Karmic score. A wayward soul may be given an opportunity to redeem itself by being drawn to a good family, while at the same time its presence there acts as a spur for the development of patience and charity on the part of the rest of the family. Similarly a relatively advanced soul may choose to incarnate in a backward family for its own discipline while at the same time the other members of this family can profit by the presence of a helpful influence in their midst.

If similarity between parents and children were due solely to heredity, it should be uniform and consistent, but this is not the case. Children may be like their parents in some respects, but differ widely from them in other ways. Children in the same family also show great differences in characteristics even though they have identical ancestry. A case is known of so called identical twins, where one was an albino with milky white skin and hair and reddish eyes, while the other had black hair and dark eyes like both parents.

Geniuses are sometimes born in families with just ordinary intellectual development, and idiots have been born to highly intellectual parents.

Napoleon showed an ability and genius completely lacking in his parents and among his many brothers and sisters. The musical ability of Bach gradually faded out from his family line.

Those who claim that our innate characteristics are caused by our heredity point to similarities, but ignore differences. A satisfactory theory must explain both. Since heredity fails to do this it is evident that the *cause* of our inherent characteristics lies deeper than the simple transfer of qualities from parents to children.

The ordinary theory of heredity also introduces problems of injustice and responsibility, which it fails to solve. Why should one child be handicapped by an unfavorable heredity, while another is aided by a favorable one? How can anyone be held responsible for his acts if his characteristics are determined by his parents and not by himself? Parents in their turn can shift the responsibility to grandparents and so on ad infinitum. Ultimately none would be responsible for any action. The criminal could then excuse his crime by blaming it on his heredity. No organized society could endure if this view of heredity were applied in courts of law.

The difficulty with the ordinary theory of heredity is that it endeavors to explain Man's inherent characteristics on the basis of a single earthlife. The problems of heredity cannot be solved unless we recognize the doctrine of reincarnation. Seen in the light of repeated existences all difficulties vanish. The Soul, the Ego, has lived before and its present characteristics are the results of its former actions. Heredity, therefore, is an effect, not a cause. It is one of the means used by Karma to bring to Man the effects of causes he sowed in previous lives. There is no injustice in the process and each one is himself responsible for what he is, and what he does.

Our environment like our heredity is the effect of our former thoughts and deeds. At birth we are drawn to such circumstances and surroundings as we made for ourselves in our past lives or to an environment where unbalanced Karma can be balanced. Environment like heredity is one of Karma's most effective working tools.

Environment is another thorn of injustice if seen from the viewpoint of a single earth-life, but is recognized as a just balancing of effects if viewed in the light of reincarnation.

CHANCE-EVENTS

When we say that an event "happens by chance" we mean either that it happens without cause or that the cause was not apparent. Used in the former sense the expression is self-contradictory, for an event can not be produced by a "cause" that by definition is no cause. There is no such thing as chance, if by chance we mean that events happen without cause. Every event in human life, from the most commonplace to the most strange and unusual is governed by the Law of Karma.

But if we use the word "chance" in its second sense it becomes a convenient term to describe events whose cause is concealed from us.

In many events the delay between cause and effect is brief. We can therefore see the connection between the two and it is easy to recognize the operation of Karma.

In the case of other events including those referred to as accidents, strokes of luck or misfortunes, chance, etc., there may be a long time period between cause and effect. In these the effect is seen, but not the cause. The Ancient Wisdom tells us that all such events are the delayed effects of causes sowed earlier in this life, or perhaps in a previous incarnation and long since forgotten. When the time is ripe for the balancing of these causes "the nick in the type" of the individual's own inner nature leads him into trouble or saves him from it. The strange outward circumstances are the means used by Karma to accomplish its ends.

Illustrations of such events are given below. They are all actual cases reported in newspapers and magazines.

Danger in Security — The home should be a safe place, but the National Safety Council reports that for one year out of 88,000 fatal accidents in the U.S., 28,000 or nearly 32% occurred in the home.

A man was seated on the front porch of his home. A speeding car picked up a pebble from some gravel on the street and threw it 80 feet, with the speed of a bullet, striking the man in the forehead and killing him.

Another man had difficulty in getting his foot into a shoe. He gave an exasperated yank, lost his balance and fell. The resultant skull fracture killed him.

A man, who had to leave his car behind on account of a flat tire, started walking to the nearest town. In order to be safe from being struck by passing cars he walked on the outside of a row of trees growing along the highway. A car trying to pass a truck got out of control, passed between two trees and struck the pedestrian, who was hospitalized.

Safety in Danger — A man plunged safely over Niagara Falls in a barrel, but broke his neck slipping on an orange peel.

A professional parachute jumper, who had made 2226 leaps from planes and balloons without injury, was hospitalized after a tumble from the back of a parked truck.

A lady flier once fell 3,000 feet in her plane and escaped unhurt, but suffered a broken nose and other injuries when her bed collapsed in a hotel.

Narrow Escapes — In an explosion in a Texas school where 413 children lost their lives, one girl leaned under her desk to pick up a piece of paper just as the blast let go. The desk shielded her from falling debris.

Just as a man drove his automobile onto a three-track railroad crossing, he saw a train bearing down on him. Thinking it was on the farthest of the three tracks, he jammed his foot on the brake. But his foot slipped, struck the accelerator and the car leaped forward to the outside track. The locomotive grazed the rear of the car, since the train actually was on the center track, on which the driver had intended to stop.

Singular Rescues — An automobile mechanic was overcome by carbon monoxide gas, while repairing the heater in a closed car. He slumped forward in such a position that his chin hit the horn button. Friends came to his rescue.

A British submarine had been lying on the bottom of the ocean two days and the crew expected certain death. The captain led them in singing the wellknown hymn "Abide With Me." Sleeping tablets were then distributed to calm the nerves of the sailors. One of them fainted soon afterwards and fell against an apparatus that set the air mechanism in motion, whereupon the submarine came up to the surface and headed for shore. All on board were rescued.

Kept from Danger — A high school boy, busy helping his father in the grocery store, just missed the school bus speeding by. He tried to hail it, but was left behind. The bus was struck by a freight train. Twenty-two of his school mates and the driver were killed.

A man, traveling with his wife and baby in the desert country of Arizona, stopped briefly to do some work on his car. A little later he came to the usually dry bed of a stream-crossing to see three other machines, just ahead of his own, swept away by a flash-flood, caused by a cloudburst, that struck without warning.

A mother used to take her four year old child for a swing in the lawn-hammock every day after dinner, but one day the mother was too busy and told the girl to go alone. The girl, however, preferred to wait inside until the mother was ready to come. A few minutes later a crash was heard and when the mother looked out into the back yard she found that a windmill and water tank, located in a neighbor's yard, and weighing many tons, had collapsed and the hammock where mother and girl used to swing was buried under heavy timber and debris.

Blessings in Disguise — A girl injured her spine falling down stairs and as a consequence lost the use of both legs. Doctors held out little hope for recovery. Five years later a truck ran into the carriage in which she was being wheeled to a theater. After the shock her condition began to improve and after a few months she was able to walk unaided.

A woman, who had become deaf from an ear infection, had her hearing restored three months later by the shock she received when her house was struck by lightning.

A fifteen year old boy suffered a leg infection after a soccer game injury, and could not walk without crutches. A year later he was kicked by a horse and this drove to the surface a bone chip which x-rays had failed to disclose. After this was removed the leg healed and the crutches were discarded.

So far — but no farther — A man, who was working near an ice saw, got his overalls entangled dragging his leg into the machinery. The saw cut off the leg, twisted the overalls into a powerful tourniquet and then jammed. The man lay helpless for an hour, the twisted clothing cutting off the flow of blood and saving his life.

A man was "hanged" for a crime he did not commit, but the rope slipped and he did not die. Later the real murderer confessed and the innocent man was saved.

A teacher who had been blind for 18 years, slowly and without any apparent cause regained her sight.

Appointment with Death — During the bombardment of a city

a business man grabbed his money and dashed off to the country in his automobile, because a house near him was bombed. Miles away he was blown to pieces by a bomb.

In an earthquake an office worker had to pass through the machine room of a laundry to reach the street. The building collapsed and the woman was killed. If she had remained in the office she would have been unharmed, for that building was not damaged.

Karma strikes or Karma saves — A gas explosion under a city street sent a heavy cast iron manhole cover five stories into the air, crashing through an elevator skylight, falling down the shaft and into the elevator, killing one passenger, but leaving the other three unhurt.

In the eruption of Mt. Pelée on Martinique on May 8, 1902, the city of St. Pierre was destroyed and all its inhabitants killed except one. A prisoner, held in the city jail, was the sole survivor.

Immunity to Disease — Some people, who are constantly exposed to contagion, do not contract disease, while others who are not so exposed, and who may use every means to protect themselves, may be stricken with it.

Accident-prone Individuals — Accidents are not uniformly distributed through the population. Statistics on this subject show that accidents in any group of individuals are mainly due to a very small number of accident-prone persons. This proneness to accidents is a relatively stable individual quality.

Circumstances do not explain — It is evidently impossible to explain these events as effects of the outward circumstances under which they happen, for the outcome is frequently the opposite to what should be expected under these circumstances. The home should be a safe place, but it may not be. Slipping on an orange peel should be less dangerous than going over Niagara Falls in a barrel. A fall of three or four feet off a parked truck should be less likely to cause injury than thousands of parachute jumps, but it was not.

The Cause must be in the Individual — Why is it that under the *same* circumstances different individuals fare differently? In the

Texas school explosion where hundreds were killed, one who was in the midst of it escaped. The same happened in the Mt. Pelée eruption where many thousands were killed; one who was in the center of the destroyed city was saved.

When we add to this the fact, furnished us by accident statistics, that certain individuals are much more subject to accidents than the average, does it not become apparent that the real cause for what happens must be inherent in the individual himself rather than in the circumstances?

COMMENTS ON CHANCE-EVENTS BASED ON THE ANCIENT TEACHINGS

No place is safe if it is our Karma to be hurt, as shown by accidents in the home.

Seeking safety may lead us into danger as was the case with the man who put a row of trees between himself and the highway, the woman who sought safety from the earthquake and the man who fled the bomb.

No danger will bring us harm if we are not due to be harmed, as shown in the case of the school girl in the gas explosion and the prisoner in the eruption of Mt. Pelée.

Karma strikes when our time is up, but not before. The parachute jumper and the man who rode over Niagara Falls both had some more time due them and escaped a greater danger only to be overtaken by a lesser one when their time was up.

We may be brought to the brink of disaster and death may seem inevitable, but Karma will provide an escape if we are due to be saved, as was the crew of the submarine, the man who fainted with his chin on the horn button and the man who was "hanged."

When our own effort to save ourselves would have brought us death as in the case of the man crossing the three railroad tracks, Karma intervenes, if we are to be spared, and, causing us to make what we think is a false step, saves our life.

We may be kept from danger by circumstances that we object to at the time, but later find were the means of saving our lives, as happened to the boy who missed the school bus, the driver who was delayed and escaped the flash-flood, and the mother and child who were unable to take their usual swing in the hammock.

When we have exhausted the measure of suffering due us, Karma finds ways and means to bring relief, means that may seem harsh, but bring the desired results as in the case of the invalid whose carriage collided with a truck, the woman whose hearing was restored by a stroke of lightning, and the boy whose infection was cleared up as an indirect result of being kicked by a horse. Or Karma may use means that are less spectacular as in the case of the school teacher, whose eyesight returned after 18 years of blindness.

Serious misfortunes may be due us, but not the loss of life, and Karma brings us the one without the other, as it did to the man who lost his leg in the ice saw, but was saved from bleeding to death. And if we are due to lose our life, death may overtake us in the most unexpected manner, as it did with the man in the elevator killed by the flying manhole cover.

We may have in our system germs of many dangerous diseases, but they are powerless to hurt us unless it is our Karma to contract the disease.

What is due us will come to us, whether good or bad. What is not due us will pass us by. The "accidents" and "chance events" of life as well as heredity and environment are tools used by Karma in balancing old and forgotten causes.

The Arabs illustrate the futility of trying to escape one's destiny with the following story:

Omar, the merchant, had been foretold that he would meet death on a certain day at 7 o'clock in the evening. When the day arrived he mounted his fastest horse and rode all day into the desert to find a safe hiding place. Just before 7 o'clock he reached an oasis and threw himself exhausted on the ground, congratulating himself at having found a safe refuge. Looking around he saw someone else lying under some trees nearby and got up to investigate. The stranger asked him: "Are you Omar, the merchant?" On receiving an affirmative answer, he continued: "I was told to meet you here at 7 o'clock. I was beginning to think that you would be late, but I see that you are just on time. I am Death; now let us go."

The real causes of accidents and other "chance-events" can not be explained on the basis of a single earth life, but are easily recognized when man's repeated earth lives are taken into account.

KARMA AND CARELESSNESS

If our destiny is inescapable is it any use to exercise carefulness in our actions?

Nature can always be trusted to balance Karma in the most merciful way consistent with Justice. When we are careless or reckless, we may interfere with Nature's plan. We are then challenging our Karma and may thereby bring down on ourselves an avalanche of effects that was not scheduled to come until later in life. If left to Nature we might have been given more time and been better prepared to face this experience when it *had* to come. We should take such precautions as common sense dictates, knowing that if we are not karmically connected with an impending event, these precautions will be effective. Excessive precautions will not save us from our destiny and may instead lead us into a situation where this destiny can be fulfilled as shown by the examples cited.

If our carelessness affects others it may hasten their Karma and force them to meet it when they are unprepared. The fact that we have caused injury to others by our carelessness makes us karmically liable to injury by the carelessness of others. We have sowed a harmful seed, which we eventually shall have to reap.

If instead of being careless we are solicitous for the welfare of others, we generate a helpful force that protects them so that their Karma may be balanced according to Nature's plan instead of being precipitated out of season.

WE MAKE OUR OWN DESTINY

We ourselves determined what our destiny was to be by our own thoughts, feelings and acts in former lives and herein lies the key to our future destiny. We cannot change our past actions and must reap the effects of these, but we can make the future brighter and happier by our present thoughts and acts.

Man is a free agent and can set new causes in motion. The motives for his actions can be inspired by his higher principles or by his personal desires. As explained earlier, the Human Ego stands as it were between these two opposing poles of its nature and has the power to choose one or the other. The impulses from the higher side of man's nature come from his spiritual source, which is the source of all life, and these impulses are therefore always of an altruistic nature. It is these impulses that should be the motives of all our actions and if followed we can never go wrong. Our actions will then be helpful to others and never injurious to ourselves.

The spiritual unity and spiritual origin of all men is the basis for the ethical teachings that have been given to men by all great Teachers of the past. They are embodied in the Sermon on the Mount and epitomized in The Golden Rule. When we do unto others as we would have others do unto us, we need not give any thought to the consequences that will follow. Karma will take care of these and our future lives will not be marred by tragedies and misfortunes.

But unfortunately we are not all capable of living up to the high ideals of the Golden Rule. We have in former existences yielded to the selfish impulses of our lower nature with the result that these are now strong and crowd out the higher motives. And when we follow the lower impulses friction and strife are the result, leading in many cases to accidents and disasters in future incarnations. Thus we make our own destiny and bring upon ourselves the tragedies that we so bitterly complain of later.

"AS ABOVE SO BELOW"

We are unable to follow the operations of Karma on inner, invisible planes, but they can be observed on the material plane. We can then apply these observations to other planes if we make use of the ancient principle known as the Hermetic axiom: "As above, so below." According to this the small mirrors the great;

the lower reflects the higher and what happens on higher planes has its counterpart on lower planes, making due allowance for the different characteristics of the different planes. We see an application of this principle in the similarity that exists between the structure of the solar system and the structure of the atom.

The Hermetic axiom in its turn is based on the oneness of all life. Since the same One Life manifests on all planes of Nature, but under different aspects, it is but natural that the same laws should govern on all these planes.

A few examples showing how the Law of Cause and Effect works in the material world should therefore illustrate how this Law operates on other planes of Nature.

In ordinary money matters it is possible to repay a debt before it is due, and it is considered fair and proper to repay it either in a lump-sum or "on the installment plan"— a little at a time. But we can become indebted to others in many different ways besides borrowing money from them. If the case is comparable to a money debt, however, it seems fair to assume that it can be repaid in advance and either all at once or a little at a time.

We learn from Physics that two equal and opposite forces neutralize each other and their combined effect is zero. If one of the forces is larger than the other the effect will equal the difference between the two and will act in the direction of the larger force. Thus in the world of human relations, if we call such actions as will bring happiness, peace and well-being to others and to ourselves "meritorious," and those that bring unhappiness, strife and suffering to others and to oneself "de-meritorious," and compare these two activities to the action of physical forces, it becomes apparent that such actions might counteract each other and leave a net result of zero, or a balance of merit or demerit, whichever predominates.

Or if we are engaged in business and charge more for our goods or services than they are worth we are doing an injustice to our fellow men. We put an extra burden on them, by whatever amount we have overcharged them, and in due time Karma will balance this by making us the victims of profiteering by others. We shall then have to pay back what we gained unduly.

We do not know how much of this or a similar nature we may have done in the past, but whatever it is, we shall have to make it up. We cannot reach each one of our victims individually to make restitution for we do not know who they are, or where they are. If we want to remedy the harm we have done, we must start a series of actions of an opposite nature and in a general way act so as to serve our fellow men without seeking selfish gain in return. By doing this we prebalance our Karma instead of waiting until Karma collects the debt we owe.

The illustration was taken from the field of commerce, but the principle applies to any human activity. We might be remiss in our mental attitude to others; we might be sulky and temperamental when we should be pleasant and even-tempered. We might be critical and cynical when we should be kindly and appreciative. We might have erred in a hundred different ways in our relations with our fellow men, but whatever may be the nature of our demeritorious acts we should start meritorious acts of an opposite nature to balance the former.

As another example we know that on the material plane we are affected by the forces of Nature, but we are not governed or enslaved by them. We cannot interfere with these forces in the sense of making them inoperative, but we can overcome their effect by interposing other and stronger counteracting forces.

The force of gravitation, for instance, tends to keep us on the ground, and if we want to get from the first to the second floor of a building, we have to overcome this force. We do this by interposing a muscular force that is stronger than that of gravitation.

If there were no stairway available, few would be able to make the ascent, but there is nothing to stop us from building a stairway and making the climb step by step — "on the installment plan."

If we want to get back to the ground floor, we can get there by jumping, in which case we might incur a serious injury, or we can use the stairway and thereby overcome the effect of the gravitational force by a number of small muscular resistance efforts. Throughout all this we were under the influence of the force of gravitation, but this did not prevent us from accomplishing our purpose.

If we can thus overcome a force on the material plane, it should be possible to overcome unexpended karmic force in any field by interposing another and opposite force in this same field.

EVERY EFFORT COUNTS

A stone placed on one pan of a scale may keep this down for a long time, but a fine trickle of sand continuously pouring on the other pan will in time balance and then outweigh the stone. In the beginning it seemed as though the sand had no effect for the stone remained unmoved, then, suddenly, it is lifted. And so it is with our own actions. We do not know how big our "stone," our accumulation of demerit, may be, and we may have to wait a long time before the results of our efforts will become apparent. But as every grain of sand did its part towards outweighing the stone, so every effort at self-improvement, even the smallest, counts, and if continued, the time will come when all demerit will be balanced.

A NEW FACTOR ENTERS

In every field of karmic guilt, meritorious action will introduce a new and beneficent force that will affect the result for the better.

The action can be compared to a ball thrown through the air. If there is no wind, the distance the ball will travel is governed by two factors: the impulse given to it by the hand and the force of gravitation.

If a wind is blowing, a new factor enters, that will change the result. If the ball moves against the wind, its travel will be shortened; if it moves with the wind its travel will be lengthened.

In either case the original impulse, given to the ball by the thrower, had its full effect. In case of the adverse wind, however, part of the impulse was absorbed in overcoming the wind-resistance, with the net result that the ball travel was shortened.

In the case where the ball travels with the wind, none of the original impulse is dissipated, and the effect of the wind is to increase the ball's travel.

If we apply this principle to human actions, and for the purpose of illustration consider that the direction in which the ball is thrown represents de-meritorious action, then the adverse wind would represent meritorious action.

As the adverse wind reduced the ball travel, so would the meritorious action counteract at least a part of the demerit and make the net effect less unfavorable than it would have been if no effort at counteraction had been made. It is conceivable that a hurricane might even reverse the direction of the ball's travel.

ALL WE NEED TO KNOW

Karma is such a vast and intricate subject that it would require super-human intelligence to understand how it works in all its various applications. But such detailed knowledge is not necessary in order to understand its application in daily life. All we really need to know is that we shall reap what we have sowed, all that we have sowed and nothing that we did not sow.

With this idea firmly in mind it is easy to see the folly of all wrongdoing, of all action that brings suffering and injury to others. It is also plain that if we apply the Golden Rule to our actions, the harvest will be beneficial to others and to ourselves and there will be no unfavorable balance that we shall have to make up later. From that time onward, life will take on a brighter and happier aspect.

NEUTRALIZING OR PRE-BALANCING KARMA

If an individual through former thoughts and deeds has built undesirable qualities into his character, he need not accept this condition with a negative, fatalistic attitude. Instead of allowing these tendencies to remain in his nature, he can take a positive attitude and, with proper counteraction, do much to modify his character for the better.

Some of the Ancient Teachings that touch on this subject follow:

Measures taken by an Ego to repress tendency, eliminate defects, and to counteract by setting up different causes, will alter the sway of Karmic tendency and shorten its influence in accordance with the strength or weakness of the efforts expended in carrying out the measures adopted.

The effects [of Karma] may be counteracted or mitigated by the thoughts and acts of oneself or another, and then the resulting effects represent the combination and interaction of the whole number of causes involved in producing the effects.*

What might be called the doctrine of the nullification of Karma is an application in this department of the well-known law in physics which causes an equilibrium when two equal forces oppose each other. A man may have in his Karmic account a very unpleasant cause and at the same time a cause of opposite character. If these come together for expression at the same time they may so counteract each other as that neither will be apparent and the equilibrium is the equivalent of both. In this way it is easy to understand the Biblical verse: "Charity covers a multitude of sins," as referring to the palliative effect of charitable deeds as opposed to deeds of wickedness, and giving a reason for the medieval knight devoting some of the years of his life to alms-giving.†

Karmic causes may interfere with each other and produce a result in our life which, while similar to neither cause, will be the proper resultant of both. It may also be exhausted by two opposite Karmic causes meeting each other and thus destroying the effect of each.‡

The nature of each incarnation depends upon the balance as struck of the merit and demerit of the previous life or lives — upon the way in which the man has lived and thought; and this law is inflexible and wholly just.§

---

* "Aphorisms on Karma." Originally published in *The Path* magazine, March 1893.

†From *Echoes from the Orient*, by Wm. Q. Judge, p. 48.

‡From an address by Wm. Q. Judge, delivered at the Convention of the Theosophical Society in Chicago, April 27-28, 1890, and reprinted in *The Theosophical Forum*, Dec. 1943 p. 551.

§From *An Epitome of Theosophy* by Wm. Q. Judge, p. 24.

[Every minute portion of Karma need not] be felt in the same detail as when produced, for several sorts of Karma may come to a head together at one point in life, and, by their combined effect, produce a result which, while, as a whole, accurately representing all the elements in it, still is a different Karma from each single component part. This may be known as the nullification of the postulated effect of the classes of Karma involved.*

POSTPONING KARMA

We can trust Nature to administer our Karma to us in the most merciful way consistent with Justice, and when we are best able to receive it. We would therefore do well to face Karma when it comes and get through with it, for whatever we endure now is that much less to be endured in the future.

If we seek to dodge it and succeed in doing so temporarily, it will return at a later time, when it may coincide with some other Karma, thus adding to the burden of the latter.

One individual may be strong enough to bear up under a heavy blow that would crush a weaker character. But as "God tempers the wind to the shorn lamb," so the second individual may receive his Karma through a series of little trials, one after another. Thus Karma can be distributed over a longer or shorter period, but the sum total of retributive Karma must balance the initial act.

GROUP-KARMA

Major accidents, such as trainwrecks and shipwrecks, plane crashes, fires, floods, earthquakes, etc., are cases where large numbers of individuals are drawn together because they have similar Karma to work off. Every participant has by his former acts created such Karma as will result in a serious accident or even the loss of life. The "nick in the type" of all these individuals is similar and this similarity psychomagnetically draws them to-

---

*Ibid., pp. 25f.

gether to that place and those circumstances where their former deeds can be balanced.

Group-Karma is therefore no different from individual Karma. If the individuals concerned had not met their destiny in a group, they would have met it sooner or later in separate accidents.

Epidemics that wipe out vast numbers of the population and famines that may affect large portions of the human race are also cases of individual Karma suffered collectively.

Nations like individuals have their life cycle. In the beginning they are strong and vigorous, then follows a period of maturity and finally disintegration and decay. They also have their Karma depending on how they have acted as nations in the past. If they have been aggressive and by brute force subjugated their weaker neighbors they will in their turn meet the same fate. The Egos that make up that nation incarnate again together, perhaps in the same nation after this has grown old and decrepit, or perhaps in another nation under a new name. This nation will now become the victim of its stronger neighbor and thus reap what it had sowed in the past.

Every individual is drawn to that nation to which he properly belongs by similarity of characteristics and by past association. National Karma as well as all other group Karma is therefore ultimately based on the Karma of its individual members.

KARMA AND THE PROBLEM OF FREE WILL*

"Behind will stands desire" said the Ancient Hermetists and behind or above desire is the Ego, the conscious entity experiencing the desire.

---

* Writers on this subject point out that the expression "free will" is not descriptive of the real problem. They generally agree that man is free to use or not to use his will in an effort to satisfy some desire, but he is not free to choose what that desire shall be. This is pre-determined by the character with which he has been endowed. Since the desire governs the will, the problem becomes: "Is man free to choose his desires?" rather than: "Is he free to use his will?" The expression "free will" has been retained here since the problem is popularly referred to by that term.

Will is a universal, impersonal, colorless force devoid of moral qualities. It is the desire that motivates the will, that determines its nature or moral quality.

The will is a driving power used by an Ego to control and direct its energies to accomplish a desired purpose. The will exists on all planes and the higher the plane, the more powerful is the will. It is possessed in greater or less degree by all entities.

"I want" is not the same as "I will." "I want" is the same as "I desire." "I will" when I strive to obtain the object of my desire.

We often hear it said of an ambitious or aggressive individual who plows through all resistance in order to attain some desired goal, that he has "a strong will," but since the "quantum" of will used depends on the strength of the desire behind the will, it would be more appropriate to say that such an individual has "strong desires."

Taking a Second Thought.

"Think twice before you speak" (or act) is an ancient rule.

When we "think once" it is our desire using the lower mind to accomplish its purpose without giving the Ego a chance to exert its influence. The Ego was then dominated by the desire.

If we stop "to take a second thought," the Ego has time to call the higher mind into action. It can then examine the desire and decide on how to act. If it decides favorably, the Ego draws upon the will and directs it to accomplish the desired objective. In this case the Ego was the determining factor rather than the desire.

CONFLICTING DESIRES*

The desires that motivate man's will come from various sources within his complex nature and are of many different kinds. Some come from the organs of the body; others from the emotional nature or the mind. These are more or less connected with the comforts and pleasures of the Personality. Still others come to

---

*Much that is said here is explained by Chapter IV, especially the sections dealing with the Human Ego, Mind, Moods and Character Building.

man from his Higher Nature. These concern his responsibilities and duties towards others and are of a broader, more altruistic type. These two types of desires naturally conflict with one another.

The active, experiencing entity, the Human Ego, stands midway between the higher and lower principles of the human constitution and feels the contrasting impulses to action from these two sides of its nature. The same individual at one time experiences a certain desire and at another time one of an opposite nature; sometimes he experiences both simultaneously.

When the Ego repeatedly yields to a lower impulse, this grows ever stronger and eventually becomes habitual. Due to lack of self-analysis the Ego has identified itself with the impulse and temporarily surrendered its power of control. When this point is reached the Ego automatically yields to the desire whenever this presents itself. The desire then uses the will to accomplish its purpose and the Ego negatively submits.

When the Ego has come to a realization that it is not identical with its thoughts or desires, it will no longer yield automatically to every thought or desire that presents itself. When confronted with conflicting desires it will instead examine them and weigh and pass judgement on them before choosing.

CHARACTER INCLINES BUT DOES NOT RULE

We know that different individuals react differently when confronted by divergent impulses, for each one is inclined in a certain direction by the qualities inherent in his character.

As an illustration let us assume the following case. Three individuals, whose daily duties are of a monotonous uninteresting nature, are unexpectedly offered an opportunity to go on an extended pleasure trip or some other amusement that would take them away from their duties and might involve the loss of their positions and incomes.

The first individual might act on the spur of the moment and accept the opportunity without considering the consequences. The desire of his personal nature for pleasure was so strong that it brushed aside the call of duty, and the Ego, being accustomed to identify itself with its desire, submits and fails to use its power of choice.

The second individual feels the same desire for pleasure as the first and the same call of duty, but after a moment's deliberation, he declines the opportunity for pleasure and sticks to his duty instead. In his case the sense of duty was so much stronger than the desire for pleasure that it naturally overruled the latter, and it required little effort by the Ego to make its choice.

The third individual is also aware of the same opposing impulses as were felt by the other two. He feels both, but he is not dominated by either. He looks beyond the present moment to the final effect of his action. He takes time to listen to the voice of conscience that whispers to him about his duties to his family and to his fellow men. He weighs and compares the pros and cons before he decides what to do. He hesitates, leaning now to one side, then to the other. He has come to a parting of the road. He cannot proceed unless he makes a choice. He cannot travel both roads. He must choose one or the other. And he does choose.

POWER OF CHOICE INHERENT IN EGO

Let us suppose that the two opposing attractions are exactly equal, for there must be such a case, since either of them may be stronger than the other. If then the two attractions are equally strong, and since a choice has to be made and is made, the power to choose must be inherent in the Ego and not in the attractions. And if the Ego has the power to choose when the attractions are equal, it also has the power to choose when they are not equal. A change in the attractions cannot take away from the Ego its power to choose, since this power is inherent in the Ego and not in the attractions.

When the attractions are unequal and the desire for pleasure is stronger than the sense of duty as in the case of the first individual, he yielded to the desire because he was negative and had his consciousness centered in his Personality. He too had the power of choice but did not use it.

If he had been positive and had his consciousness centered in his Higher Nature, he could have refused to submit to the lower impulse, used his power of choice and resisted the lower impulse, even though this was stronger than the higher. This requires effort, for the Ego has to furnish the will that is necessary to over-rule the stronger desire. The Ego is not under compulsion to make this effort, for the upward attraction does not force itself on the Ego. It is felt merely as an appeal to the better side of the Ego.

In this case the higher appeal by itself would have been ineffective, and would have been overruled by the stronger desire unless the Ego chose to ally itself with the appeal and add its force to this side of its nature. If a man resists a desire for something that he likes to do, and that is easy to do, and instead does something that is drudgery and requires effort on his part, such action must be the result of a conscious and deliberate choice and a resolutely applied will.

We can slide down hill without effort. We do it from sheer inertia, but we cannot stop that downward slide without determination to do so, and we cannot climb uphill without effort. That determination and that effort are not forced on us, but are the results of choice and a strong will.

NOT PREDESTINATION OR FATALISM

The different manner in which the three individuals reacted to the same impulses was due to differences in their characters. It has already been explained how man builds his own character by his thoughts, acts and habits. A part of this work has been done in his present life, but by far the greater part he carries with him from former existences.

His character gives him an inclination in a certain direction, but he is not obliged to follow this. He has the power of choice as we have seen and the opportunity to choose is given him by his dual nature. This opportunity has always been his for man's nature has been dual as long as man has existed. By his choice and the acts that follow he creates causes that Karma later returns to him as effects. Since man is the maker of his own character, he alone is responsible for his desires, preferences and consequent reactions.

Man is free to choose, but he must reap the consequences of his choice. It is a destiny he cannot escape, but it is self-made, and since it is not imposed on him by anyone else it is not "predestination." Neither is it "fatalism" for it is not the result of blind, mechanical forces.

When man by his own choice initiates an act, he thereby calls the forces of Nature into operation. He invokes the Law of Cause and Effect, which thenceforth takes over the operation and adjusts the effect to the cause. The conception of free will is therefore in full accord with the Law of Cause and Effect. Neither one invalidates the other and both are factors necessary to man's evolution.

THEORIES OF FATALISM

From the remotest antiquity to the present time, the problem of free will has been a subject of heated debates and much controversy. Many philosophers have come to the conclusion that man is not free to determine how he shall act, but that his choice is predetermined by his inherent characteristics, his desires, his likes and dislikes.

The theologian and the materialist both assume that man came into being at birth and must therefore conclude that he had no part in the making of his character. This must have been made for him by the power that brought him into being, whether that power was God as the theologian believes or blind forces operating in Nature as the materialist holds.

Given a certain character a man must act in a certain way. If he has a noble character, his acts must be good; they cannot be otherwise. If his character is evil his acts must also be evil. He has no choice in either case. He thinks he is free to act because he is free to follow his desires, but since these desires were implanted in him, this sense of freedom is only imaginary. Actually he has no freedom of choice or free will as it is popularly called. These are some of the theories of fatalism. If they were true, man would be an automaton without initiative, a robot compelled to move in a pre-determined groove.

Under these conditions man connot be held morally responsible for his acts. This responsibility must be placed on the power that brought him into being.

A NON-FATALISTIC SOLUTION

The fatalist takes for granted that man only lives a single life on earth and it is this assumption that leads to all the difficulties that follow. The Ancient Wisdom on the other hand teaches that man has lived on earth before. The character, that now inclines him to a certain line of action, was not made for him; he made it himself in former lives. In this life he reaps the effects of his former actions through the medium of this character.

The fatalist also assumes that man is a single, unitary being, identical with his desires, for he makes no distinction between the man himself, the Ego, and the desires he experiences. If this assumption were true, then there would be nothing to offer resistance to these desires and they would dominate man's life completely. In that case fatalism becomes the inescapable conclusion. But there can be no desires felt unless there is an entity, a center of consciousness, that experiences these desires. This entity, says the Ancient Wisdom, is the Human Ego, and the desires are only part of the many-sided vehicle used by the Ego.

They are not identical with the Ego any more than the cocoon is identical with the larva that spun it around itself.

The single earth-life theory is totally inadequate in solving the problem of free will, but with an understanding of man's complex nature and an acceptance of the doctrine of Reincarnation this problem can be solved in conformity with Justice and the Law of Cause and Effect.

FREEDOM OF CHOICE VARIES

The degree of freedom to choose, varies in proportion with the degree of development attained by the individual.

Small children, whose minds are immature have very little

freedom of choice and act almost wholly from impulse. They are therefore not karmically responsible to the same extent as adults. But as the years pass, mind and self-consciousness develop. With these comes the power to tell right from wrong, man's choice becomes deliberate and he is thenceforth morally responsible for his acts.

The less evolved man feels the same opposing attractions as his more developed brother and has the same opportunity to choose, but is less likely to make use of this opportunity. By sheer inertia he allows himself to be swayed by his impulses instead. In this respect some human beings are not far above the animals who obey any impulse that comes upon them.

It is the kind of character we have made for ourselves that determines the degree of freedom of our will.

In the Kingdoms of Nature below the Human, the freedom of choice is very limited, but even in these there exists a certain freedom within the limited range of each one's activities.

FREE WILL A FACTOR IN EVOLUTION

The Ancient Wisdom teachings regarding evolution are treated extensively in such works as *The Esoteric Tradition* and *Man in Evolution* by G. de Purucker. It will here only be touched on in its relation to Karma and free will.

The Universe exists for the evolution of the Soul and the method used to attain this objective, the "scheme of Evolution," is to place man in a series of circumstances where he has to choose between conflicting interests and learn by the experiences that follow upon his choice. Freedom to choose is an indispensable factor in the operation of this plan.

Even the most insignificant act of ours is the result of choice, either made consciously or by force of habit, and that habit was the result of un-numbered choices in the past.

In the business affairs of everyday life we are constantly faced with situations that require choice on our part. In many cases we cannot foresee the consequences of our decision, but have to choose more or less blindly. We may choose wrong, but if we had not chosen we would never have found out our mistake. We learn by a process of trial and error in which mistakes are valuable lessons.

Man often allows himself, even against his better judgement, to be governed by his lower nature rather than by his higher, because he thinks it is easier and more to his advantage. He is short-sighted and grasps at the immediate reward, the pleasant experience close at hand, which this choice seems to offer. If he had taken the long-range view he would have seen that the easy advantage he gained would have to be made up for later by some counter-balancing labor or other compensation, and he would have seen that the selfish pleasure he enjoyed may bring suffering or some other misfortune in its train.

If one such experience is insufficient to teach him the lesson, the individual will repeat his mistake and Karma will reproduce the same effect. After a series of such actions the memory of the experience will associate itself with the selfish impulse, and when this returns, the Ego, even if it has forgotten the details of its experience will, subconsciously, be forewarned and refuse to submit to the impulse. If we choose what we know is beneficial for others and for ourselves, all goes well. If we choose unwisely or selfishly, nothing can stop us from doing so, but we have to reckon with the consequences of our choice.

Thus we see that Nature's methods are beneficent, for the suffering she brings helps us to break up selfish impulses before they become permanent. It helps us to get a grip on ourselves and to make a new start in the right direction.

It has often been asked: "Why were not all men created so that they would always choose what was good for others and for themselves?"

If man were "only able to choose good" he would not be choosing at all; he would act under compulsion. He would be an automaton and would have no opportunity to develop free will and this is a faculty that belongs to a fully developed man. If he is to evolve, man must be free to choose evil as well as good, right as well as wrong. He can not develop strength of character except by repeated victories over his lower nature. If man had no freedom to choose wrong, there would be no merit if he chooses right.

A child that learns to walk could never accomplish this feat if he had to succeed at his first attempt. He must be free to take his tumbles, get bruised and gradually gain control over himself. Likewise man must be free to make mistakes in order to learn by them; and man's nature is made with dual tendencies in order to give him this opportunity.

Struggle is a temporary phase of evolution says the Ancient Wisdom, and once man has won his battle over his lower nature and allied himself permanently with his Higher Nature his struggles will cease. From that time onwards his evolution, directed by his Higher Nature, proceeds smoothly and his higher faculties unfold as a bud unfolds into a flower.

DELAYED EFFECTS AND FREE WILL

The effect of an act does not always follow immediately upon its cause; there is often a long delay between the two. If we are to learn by experience, it might be asked: "Would not the lesson carry more weight if the effect followed immediately upon the cause, for we would then see the connection between the two?"

If the effect did follow immediately upon the cause, as the thunder clap follows the bolt of lightning, an individual with selfish tendencies would never dare to let these out through fear of immediate retribution. He would be prevented from giving an outlet to these tendencies, and they would be repressed but not eliminated. They would then force themselves to the surface at some later date.

In the hope that the effect may be long delayed, or led by ignorance to believe that no effect will follow, the individual will take a chance and try his evil ways. In due course the effect follows and the experience becomes a lesson. The inherent tendency is thus "worked off" instead of being merely repressed.

But it is not necessary that man should give vent to his evil tendencies in order to evolve. They can be faced and conquered on the mental plane and would not have to lead to physical results. It is only when we refuse to do our battles on the mental plane that we have to fight them on the outer plane.

DUAL ASPECT OF FREE WILL

Free will is a tool that man must learn the use of. It is a valuable tool, but like so many other tools, its use is accompanied with certain risks. To an experienced user it is of great benefit, while in the hands of the inexperienced it can cause injury to the user as well as to others.

The man whose consciousness is centered in his personal nature feels his separateness from his fellowmen more strongly than his oneness with them. His motives are therefore often selfish and he acts without due regard for the welfare and the rights of others. By his actions he encroaches on their rights just as other similarly-minded persons encroach on his rights.

When hosts of human beings act in this manner the result is the strife and conflict that is so prevalent in the world today.

Children a few years of age are usually willing to follow the advice and guidance of their parents without much opposition. After a few more years, however, they enter upon a period when they want to have their own way. Then they get themselves into mischief of many kinds and cause trouble for themselves and their parents. When more years have passed they begin to develop responsibility and become more helpful members of their respective families, later to develop into fully responsible men and women.

It would have been stagnation for them, if they always were to be led and directed by their elders. Maturity requires a self-directed life and development of initiative. Lacking in experience the child has to learn its lesson at the cost of much friction and strife. It is a trying period for child and parents, but it is a necessary phase in the child's evolution. The process is made easier to the extent that the child voluntarily accepts the helpful advice of its elders.

Like the child the whole human race is now passing through its "trying age" as it begins to exercise free will. It has not yet learned to do this wisely. Through weakness or ignorance it chooses to follow selfish impulses, and this, done on a grand scale, has brought the whole world into a state of turmoil.

The "trying age" of humanity would be less trying if men followed the Golden Rule and other ethical teachings given them by Jesus, Buddha and other great teachers, for humanity has also had its "Elders" that have tried to lead man through this period with the least possible suffering and strain.

But for humanity, as for the child, this period is only a rung in the ladder of Evolution, that must be surmounted before greater progress can be made. After this phase has been passed and man has reached a point in his evolution where he allies himself with his Higher Nature, he will realize his oneness with his fellow men and his responsibility to them. He will have learned to use his free will more wisely. He will choose to work in harmony with his fellows and for the common good.

There are signs in the world of a growing realization that we are all mutually dependent on one another; that this is "One World" in which there can be no lasting prosperity or happiness in one part if there is misery and unhappiness in another.

GOOD AND EVIL

The presence of evil in the world presents a problem that can not be solved on the assumption that a beneficent, all-wise and all-powerful God is the creator of man. The problem could not be better stated than in the words of the Greek philosopher Epicurus, written some twenty-two centuries ago:

Either God wishes to remove evil from this world, and cannot, or he can and will not, or he neither can nor will, or, to con-clude, he both can and will. If he will and cannot, it is impotence, which is contrary to the nature of God; if he can and will not, it is wickedness, and that is no less contrary to his nature; if he neither will nor can, it is wickedness and impotence at once; if he both can and will (which alone of these conditions is suit-able to God), whence comes the evil which exists in the world?

What we call "evil" or disharmony, strife, greed, oppression, tyranny, together with the misery and suffering that result from such conditions, can be traced directly back to man's belief that he is separate from his fellows and can act without regard for their welfare. The belief that he can do this without having to reap the consequences thereof, gives free reins to his selfish impulses and he acts accordingly. When this attitude of "each one for himself" is taken by vast multitudes of individuals, whose interests conflict, the result is the evil that is so prevalent in the world today.

The duality of spirit and matter that exists in the Universe and in man creates a series of situations in which man has to choose between obeying the impulses of his higher or lower nature. Later he experiences the effects of his choice, and it is by these experiences that Nature teaches man whether he is breaking her laws or living in harmony with them. Good and evil are the end-products of actions inspired by man's higher or lower nature, and it is by comparing these contrasting results that man gradually learns to recognize that the path of altruism is better than that of selfishness.

Standards of good and evil are not fixed conceptions, but vary according to the development of evolving entities. What is "good" for one degree of development is "evil" for a higher degree, and what is "evil" for a lower degree is "good" for one still less developed.

The flame of a candle is a bright, luminous object when placed in a dark room, but it is a dark body when compared to the sun, for it actually throws a shadow when placed in bright sunlight. Good and evil like light and darkness are likewise relative conceptions, but for each degree of development there is a standard of good and evil. Anyone who acts, or tries to act in accord with his best knowledge and belief, is doing what is right or "good" for him, while anyone who acts contrary to this belief, is doing wrong, or "evil." A person who centers his consciousness in the material side of his nature has as yet little control over his appetites, whereas another man, who may be further evolved, centers his consciousness in the spiritual side of his nature and has his appetites under control. More would be expected of the latter and for him to act selfishly would be inexcusable, while to the former it would be understandable, even if not excusable.

Many qualities and quantities in Nature exist "in pairs" or as opposites. For instance there could be no mountains unless there are lowlands or valleys above which the mountains rise. The hand could not feel either heat or cold if all objects were the same temperature as the hand. When compared to a hot object, the hand is cold, while to a cold object it is warm.

There can be no shadow unless there is a light to produce it. If the sun were shining on us day and night, year after year, we would not look upon it as light, for we would have nothing to compare it with. It is only when the darkness of night replaces the sunlight that we learn to appreciate the value of the latter.

The two conceptions of good and evil form a duality on the moral plane, just as the examples cited are dualities on the material plane. We cannot think of good except as a contrast, an improvement on something that is not good, or "evil."

Man is here to progress, and the very idea of progress implies a moving forward from something outgrown and therefore no longer "good," to something better seen ahead; a climbing upward from something inferior to something superior. If there were no such contrasts as forwards and backwards, up and down, good and evil, there would be no "ladder" up which to climb, no resistance to be overcome.

Good and evil are states through which entities pass as they progress from imperfection towards perfection. In the present stage of man's evolution such contrasting states are necessary to his progress, for they involve experiences that man must have in order to round out his character. By experiencing the adverse effects of evil, man fortifies himself against future failures, but to choose evil deliberately for the purpose of experiencing it, is to slide down hill, and is not progress, but retrogression.

When men have learned the lesson of good and evil, they will naturally and automatically act from altruistic motives, and the gross evil that is prevalent in the world today, will be a thing of the past. The duality of good and evil as we know it, will then have served its purpose and will be discarded as a piece of training apparatus in a gymnasium, that is no longer needed. Humanity will then have reached a higher grade in Nature's school of experience. This higher grade will not be free from all problems and difficulties, for man's nature will always be a duality of spirit and matter with its consequent contrasts, but such difficulties as may arise will not lead to the gross evil that plagues the world today, but will take a form appropriate to the higher plane on which humanity will then exist.

It will be seen from what precedes, that the presence of evil in the world is due to the actions of imperfect, unevolved human beings, who break Nature's laws of harmony, and not to any force outside of man, neither God nor blind chance. Man made the evil in the world, but it is also in his power to restore harmony.

In the words of H. P. Blavatsky: "Neither good nor evil would exist were it not for the light they mutually throw upon each other." *

"If we would discern good from evil, light from darkness, and appreciate the former, we can do so only through the contrast between the two."†

Or in the words of Plotinus: "The experience of evil produces a clearer knowledge of good."

SUFFERING AND ADVERSITY AS TEACHERS

Suffering.

Those who believe that our existence here is limited to a single earthlife and who see no purpose in life except the pursuit of pleasure naturally look upon disease and suffering as misfortunes without specific cause and with no useful purpose. To them such misfortunes are but evil intruders that should be eliminated as quickly as possible, since they interfere with a full enjoyment of life.

According to the Ancient Wisdom, however, the purpose of life is not the pursuit of pleasure, but the evolution of the soul; the strengthening of character, and the misfortunes that befall us in life are not accidental, but are the karmic retributions for our

---

*Lucifer, Vol. I, No. 2, October, 1887.
†Ibid.

former acts. While such retributions are painful to endure, they compensate for this by hastening our evolution, for they teach us lessons that we do not learn while life runs smoothly and without difficulties.

Is it not often the case that when life is all pleasant, we settle down to enjoy it and neglect to search for anything beyond our own comfort? We become more self-centered and live a life that is stagnation so far as evolution of our higher faculties is concerned. But Nature will not long tolerate such a condition to exist. A continuous indulging in pleasures is an invitation to disease, and when disease comes pleasure-seeking has to stop and the consciousness turns to more serious subjects. The impaired condition of the physical nature reduces the power of the lower principles to dominate the Ego, and gives the higher principles in man's nature an opportunity to exert their elevating influence.

The breaking up of the everyday routine caused by the disease, the enforced quietness, the time for reflection, all help to give a new outlook on life. What formerly seemed so important may now be recognized as quite insignificant, and the really important things in life may be seen at their true value.

By making the physical nature uncomfortable, suffering forces man to direct his interest and attention towards his Higher Nature. It frees him from the grip of the lower nature and drives him to seek a refuge in the peace of his Higher Nature. Never again, even after health is restored, need the grip of the lower nature be as strong as it was before, if the man takes advantage of the opportunity for a new start that the suffering has opened up for him.

Suffering has another important function. It awakens compassion in our hearts. It enables us to understand the suffering and hardships that others have to pass through, and thus we become ready to extend sympathy and offer them such help and comfort as it may be in our power to give.

If we are cold and indifferent to the distress and suffering of others it is a sign that we ourselves have not had the experience that they are now passing through. If we are callous and hard, how can sympathy be awakened in us except through suffering? We too must suffer in order to understand.

Patience, endurance and fortitude are other faculties that suffering helps to develop.

Besides the beneficial effect that suffering has in improving man's character it is also a help to him on the physical plane, for disease is a purifying process whereby the disharmony, which man created by former wrongdoing, is eliminated and balance and harmony restored.

Poverty.

Poverty and prosperity are other experiences necessary to a rounded-out character.

If a prosperous individual lives in luxury and comfort, without making an effort to relieve the poverty and misery by which he may be surrounded, or which he knows exists, it is evident that he has not yet had the experience of being poor. Since the sight of the misery of others is not enough to arouse his compassion, he must himself pass through this experience in order to understand. It is one of the "grades in the school of experience" that cannot be skipped, and poverty will exist as long as there are individuals that have not learned the lesson thereof. After he has had the experience and knows the hardships it entails, he will no longer be indifferent to the misery of others, but will, with sympathetic understanding for their situation, do something to improve it. A broad, generous, sympathetic nature is characteristic of one who has learned the lesson of poverty and profited therefrom.

Poverty comes to individuals as the result of their Karma, but this is no excuse for the more fortunate to refuse aid if they are in a position to give it.

Poverty teaches lessons to both rich and poor. It is a challenge to the prosperous to show compassion, to practice generosity. The prosperous of today, may have been the poor in the last incarnation. This is their opportunity to show if they have learned their lesson. For the poor the experience is an opportunity to learn the value of little things, to curb wastefulness, to practice economy, to reduce one's wants.

Those who have had to ask for charity report that their requests are much more frequently answered in the districts of the poor than among the well-to-do, even though the amounts received in the former case were smaller, showing the effectiveness of poverty as a teacher.

Adversity.

Experience of success and adversity are both needed for man's training, just as sunshine and rain are necessary for the growth of plants. The oak grows strong by resisting the wind and man grows strong by overcoming the obstacles he has to face. Benefits can be extracted even from unfavorable situations. Every difficulty that we meet can be used as a stepping stone. A ship can be sailed against an unfavorable wind by skilful use of sail and rudder. Periods of success, ease and comfort are not growing periods but interludes for rest between trials.

Mencius, the Chinese philosopher (Third and Fourth Century, B.C.) writes: "When Heaven is about to be gracious to any man, it first exercises his mind with suffering and his sinews and bones with toil. It exposes his body to hunger, subjects him to extreme poverty, and confounds his undertakings. In all these ways it stimulates his mind, strengthens his nature and supplies its incompetences."

And Buddha says: "He who has learned to suffer with patience will be purified and will be the chosen instrument for the alleviation of suffering."

And Socrates, speaking of pleasure and pain, says: "How singular is the thing called pleasure, and how curiously related to pain, which might be thought to be the opposite of it; for they never come to a man together and yet he who pursues the one is generally compelled to take the other. They are two and yet they grow from one stem — and this is the reason why when one comes the other follows."

Understanding Lightens Burden.

Suffering is hard to bear under all circumstances, but an understanding of its cause and purpose makes the burden easier to carry.

The knowledge that it is karmic, and not the result of blind chance, that we have brought it upon ourselves, removes the sense of injustice that would otherwise add to our burden.

What we have made for ourselves must come to us — we can not escape it — but on the other hand *no more* will come to us than is our own.

The karmic suffering that we are now working off will never return and we shall have that much less to face in the future.

When we experience prolonged suffering and pain we are apt to think that this condition will be permanent, but this is not so. When that particular "karmic deposit" is exhausted, the suffering will cease, that account will be closed and will remain so if we do not open it up by sowing new seeds of disharmony.

It helps us to endure suffering if we realize that it is not a meaningless accident without purpose, but that it is a process of purification and helps to restore harmony and health.

It is difficult to recognize the value of suffering while we are experiencing it, but after the ordeal is over, many who bore it bravely have said: "It was hard, but I would not have missed that experience for any price."

It also helps us to realize that while the suffering is temporary, the gain in character development is eternal.

Is suffering necessary to evolution?

The Ancient Wisdom tells us that on higher, more spiritual planes of existence, planes closer to the universal source of life, evolution proceeds as normally and painlessly as the growth of a bud into a flower.

Man's evolution could also proceed without suffering, if his actions were always governed by his Higher Nature, for this never prompts him to act contrary to Nature's laws of harmony.

Man has always had Teachers who, through the various religions of the world, have taught him how to live, and he has had his conscience to warn him when he was in danger of doing wrong. But in the past, as at the present time, man has ignored the ethical teachings that have been given him, and the result is the widespread suffering that we see in the world today.

Man was meant to fight his battles on the mental plane and if he wins his victories over his lower nature there, he will not have to go through his struggles on the physical plane. If he allies himself with his Higher Nature, he avoids painful consequences; if not, he invites misfortune. He himself calls into operation the suffering he needs to learn his lesson.

"GOOD" KARMA AND "BAD" KARMA

The great variety of circumstances under which people live, such as wealth, social position, poverty, sickness or health, etc., are all due to the Karma of the individuals experiencing them. It depends on how the individual reacts to the impact of these circumstances whether they will prove to be a benefit or a detriment to him, for his present reaction determines his future Karma.

Circumstances of wealth, position and power, if used wisely, can be the means of doing much good in the world. They enable their possessor to relieve suffering, spread happiness and promote enterprises that are of general benefit. If used in this manner these circumstances afford an opportunity for man's Higher Nature to express itself. In that case they tend to advance man's evolution and can therefore properly be called "good" Karma.

But such favorable circumstances are not always used in this manner. They can be a temptation to lead a life of idleness and smug comfort. They offer opportunities for an unrestricted pursuit of pleasures, which may lead to dissipation. When reacted to in this manner they are apt to increase the selfishness of the individual, thereby retarding his evolution. Under these conditions what seemed like favorable circumstances actually turned out to be "bad" Karma.

Poverty, hardships, ill health likewise may be either "good" or "bad" Karma according to the reaction they produce in the individual experiencing them. Adversity is a more effective teacher than success, and may, if it develops fortitude, patience and endurance, strengthen a man's character. If reacted to in this manner, adversity promotes man's evolution and, even though it is not pleasant to experience, is in reality "good" Karma.

Whether Karma is "good" or "bad" therefore does not depend so much upon the circumstances we find ourselves in, as on the manner in which we react to them.

What is pleasant Karma, therefore, is not necessarily "good" Karma, and what is unpleasant is not necessarily "bad" Karma.

KARMA AND REVENGE

When the effect of a former deed returns to us we can react in different ways. Suppose it is an unfriendly remark that comes back. If we can accept it without striking back, if we "absorb the shock" without trying to retaliate, we have then and there balanced the effect and closed the account. But if we resent the reaction, if we "toss the ball back" to our adversary, we have set a new cause in motion, which in due time will return to us, and the process will repeat itself until we learn not to strike back. "For hate never is overcome by hate at any time. Hate passes away through love. This is the ancient rule," says the old Buddhist scripture, the Dhammapada.

The desire to retaliate arises from a feeling that we have suffered some injustice, which we feel should be returned in order to restore balance. But if we realize that every event is governed by Karma, we see that the suffering was due us, and that there was no real injustice involved. We also see that the one who caused us injury has thereby set the stage for a similar injury to befall himself, and Karma will inevitably bring this to him without any action on our part.

"To me belongs vengeance and recompense" says the Lord according to Moses.* In other words, it is not for man to revenge himself, but to leave it to Nature and the Law of Cause and Effect. If man insists on taking revenge, he is thereby sowing the seed for the return to himself of the same injury in the future. He is repeatedly striking his head against a stone wall. The only way out is to return good for evil, as taught in the Dhammapada and likewise taught by Jesus.

---

* *Deuteronomy* XXXII, 35.

In the Sermon on the Mount Jesus says: "Ye have heard that it has been said, An eye for an eye, and a tooth for a tooth: But I say unto you, that ye resist not evil: but whosoever shall smite thee on the right cheek, turn to him the other also."* And in the verses that follow there are many other precepts, all based on the principle of returning good for evil.

The saying referred to by Jesus is found in *Exodus* XXI, 23-25. Here, in referring to the punishment that will follow upon evil-doing, it is stated that: ". . . then thou shalt give life for life, eye for eye, tooth for tooth, hand for hand, foot for foot, burning for burning, wound for wound, stripe for stripe."

This, it will be noted, is a concise statement of the Law of Cause and Effect or Karma for it affirms that for every evil done an equal punishment will follow. But, as Jesus says, this Mosaic maxim is not to be taken as a guide for our actions. These should be governed by the principle of returning good for evil.

"INTERFERING WITH KARMA"

If the suffering of an individual is due to his Karma, is it right to interfere with this by trying to relieve the suffering?

The first rule for all our actions should be the Law of Compassion; it is our duty to follow the natural impulse based on human solidarity and render all possible aid to the sufferer.

Furthermore we are not in a position to judge what is or is not someone else's Karma. How do we know but what it is the sufferer's Karma to be relieved by us and failure on our part to render aid may be an interference with Karma rather than the act of rendering such aid? "Inaction in a deed of mercy becomes an action in a deadly sin," says an ancient Hindu scripture.†

When we have rendered such aid as is within our power, our duty is fulfilled. It will then depend on just what is the Karma of the sufferer. If it is to be relieved, our aid will be effective; if not it will fail in its purpose.

---

*Matt. V, 38, 39.

†*The Book of the Golden Precepts.* See *The Voice of the Silence* by H. P. Blavatsky.

It is not possible to interfere with anyone's Karma in the sense of removing it as a cause, but even if the Karma must be experienced it can be made more endurable by compassionate love from some sympathetic friend. This generates a beneficent force that touches and is felt by the sufferer and helps him to bear up under his suffering. It "mixes" with the pain and makes this easier to bear.

KARMA AND FORGIVENESS OF SIN

There is a belief held by many, that we can by prayer to some higher power, or by the adoption of some formula of salvation, be relieved from experiencing the effects of our evil deeds. The ideas we hold influence our actions and a belief that we can escape the consquences of our acts leads us to think that it is not vitally important how we act, since the effect of wrongdoing can always be eliminated by prayer for forgiveness. Those who hold this belief act without serious forethought of the consequences and may thereby bring misfortune on themselves and others.

Since a belief in the forgiveness of sin has this detrimental effect, it becomes important to determine if this is a reasonable assumption on which to base one's future and one's destiny.

It will be noted that the doctrine of the forgiveness of sin contradicts that of Karma. Both doctrines can not therefore be true.

The effect of evil deeds could never be erased unless it were possible to suspend the Law of Cause and Effect, and since this is a law of Nature and not a man-made dictum, it can not be suspended. We know that this does not happen in the material world and would not base our actions in the practical affairs of everyday life on such a belief.

Yet this is in effect what we expect Nature to do when we pray to be freed from the consequences of our wrong-doing. We then ask Nature to break her own laws and make exceptions in cases where we would like to have them made. But in cases where we have done something commendable we would want the same law to operate so that we would receive the fruit of our labor.

If we were successful once in evading the consequences of our acts we would try it again and again and others would do the same.

If Nature's laws could be thus turned aside, man would not learn the lesson which he called forth by his unwise action. A Universe in which this could happen would be a Universe without law, in which all evolution would be impossible.

When man is faced with the ever recurring necessity for choice which daily confronts him, Karma gives him the information he needs to make a wise choice and it tells him what will happen if he does not. After that it is up to the man himself to use his free will and later get his experience.

A wanderer, who comes to a parting of the road, and there finds a road-sign which tells him that the road of selfishness leads to a swamp of misfortunes, while the road of altruism leads to the firm ground of a happy and harmonious life, can save himself much needless suffering and make his evolution easier if he heeds the warning given by the sign.

If he does not heed it but, because he hopes to gain a temporary advantage, deliberately chooses the road that in the end leads to unhappiness and misfortune, he has no one but himself to blame for the result, for he was forewarned and was free to take the other road.

When the effect of his ill-advised deed overtakes him he suffers, and this suffering, if meditated on in the light of Karma, will aid him in making a wiser choice the next time he is faced with one. Paradoxically, he realizes that the time for "after-thoughts" is *before* the choice is made.

The doctrine of forgiveness of sin is also a sign at the parting of the road. It does of course tell the traveler to take the road to firm ground, but it adds that, if he takes the road to the swamp and begins to sink, he can get out of his trouble by asking someone else to come in and take his place. This sign may make comforting reading, but will Nature be satisfied with this arrangement? Will she receive an impulse from a certain direction and return it in a different direction? Will she change her laws because a certain sign says so? Where do we see any evidence of this in the material world? We would not risk our material welfare on such a belief; is it not still more important not to risk our moral welfare on it?

KARMA AND MENTAL HEALING

Our diseases are the results of wrong thinking, feeling and consequent acting on our part either in this life or in a former one. The disturbances thus produced in our inner nature gradually work their way from the mental plane, through intermediate stages, down to the physical plane, where they appear as disease. Instead of looking upon disease as something to be shunned, we should look upon it as a beneficent process of purification aimed at restoring inner harmony and health. It is the last stage in Nature's effort to rid the system of the effects of former wrongdoing.

When the disturbances manifest in the physical body as disease, we can aid Nature in her work by using such medicines as are known to be helpful in leading the disease out of the body without permanent injury to the body. A cheerful and optimistic frame of mind can also be a great help to this end.

To "cure" disease by thought, or so-called Mental Healing, which usually takes the form of a denial of disease and an affirmation of health, can prevent the disease from manifesting through the body. But this has not removed the cause. It has reversed the natural process and returned the effect to the mental plane where it is re-planted as a cause. Here it lies in wait for another opportunity at expression and may be reinforced by a new crop of similar causes, the result of more wrong thinking and acting. Thus growing in strength, the time will come when it will burst all barriers and eventually force itself out as a disease that may be far more disastrous than the one that was dammed back originally.

"UNMERITED SUFFERING"

It is difficult for us to recognize the justice of suffering that we may have to endure, when we are unable to recognize its cause. Especially is this the case when we see an individual who has lived a spotless life suddenly afflicted with some painful or fatal disease. To a Human Ego, that identifies itself with its Personality, and therefore sees only what has happened during its present existence, such suffering does of course seem unmerited. But to the Higher or Reincarnating Ego, which is the same throughout the series of incarnations, it is known to be karmic justice. It was the Reincarnating Ego, that jointly with its former Personality sowed the seed of suffering in the past, and it is the same Reincarnating Ego, that, jointly with its new Personality, suffers the effect in the present incarnation.

But since the *feeling* of injustice experienced by the Human Ego during life, although not based on fact, yet *seems* very real to the Human Ego on account of its limited vision, it is entitled to have a compensation for this apparent injustice, and this it receives in the blissful post-mortem dream state.

Continuous Adjustments.

Karma is constantly making adjustments between causes and effects. These adjustments do not always, and in a single operation, restore an exact balance, but may hit the target a little above or below the mark. Especially is this true in the case of "Group-Karma," where it is only reasonable to suppose that there must be differences in degree between the karmic guilt of the group members. The Karma is just for the average of the group, but may be too harsh on some while it is too lenient on others. Any such unbalanced remainders would then be taken care of by future events, favorable or unfavorable as the case might be.

Karma is like the man who reads our gas-meter; if he overcharges us one month it is compensated for on next month's reading, but when the final reading is taken there will be no remainder. Like the pendulum, that stops in the exact mid-position, so Karma will come to rest when cause and effect balance exactly.

Judging Others by Their Karma.

In case we are inclined to judge our fellow men by their Karma, it would be well to remember that one who is experiencing suffering and pain may have sowed the seeds for this many incarnations ago, and may since that time have changed his character for the better. Furthermore, by unkind judgement of others, we sow the seed of criticism to be directed against ourselves when we may have to experience some karmic suffering.

Hastening Karma.

There is another reason why outward experiences are no criterion to judge a person's character by. An individual who makes an earnest effort at self-discipline and self-improvement is by this action challenging his old Karma to come to the surface. The more unselfishly this is done, the more will his Karma be hastened and bring down upon him an accumulation of effects, which under normal conditions might have been distributed over a long period of time. The case is comparable to that of a student who takes up a serious program of training that requires much hard work. His life may seem bleak and austere when compared to that of another who is drifting along comfortably and without effort. Judging superficially, we may conclude that the drifter's life was to be preferred, when in reality it is one of stagnation. Seen in its true light a life of suffering may be an indication that here is a Soul that is hastening its evolution and fitting itself for some great work to be done in the future.

Abnormal Cases.

Sometimes our Karma comes to us through impersonal processes of Nature and other times through the actions of our fellow men. Nature makes no mistakes and returns to us all that is due us and nothing that is not due us. In all normal cases when Karma reaches us through our fellow men the effects are also in full accord with what is due us.

But there may be abnormal cases. It is conceivable that a perverted human being might deliberately and with malicious intent do injury to others, which, in some cases, it might not have been their Karma to endure.

If this should happen Karma will make adjustments by a suitable compensation to the victim. The perpetrator of the deed, on the other hand, has by his evil act sowed the seed of a similar experience, which sometime in the future he shall have to reap.

IS IT UNFAIR TO SUFFER FOR FORGOTTEN DEEDS?

The following objection to Karma is frequently made:

"It is unfair that we should suffer for deeds that we have long since forgotten."

If we object to Karma on the ground that we sometimes have forgotten the cause of our suffering, we should ask ourselves if we also object when Karma brings us benefits which we earned by some long forgotten deed. If we do not object to the benefits, is it fair to object to the misfortunes?

If we act contrary to our sense of right and our better judgement, and if the effect follows swiftly, we see the connection between our act and the suffering that follows, and we recognize the justice of what happens to us. But suppose the effect is delayed, even beyond death, does that alter the intrinsic justice of the suffering that must eventually follow?

Is it not of common occurrence that individuals who do what they know is wrong, if the effect is delayed, want to forget, and soon do forget their misdeed, confident in the belief that no unfavorable effect will follow? Long after the deed is forgotten, perhaps later in this life, perhaps in a succeeding incarnation, the effect does materialize in the form of suffering or some misfortune. Then the "victim" of this suffering asks indignantly: "What have *I* done that this should come to *me*?" He does not know, but he did know he was doing wrong at the time he committed the deed. The misfortunes that come to us today, and that seem so undeserved, are the results of our former misdeeds, and our misdeeds of today will return to us as similar unpleasant surprises in the future.

If the mere forgetting of an act would nullify its effect and relieve us of responsibility for it, then a poor memory would be a valuable asset.

We know better than this, however, and prove it by our actions in ordinary business affairs. For, if a person has borrowed some money from us, and when it is due, pleads that he has "forgotten all about it," and that it is unfair that he should have to pay, we do not accept this as a valid excuse for non-payment. How then can we expect our forgetfulness to interfere with the operation of the Law of Cause and Effect?

If we do not accept the doctrines of Karma and Reincarnation, how shall we then account for suffering that has no visible cause?

If we accept heredity as a cause, we suffer for the sins of our ancestors, which we could not even forget, since we never knew anything about them. This makes heredity a more unjust explanation than Karma.

If we accept the theory of the theologian that God created man at birth, then we had no part in producing the suffering that we now endure, but God is responsible for it.

If we take the view held by the materialist, that man is the product of blind natural forces, then our suffering must be due to the imperfect work of these forces, over which we had no control.

The explanations offered by heredity, by the theologian and the materialist allow man *no part* in causing the suffering he has to endure. Are not these explanations more unfair than that of Karma, which teaches that man himself is the cause of both his own suffering and his own good fortune, even though he has forgotten the originating acts?

ARE DELAYED EFFECTS CONDUCIVE
TO WRONG-DOING?

Objections have been raised to Karma on the ground that, since the effect of evil deeds may be long delayed, the temptation to disregard the future retribution and accept the present advantage would be too strong and this would result in unchecked evil-doing.

Does not this objection apply still more strongly to the doctrine of forgiveness of sin, or to a belief in chance? If either of these theories were correct, effects of evil-doing might be avoided entirely.

Karma teaches what every observer knows to be a fact, namely that the effect does not always follow immediately upon its cause. But Karma gives no assurance that the effect will be delayed. It may follow immediately, but whether delayed or not, it is inescapable. Anyone who still is inclined to gamble with destiny should review his past experiences and see if he has not met with accidents or misfortunes for which he could assign no cause. Such experiences are the delayed retributions for past misdeeds that now catch up with him. In some long-forgotten past he reasoned, as he does today, that the retribution would probably be so long delayed that he might ignore it. But now when the effect of his misdeed comes home to him, he resents it and feels that he has been singled out by fate to suffer unjustly. The "future," that seemed so far away when the deed was committed, has arrived: it is the present time, and the effect was no less painful because it had been delayed. The self-deceiving reasoning of the past was no help in avoiding his present misfortune. Should he then apply it again to the future?

With our present experience before us and realizing that we may have many more such misfortunes awaiting us, "just around the corner" perhaps, any temptation to wrong-doing based on the hope that the effect might be postponed should lose all its attractiveness.

When we plant a seed we do not expect immediate results, but we know what the fruit is going to be and choose the seed accordingly. Should we use less judgement in something that affects our own future welfare?

KARMA-NEMESIS, AND KARMA-THE-FRIEND

Those who consider Karma a harsh and cold doctrine, because it teaches that we must face the consequences of our acts, think only of its punitive aspect.

In Greek Mythology this aspect of Karma was symbolized by Nemesis, the goddess of retributive justice, who was represented as relentlessly pursuing the guilty until punished. But this is only one half of the doctrine, and Karma can be looked upon as a guardian angel just as much as an avenging deity for it protects the innocent from harm just as surely as it punishes the guilty. It is our friend as much as a stern teacher for it rewards our good deeds just as surely as it punishes our misdeeds. The friendly,

happier aspect of Karma is of course just as important as the
Nemesis aspect, and should be emphasized just as strongly as its
negative counterpart. The only reason so much has been said about
Karma-Nemesis and so little about Karma the friend, is the fact
that almost everyone will accept the latter as needing no explanation, while objecting to the former as being unjust.

KARMA AND ITS COMPANION DOCTRINES

The doctrine of Karma is only one out of many teachings which
collectively form the Ancient Wisdom. None of these teachings
is complete by itself; all mutually shed light on their companion
doctrines. Each one of them should therefore be studied in its
relation to the others in order to be seen in its right perspective.

Karma, for instance, if viewed by itself alone, may seem like a
cold, mechanistic doctrine. But when it is realized that the purpose
of life is the evolution of the Soul, then it can be seen that Karma
is of inestimable value to man for it is a statement of the law that
governs his evolution. It points out the right road and warns him
of the pitfalls.

The fundamental unity of all life is another doctrine closely
related to Karma. The fact that all men are inwardly united and
all have the same ultimate goal makes harmony the natural condition in men's relations with one another. Karma promotes this
harmony, by teaching that our own deeds return to us, thereby
proving the wisdom of altruistic action.

Evolution, the oneness of all life and Reincarnation are all links
in the same chain of ideas and all are necessary in order to present
Karma in its true light.

In Karma lies the hope of building a better world, for it teaches
that every effort counts and will bear fruit. We can make Karma
our friend and it need not be harsh unless we make it so.

KARMA AND THE SINGLE EARTH-LIFE THEORY

Any thoughtful individual, who observes life around him, must
have been struck by the inequalities, injustices and misfortunes

of various kinds that afflict so many human beings. He notes instances where the innocent suffer, while the guilty go free, where the honest fail while the dishonest prosper. He observes that some men are gifted and talented, while others have very limited capacities; that some have robust health, while others are invalids for life. He sees these and a variety of other inequalities and he asks: Why all this injustice? Why are not all healthy, gifted and prosperous?

Seeking an answer to these questions he examines current theories in regard to man and the world he lives in. He finds two principal lines of thought, one presented by orthodox religion, and the other held by the materialists. These two groups have widely divergent views in some respects, the theologian believing that man is created by God, the materialist holding that he is the product of material energies operating in Nature. In other respects they hold similar views. Both might be called "Creationists," for both assume that man is created at birth. They are also in agreement by both taking for granted that man is limited to a single life on earth.

If these latter assumptions are true, man is not responsible for what he is or what he does or the circumstances of life in which he finds himself. All this was predetermined for him by the power that brought him into being, whether that power was God or Nature with its forces.

The misfortunes that befall man are under these conditions actual injustices inflicted on him by extraneous agents, and he suffers effects which he did not cause; he reaps what he did not sow. In other words the assumption that man is created at birth and is limited to a single earth-life leads to the inescapable conclusion that man's life is not governed by the Law of Cause and Effect. And vice versa: If the Law of Cause and Effect governs man's life, then the preceding assumptions must be wrong.

The belief in creationism and a single earth-life is incompatible with a belief in Justice and a Law of Cause and Effect as governing principles in human life. The two propositions are the antithesis of each other.

No misfortune can befall a man justly unless he brought it on himself, and since some misfortunes begin with birth, how could man have brought them on himself unless he existed prior to birth?

Likewise there are many causes set in motion by man, that do not come to fruition before death. How can these be equitably balanced if the death of the body meant the death of the Soul?

An explanation of the inequalities of life in conformity with Justice, makes an existence of the Soul both before birth and after death imperative requirements.

The doctrine of Reincarnation fulfills these requirements. It explains the apparent injustices man now suffers as the effects of his own former deeds, and that eventually he shall reap all that he has sowed.

We notice then that the doctrine of Reincarnation is a corollary to the Law of Cause and Effect. If the latter operates in human life, Reincarnation must be a fact.

There is no disagreement between Creationists and Reincarnationists in regard to our present earth-life. The disagreement concerns what precedes birth and what follows death.

The Masters of Wisdom, who have reached a higher stage in evolution and can enter inner planes of existence in full possession of their consciousness, tell us that Reincarnation is a fact, but until the ordinary individual has reached this stage, he has to be satisfied to theorize on what takes place on these planes. If Reincarnation to him is only a theory, it should be remembered that the beliefs of the Creationist and the materialist also are no more than theories, unsupported by direct observation.

The comparative value of these theories will have to be determined by their ability to explain life and their agreement or disagreement with such facts of Nature as are known.

The assumption that man's Soul was created or came into existence at birth is not in accord with the knowledge we have of the material plane. On this plane it has been established that matter and energy are indestructible, a fact referred to as The Law of Conservation of Energy. Matter and energy can undergo many transformations, but were never created and can never be annihilated or destroyed.

Man's Soul or consciousness is energy of some kind belonging to inner, unseen mental-spiritual planes of Nature. These inner, unseen planes are just as much a part of Nature and subject to its laws, as is the outer material plane. The Law of Conservation of Energy must therefore have its counterpart on the unseen side of Nature and the higher mental-spiritual energies must be as indestructible on their respective planes as their counterparts are on the material plane. And if they are indestructible, they could not have been created, but must have existed always. What has no end can have had no beginning. What is to be of infinite duration in the future must have been of infinite duration in the past.

The conclusions to which the single earth-life and repeated earth-lives theories lead, can now be compared.

The belief that man begins his existence at birth cannot be reconciled with a belief in Justice or that man reaps what he sowed and is therefore contrary to the Law of Cause and Effect.

A belief that the Soul existed before birth harmonizes with a belief in Justice, for it explains when and where man sowed the seeds that resulted in the inequalities and "injustices" of birth, and is therefore in harmony with the Law of Cause and Effect.

The belief that man is created at birth conflicts with the Law of Conservation of Energy, which states that energy can neither be created nor annihilated.

A belief in the pre-existence and indestructibility of the Soul is in accord with the Law of Conservation of Energy.

A belief in repeated earth-lives explains how causes, sown by man, that have not yet been balanced, will bring their effect in some future earth-life.

It is apparent, then, that the doctrine of Reincarnation conforms to known laws in Nature, while the theories of the Creationists are contrary to these laws.

It is difficult to understand how a belief, that is so illogical as the single earth-life theory, can have held such sway over men's minds as this idea has in the Occident. The only plausible explanation for this is the fact that no alternative theory was available.

After the condemnation by the church-authorities in the 6th Century of the doctrine of Reincarnation, no reference was made to it in the church teachings. This left the single earth-life theory without a competitor and thenceforward it was accepted by generation after generation without challenge as to its validity. But since the Ancient Wisdom teachings have again been brought to the attention of the West, the single earth-life theory is no longer alone in its field. It must now face a comparison with the doctrine of Reincarnation.

A belief that we are here only once has no basis for its existence other than the fact that we have inherited it from our ancestors and that certain surface indications seem to be in its favor. Chief among these is the fact that we do not remember our past lives; neither can we peer into the future and see what is in store for us. All we are sure of is our present earth-life and without investigating further we have taken for granted that this is the only life we have had or will have here.

But surface indications can be misleading. We have been deceived before by ideas that at one time were generally accepted and considered unassailable, but later were proved to have been entirely wrong.

There was a time, for instance, when man accepted as self-evident and beyond argument the belief that the earth was flat and was the center of the Universe. Pythagoras, who taught that the sun was the center of the Universe and that the earth was a sphere, was vigorously attacked and ridiculed by the Church Father Lactantius (260-330 A.D.) for holding such views.

In rejecting Pythagoras' ideas Lactantius writes as follows:

The folly of this foolish old fellow ought to be laughed to scorn!

How can people believe that there are antipodes under our feet? Do they say anything deserving of attention at all? Is there anybody so senseless as to believe that there are men living on the underside of the earth, whose feet thus are higher than their heads? Or that the things which with us grow upright, with them hang head downwards? That the crops and trees grow downwards? That rains, and snows, and hail, fall upwards to the surface of the earth? . . . These people thought that the earth is round like a ball . . . and that it has mountains, extends plains, and contains level seas, under our feet on the opposite side of the earth: and if so, it follows that all parts of such an earth would be inhabited by men and beasts. Thus the rotundity of the earth leads to the idiotic idea of those antipodes hanging downwards! . . . I am absolutely at a loss to know what to say about such people, who, after having erred in one thing, consistently persevere in their preposterous folly, and defend one vain and false notion by another . . .*

We now know that the idea Lactantius so effectively ridiculed was right, and that the flat-earth theory which he accepted, was wrong. Lacking evidence to the contrary, he based his opinion wholly on outward appearances and was led to a wrong conclusion.

The single earth-life theory is another belief generally accepted in the Occident today. It dominates our thinking in its own field as completely as did the flat-earth idea some centuries ago.

But the single earth-life theory leads to conclusions that are impossible to reconcile with Justice and an orderly Universe governed by law. It is incapable of solving the problem of free will and of showing that man is morally responsible for his actions. It fails to explain heredity, environment and accidents in harmony with Justice. It is the great obstacle that confuses our thinking and prevents us from seeing that we create our own misfortunes.

Since the single earth-life theory has caused such havoc in our thinking and has produced such disastrous results by depriving man of his faith in law and Justice, is it not time that this theory should be challenged and an effort made to determine what justification there is for its existence?

All that can be said in its favor is that it has been accepted by past generations and that there is no outward evidence to contradict it, and so, in the absence of alternatives, it has been left unchallenged as to its validity.

The doctrine of Reincarnation, on the other hand, solves all the problems that the single earth-life theory leaves unsolved, in harmony with Justice and law in the Universe.

In the light of repeated existences the sequence of cause and effect can readily be understood. Man himself is responsible for his heredity, his environment and the good or evil fortune that may befall him and he is morally responsible for all his acts.

---

* From *The Divine Institutes* by Lactantius, Bk. III Chap. XXIV. Quoted from *The Esoteric Tradition* by G. de Purucker.

A Fragment of a Long Story—Trying to understand life on the basis of the single earth-life theory is like trying to understand a book by reading a page in the middle of it. Events that are narrated on this page are the effects of causes described on preceding pages and can not be understood unless these pages are read. The effects of new activities described on this single page will appear on some following page or in a later chapter. The full significance of what the single page relates can only be understood when the book is read from start to finish. A single earth-life is but a "page" in the endless story of a Soul on its pilgrimage towards perfection. If we could read the record of our past lives, we should have the explanation to all that happens to us in this life. If we could look into the future and see what will take place there, we would see the result of our present actions.

Can there be a reasonable doubt in the mind of anyone, who makes a fair comparison of the two theories, that the doctrine of Reincarnation solves life's problems more in accord with Justice and law, logic and reason, than does the single earth-life theory?

The single earth-life theory may be strongly entrenched in men's minds today, but let us not forget what happened to the geocentric theory. History may repeat itself and the day may not be far distant when the single earth-life theory will join the geocentric one in some "museum" of obsolete ideas happily no longer darkening our mental horizon.

Reincarnation is the "Lost Chord" in modern thought that must be restored before man's faith in Justice can be re-established.

Karma is the law that governs man's life. Reincarnation is a companion doctrine to Karma that explains how Karma operates.

KARMA AND SCIENTIFIC PROOF

The great success achieved by scientific research on the material side of Nature has given rise to a popular belief that scientific theories are infallible and have been proved beyond possibility for doubt.

The scientific method of proof consists in gathering all known facts in regard to some phenomenon in Nature and then in assuming some theory, that fits these facts and explains the phenomenon. If no new facts are discovered that contradict this theory, it is considered proved.

No responsible scientist will claim that such proof is final for it is recognized that there is always a possibility that new facts may be discovered that call for a change in the theory or perhaps its complete abandonment for a new and better one.

The author of a textbook on Physics used in one of our largest universities, referring to one of the most important and generally accepted laws in Physics, expresses himself as follows: "Like all the fundamental physical laws, the law of conservation of energy is not capable of direct proof, but is *an assumption consistent with all known facts*, and is to be accepted until some phenomena are discovered with which it is inconsistent."

Scientific knowledge, then, is not in a class by itself as being infallible, but such theories as are based on actual facts, correctly interpreted, are strong probabilities and the nearest possible approach to truth, based on the information available.

If we were to apply the scientific method of proof to Karma as it affects us human beings, we should take note of all the experiences we meet during life. These are the "facts and phenomena" that have to be explained in conformity with the Law of Cause and Effect. Since every experience we meet can be explained by Reincarnation and Karma as the effect of our own acts, it is apparent that the doctrine of Karma with its companion doctrine of Reincarnation "fits the facts" and therefore should be accepted until some new facts are discovered with which it is inconsistent. Karma can therefore be considered proved by the same method that the scientist uses to prove his theories.

THE STRONGEST PROOF FOR KARMA

Man's moral instincts, his sense of "the fitness of things," experience, analogy, reason and logic tell him that this Universe is governed by the Law of Cause and Effect.

The strongest proof for Karma, however, lies in the fact that there are no alternatives. It is logically impossible to imagine an event that happens without a cause.

KARMA AND THE GREAT RELIGIONS

In the Bible there are many statements to the effect that man shall "reap what he sows," that he shall "receive according to his works," and this is the doctrine of Karma:

Be not deceived; God is not mocked: for whatsoever a man soweth, that shall he also reap.

—*Gal.* VI, 7

For verily I say unto you, Till heaven and earth pass, one jot or one tittle shall in no wise pass from the law, until all be fulfilled.

—*Matt.* V, 18

Judge not that ye be not judged. For with what judgment ye judge, so shall ye be judged: and with what measures ye mete, it shall be measured to you again.

—*Matt.* VII, 1, 2

. . . for all they that take the sword shall perish with the sword.

—*Matt,* XXVI, 52

Cast thy bread upon the waters: for thou shalt find it after many days . . . [lives]

—*Eccl.* XI, 1

But this I say, He which soweth sparingly shall reap also sparingly; and he which soweth bountifully shall reap also bountifully.

—*II Cor.* IX, 6

Sow to yourselves in righteousness, reap in mercy . . . . Ye have ploughed wickedness, ye have reaped iniquity.

—*Hos.* X, 12, 13

He that leadeth into captivity shall go into captivity: he that killeth with the sword must be killed with the sword.

—*Rev.* XIII, 10

Ye shall know them by their fruits. Do men gather grapes of thorns, or figs of thistles?

—*Matt.* VII, 16

Blessed are the merciful: for they shall obtain mercy.

—*Matt.* V, 7

Similar statements are also found in: *Matt.* XII, 36; *Matt.* XVI, 27; *Job* XXXIV, 11; *Ps.* LXII, 12; *Prov.* XXIV, 12; *Jer.* XVII, 10; *Jer.* XXXII, 19; *Rom.* II, 6; *Matt.* XVI, 27; *II Cor.* V, 10; *Col.* III, 25; *Rev.* II, 23; *Rev.* XXII, 12.

In the *Anugîtâ*, Ch. III, one of the *Upanishads*, we find the following:

Whatever action he [man] performs, whether good or bad, everything done in a former body must necessarily be enjoyed or suffered.

In the beautiful poem *The Light of Asia*, Sir Edwin Arnold tells the life story of Gautama, the Buddha, and also gives some of his teachings. Referring to Karma he writes:

KARMA—all that total of a soul
Which is the things it did, the thoughts it had,
The "self" it wove with woof of viewless time
Crossed on the warp invisible of acts.

·   ·   ·   ·   ·   ·   ·   ·   ·   ·

Before beginning and without an end,
As space eternal and as surety sure,
Is fixed a power divine which moves to good,
Only its laws endure.

·   ·   ·   ·   ·   ·   ·   ·   ·   ·

It will not be contemned of anyone;
Who thwarts it loses, and who serves it gains;

The hidden good it pays with peace and bliss,
The hidden ill with pains.

It seeth everywhere and marketh all:
Do right—it recompenseth! Do one wrong—
The equal retribution must be made,
Though Dharma* tarry long.

It knows not wrath nor pardon; utter true
It measures mete, its faultless balance weighs;
Times are as nought, tomorrow it will judge,
Or after many days.

By this the slayer's knife did stab himself;
The unjust judge hath lost his own defender;
The false tongue dooms its lie; the creeping thief
And spoiler rob, to render.

Such is the law which moves to righteousness,
Which none at last can turn aside or stay;
The heart of it is love, the end of it
Is peace and consummation sweet. Obey!

. . . .

The books say well, my brothers! Each man's life
The outcome of his former living is;
The bygone wrongs bring forth sorrow and woes,
The bygone right breeds bliss.

That which ye sow ye reap. See yonder fields!
The sesamum was sesamum, the corn
Was corn. The silence and the darkness knew!
So is a man's fate born.

He cometh reaper of the things he sowed,
Sesamum, corn, so much cast in past birth;

---

* The Law.

And so much weed and poison-stuff, which mar
Him and the aching earth.

If he shall labor rightly, rooting these,
And planting wholesome seedlings where they grew,
Fruitful and fair and clean the ground shall be,
And rich the harvest due.

Chapter IX

BROTHERHOOD

[W]hen men have no standard of right and wrong, which they can prove to be based on natural law, there is always widespread immorality, not sexual immorality alone, but also political immorality, social immorality, ethical immorality in general. In such case men have no guide in life, and the consequence will be corruption, deceit, self-seeking, war and all the other evil things that follow in the train.

Our Theosophical doctrines give to man not only a great and sublime hope, but they also give to him ethical principles, by which he will live, and a grand philosophy, which adequately explains those principles. Hence, wars will automatically cease when the world is finally Theosophized; corruption in high places and in low will become an awful memory of the past. This regeneration, among other things, is what we are working for. This . . . is one of the fundamental reasons for the founding of the Theosophical Society.

G. DE PURUCKER
(*The Theosophical Forum,* Feb. 1932)

BROTHERHOOD — A FACT IN NATURE

Brotherhood is a fact in Nature declares the Ancient Wisdom. This affirmation is based on the inner spiritual unity of all life. Every life-unit or Monad is an emanation from the One Universal Life, which is the unseen cause behind the visible universe.

We human beings constitute one group of Monads, linked with one another through a common origin and a common destiny — fellow travelers with a common goal. The basis for harmony and cooperation already exists therefore, and a brotherhood in actu is the natural and normal relationship between men.

OUTWARD INDICATIONS OF UNITY

The extent to which our spiritual unity is recognized depends on our development and differs vastly with different individuals.

Indifference to the suffering and hardship of others shows a lack of spiritual development. A sense of oneness, compassion, fellow-feeling and sympathy for the one who suffers shows a realization of inner unity. A witness to an accident, although not affected physically, may feel sick and even faint as a result of this feeling of inner unity with the victim.

When we see or hear of some heroic deed, or some act of self sacrifice, some duty done in the face of difficulty or danger, we experience a warmth of heart, and a renewed faith that there is something noble or divine in our fellow men. There is a chord in our nature that responds when a true note is struck by someone else, and why should this chord vibrate in unison with the note struck unless there is something of divinity in all human hearts?

The separateness we feel outwardly is not as complete as may appear on the surface. When we step on a bus or a train for instance our safe-keeping is in the hands of those who drive these conveyances. Our life may depend on the mechanic who repaired

243

our auto and when we are riding in it, our life is almost as much dependent on the care of other drivers as it is on our own. When we cross a bridge or use an elevator we are entrusting our lives to those who designed and built it. What we do affects others and what they do affects us. We *are* our "Brother's Keeper," and he is our "Keeper," and we are responsible to each other for our acts.

In Nature we find that certain animals such as bees and ants have developed a type of group-consciousness for they form large colonies in which they cooperate for the common good. As a result the colony prospers and the individual units are enabled to survive, which they could not do if working for themselves alone.

We human beings find ourselves placed by Nature as parts of various combinations such as families, towns, nations, etc. As members of these groups we do much of our work collectively. We recognize that we are parts of something greater than ourselves and that there is something to be gained for the individual and the group by such cooperation.

The human body is a marvelous example of cooperation between various cells and organs, all working together for the benefit of the body as a whole. Unwittingly man copies Nature's method of cooperation when some great public work has to be done and finds that he profits thereby. He then joins with others to form what he calls an "organization" with someone as its "head" and various committees and subordinates to carry out the details, much as the organs in the body perform their various functions. When we refer to our community or state as a whole and call it the "social body" or the "body politic" we sub-consciously recognize an inner fact.

Whatever the objective, whether religious, political, scientific, commercial or other, and whether the motive be selfish or altruistic, men realize that they can accomplish more by acting collectively than they can by acting as individuals.

We can not expect much evidence of unity on the outer plane, where our separateness is most pronounced; yet, as we have seen, indications that we are in some way united with one another are not entirely lacking. The real oneness of all life is to be found on the spiritual planes of Nature, however, and since the ordinary man has not as yet become conscious on these planes he is unable to prove this unity by direct observation.

INDIRECT EVIDENCE OF UNITY

Outward and direct indications of oneness may not be plentiful, but there is an abundance of indirect evidence that we are not separate, for we see the disastrous results that follow when men act selfishly and contrary to the laws of harmony.

These laws can not be broken with impunity for they are self-enforcing. If we are to build a stone arch the stones must be shaped and placed according to the laws of mechanics. There is no outward authority to force us to obey these laws, but if we fail to do so, the arch will collapse. Neither does Nature compel us to live in harmony with our fellow-men, but failure to do so results in the collapse of a well organized society, just as failure to observe the laws of mechanics results in failure of the arch.

We see examples of this on every hand, in the small and in the great, in the family and the community, in the nation and internationally. Selfishness and disregard for the rights of others practiced by some individuals brings suffering and unhappiness and increased burdens on others. With every passing year our oneness becomes more and more apparent. Modern inventions have brought us all so close together that acts of selfishness and aggression, which formerly were localized and passed unnoticed outside of a small circle, now affect the whole human race. If an aggressor nation attacks a weaker neighbor in some remote part of the world, we may think that it does not concern us, but before the chain of events thus set in motion comes to rest, we may have been dragged into the conflict and found that it did concern us too.

THE STUMBLING BLOCK IS SELFISHNESS

The ideal of Brotherhood has always appealed to man's imagination. In his better moments he dreams of the Millenium and something within tells him that it is not an unattainable Utopia, but that some day it shall become a living reality.

The ethical teachings of the great religions also teach Brotherhood. In the Sermon on the Mount Jesus urges men to practice unselfishness, forgiveness, generosity, to love one's neighbor as oneself, to apply the Golden Rule in everyday life and thus make Brotherhood a living reality. Other spiritual teachers have taught the same ethics.

It is generally agreed that the simple teachings in the Sermon on the Mount, if taken seriously and applied in practice, would be sufficient to establish Brotherhood, and man's failure to do this has not been due to a lack of ethical teachings on the subject.

The altruist and the humanitarian do take these teachings seriously and seek to benefit their fellow men without selfish motives. Many sincere attempts have been made by religious and other groups to practice Brotherhood, and if it were not for such efforts by people of good will this world would be in a far worse condition than it is. But those who try to practice Brotherhood meet with difficulties. They have to deal with others, who by their selfishness hamper the efforts for Brotherhood, and make these ineffective.

It is the selfish man who causes the strife and disharmony in the world. He too has had the ethical teachings of religion presented to him, but has ignored them for ages past and is doing the same today. Unless he can be induced to change his selfish attitude, Brotherhood will not become a reality. Evidently ethical teachings, wonderful as they are, are not sufficient to accomplish this when standing alone and are ineffective where they are most needed.

The selfish man feels that selfishness offers immediate and concrete advantages, while the benefits resulting from altruism are uncertain and may never materialize. He sees others practice selfishness with apparently favorable results and hence concludes that selfishness "pays" better than altruism and that is his reason for acting selfishly.

Selfishness and crime can not be eliminated as long as man believes that they are profitable. Unless it can be shown that they are unprofitable and injurious to man's welfare, selfishness, corruption and crime will continue, become more aggravated and eventually wreck our civilization as they have done with so many others in the past.

The elimination of selfishness, then, depends on eliminating the profit motive behind it, and the solution of the problem of selfishness depends on the question: Does selfishness pay?

DOES SELFISHNESS "PAY"?

If we are to profit by selfishness we must get from others more than we give in return, or better still "get something for nothing." We must be able to reap benefits that we have not earned and we must be able to escape the consequences of our evil deeds.

It will be noted that all success gained through selfishness is based on the assumption that we can reap benefits without sowing, and sow evil without reaping, in other words, it depends on our ability to defy the Law of Cause and Effect. If we can defy this law, we can profit from selfishness. If not there can be no profit in selfishness.

To demonstrate that human actions are governed by the Law of Cause and Effect, therefore, is to demonstrate that there is no profit in selfishness, and hence no reason to practice it.

Anyone who accepts the Law of Cause and Effect must reject selfishness as a means of gaining advantages.

Anyone who acts selfishly, hoping to gain thereby, proves by his action that he does not believe in the Law of Cause and Effect. He may pay lip-service to it, but by his act he says in effect: "I am sure I won't have to suffer from the evil effect of my deed. There may not be any effect at all, and if there is I can side-step it." An evil act can only be based on a belief that the evildoer can escape the consequences of his act, in other words on his ability to defy the Law of Cause and Effect.

AN APPEAL TO THE SELFISH

The selfish man lives on a lower plane than the altruist. His consciousness is centered in his Personality and he is therefore more aware of his physical separateness from his fellow men, than he is of his spiritual oneness with them. The ethical appeal of religion goes over his head. If we hope to change his selfish attitude, we must deal with him on the plane where he functions; we must appeal to his self-interest.

The Law of Cause and Effect, besides appealing to the altruist, also has an effective appeal to the selfish man.

When the selfish man becomes convinced that he shall reap what he sows, he realizes that any act he performs to the benefit of someone else, will inevitably result in a similar benefit returning to himself and that in benefiting others he therefore also benefits himself.

Similarly he realizes that any suffering he may have caused, any harm he may have done to another, shall also return to him, and that in injuring others he therefore also injures himself. Under these conditions it is only common sense to practice Brotherhood and avoid injuring others. To do otherwise is to act contrary to one's own interest. The knowledge that we shall reap what we sow has a double effect; it restrains selfishness and promotes Brotherhood.

It is the illogical notion that we are here for one single earthlife that misleads man into believing that he can gain advantages through selfishness. Seen in the light of Karma and Reincarnation it is apparent that such gains are only temporary and imaginary. Instead of being real they are no more advantageous than the incurring of debts, which eventually must be repaid.

The importance of the doctrines of Karma and Reincarnation in their effect on human behavior can not be overestimated, for they hold the solution to the problem of selfishness, the greatest obstacle to human progress.

SELFISHNESS REVERSED

When the selfish man realizes that altruism is advantageous to him, he will begin to practice it. We can not expect him to alter his character all at once, for old habits and thought-forms are difficult to change. His first attempts will be made with a view to the benefits he expects to derive therefrom. His motive is still selfish, but the direction of the selfishness is reversed; it no longer injures others, it benefits them. He has made a start in the right direction, which is better than no start at all, and he has not stored up future trouble for himself.

The results so far as direct benefit goes may be disappointing, but he has opened a new door to the better side of his nature. He has the novel experience of making others happy, and this brings happiness to him in return.

As he gradually advances in his evolution, the happy experience of benefiting others will be its own reward, or blot out all thought of either reward or punishment. Altruism will then become the natural way of life.

ETHICS BASED ON NATURE'S LAWS

In his effort to determine the validity or truth of a doctrine man has three methods by which he can investigate the subject. These are religion, philosophy and science and each of these reveals a different phase of the subject under consideration. If a doctrine is true it must have an explanation that is satisfactory from all three of these viewpoints.

In its religious aspect the doctrine must satisfy man's moral intuitions, his aspirations and longings for a higher, nobler life; it must teach him how to adjust his life in harmony with his fellow men. But religion alone, without philosophy and science can lead to dogmatism and superstition.

In its philosophic aspect the doctrine must satisfy man's reason and logic. But philosophy without religion and science can lead to cold and barren intellectualism remote from human understanding and sympathy.

In its scientific aspect the doctrine must harmonize with established facts and laws of Nature, but unless it also satisfies man's religious aspirations, his reason and logic, its presentation is incomplete and may lead to irresponsible materialism.

"There is no religion higher than Truth" says the Ancient Wisdom and adds that there can be no conflict between true religion, true philosophy or true science. A doctrine that fails to satisfy all three methods of investigation is either erroneous or incomplete in its presentation.

When we seek to determine why ethical teachings have not had a greater influence on man's behavior than they have, we find that they have been presented from the religious viewpoint only. What is lacking is a philosophy that shows *why* man should practice ethics and a science to demonstrate that this philosophy is based on facts in Nature.

The doctrines of Karma and Reincarnation give the philosophic basis on which ethics rest. These doctrines in their turn are based on Nature, for science has demonstrated that the material side of Nature is governed by law, and reason and logic tell us that this law must apply everywhere in the universe.

If we examine ethical teachings we find that even if they do not refer to the Law of Cause and Effect, they are based on it. In the Sermon on the Mount Jesus teaches men to "first seek the Kingdom of God and his righteousness" and then the needs of the body will be provided for. What is "the Kingdom of God and his righteousness" but to practice unselfishness, generosity, in brief to live according to the Golden Rule? Such actions must have their effects, for Nature will react in kind to our actions, and the effects are bound to return to us. Therefore Jesus says in effect: Give, and the getting will take care of itself, a statement that is based on the Law of Cause and Effect.

There are many old aphorisms or rules pertaining to human conduct that have been passed on from generation to generation, because men feel intuitively that they are true. When analyzed it is found that they too are based on Karma.

"The more you give, the more you have, that is the law of love." is one such saying. The more we give out, the more we do unselfishly and without seeking reward, the more good Karma we have "stored up" for ourselves, to be reaped in the future.

"Honesty is the best policy" is another. Both honesty and dishonesty will bring their appropriate effects in accord with the Law of Cause and Effect. The former naturally will be favorable, while the latter will be unfavorable, hence honesty is the better policy.

Another aphorism tells us that "It is only what you have given away that you can hold in your cold dead hand." What we have given away without receiving compensation Karma is bound to return to us in due time.

Man's intuition tells him that there is truth in these old sayings, but his reasoning mind must also be convinced of this before he will put them into practice.

To summarize:

Religion teaches ethics.
Philosophy shows why man should practice ethics.
Science shows that ethics are based on the laws of Nature.

Taken all together they give the knowledge and understanding that are necessary to make Brotherhood a reality.

UNITY IS THE CAUSE — BROTHERHOOD THE EFFECT

As stated previously the basis of Brotherhood is the oneness of all life. When this oneness is fully realized, Brotherhood will follow of its own accord. It will come as the outward manifestation of a condition that already exists on inner, spiritual planes of Nature.

It is man's failure to recognize this unity that leads to all the strife and disharmony in the world. In his inner Higher Nature man feels a bond of union with his fellow men, and when he is under the influence of this feeling he acts in harmony with them. A great calamity of Nature brings out this better side in man and he recognizes immediately his duty to help those in distress.

But he has not yet evolved to the point where he recognizes this unity when the suffering and hardships take a less spectacular form. He then isolates himself by retreating into the shell of the lower self-hood and takes refuge in the separateness that exists there. He does not realize that the separateness, by which he tries to shield himself, is a delusion caused by the fact that his vision is limited to the material plane of Nature only, but fails to inform him of the unity that exists on inner planes.

If he had the inner vision, he would see that his isolation was no more real than that of a tenant in a large apartment house, who takes comfort in the thought that a fire in someone else's apartment is no threat to his own security.

We *do* live in "the great apartment house of Nature" and "a fire in any apartment," if not checked, will ultimately affect all. As nations we are beginning to learn that our peace, liberty and prosperity depend on other nations also enjoying these privileges; that an attack on one of our sister nations is an attack on all, that "the fire in our neighbor's apartment is our fire."

As man evolves and becomes more fully aware of the links that bind him to his fellow-men, he can no longer feel indifferent towards them. His understanding of their problems and hardships becomes so vivified, so keen that they seem like his own problems and hardships. He would have no peace of mind until he had done all in his power to bring relief to those in need.

When we have reached this point the "Social Body" will no longer be a mere figure of speech, it will be a living reality. In such a society slum conditions and lack of opportunity for the underprivileged and other social injustices would be looked upon as diseases of the Social Body and everything possible would be done for the elimination of these, just as an individual would seek to cleanse and heal a festering sore lest it bring disease to the rest of the body.

Members of such a society would not compete with one another for selfish advantages, but rather cooperate in an effort to contribute something to the common welfare. Instead of the jungle law "each one for himself" the motto would be: "each one help those less advanced than himself" and there would be no one to fall behind in the march of progress. Even the least has something to give, and the laggard of today may, after lives of effort, be the leader of the future and then return the help that was rendered him.

Brotherhood will not come as the result of any artificial man-made arrangement imposed from without, but it will come when men realize their oneness with their fellow-men. They will then act and live as the brothers, which in fact they are. When this takes place the Kingdom of Heaven will no longer be a utopian dream, but a living reality "on earth as it is in Heaven" or on the spiritual planes.

IDEAS RULE THE WORLD

If the idea that selfishness is profitable has resulted in the prevalence of selfishness, it is evident that the idea that selfishness never can be profitable, but always must be injurious, will result in the elimination of selfishness. This result will not come all at once. The Law of Karma, on which the idea is based, would have to be understood and assimilated first. In matters like these we should "think in centuries" to quote a Theosophical Teacher, rather than in years and decades.

Let us go forward a hundred years in imagination and let us assume that during those years the doctrine of Karma has been understood and assimilated, first by the serious minded and thoughtful, and from them gradually imparted to others until it finally has permeated all strata of society. It will then be accepted as a self-evident fact, just as we today accept the law of gravitation, and it will be taught in our churches and schools.

The children growing up in such a society would imbibe from their earliest years, from parents and all their elders, the idea that they are responsible for all their acts and that they shall inevitably suffer for any injury they may cause others.

Can there be any doubt that these ideas would produce a generation of individuals with their selfish tendencies largely under control? Think of the advantage of just the negative aspect of Karma, the restraining effect it would have, and think of the suffering and misery that humanity would be spared thereby!

Once selfishness is subdued, the higher faculties in human nature will be liberated and begin to express themselves. Add to this the positive assurance that Karma gives that the benefits we sow shall also return to us, and can there be any doubt that the result will be harmony and good will among men — the first step towards Brotherhood?

ANSWERS TO SOME OF THE RIDDLES OF LIFE

We can now return to the questions presented in the beginning of this volume, which make up part of the "Riddle of Life," and see how they are answered by the teachings of the Ancient Wisdom.

A summary of these answers is given below.

Why is there so much suffering in the world?

It is the result of men's wrong thinking, wrong living and wrong acting in the past. It is Nature's reaction to our lack of self control, our selfishness and the suffering we have caused others. It is not inflicted on us by any extraneous power, or by chance; we brought it on ourselves.

If we persevere in right thinking and right acting suffering will gradually cease.

Why is there so much injustice?

There is no injustice. The circumstances in which we find ourselves, the experiences we meet, we have made for ourselves. It is only our belief in the single earth-life theory that prevents us from recognizing the justice of all that happens to us.

Have we free will or are we the puppets of destiny?

Man has free will or freedom of choice. His character, which seemingly guides his choice, he has made for himself. By changing his character he can change his destiny. His destiny being self-made, he is not predestined by anything outside of himself.

Are we responsible for our acts— *Shall we reap what we sow?*

Man is a free agent with a sense of right and wrong. He can act as he chooses, but he can not escape the consequences of his act. He shall reap what he has sowed, no more, no less; no better, no worse.

Is there a life after death?

There is. Death is but a sleep — the *real Man* still lives. All that was best and most lovable is eternal. Age is but a condition of the body — the Soul never grows old. The life of the Ego is continuous and it exists after death as it also did before birth.

Birth and death are portals through which the Ego passes as it changes from one state of consciousness to another. At death the Ego recedes from an active self-conscious state to a passive dream state. After a long rest-period the Ego returns to the active, self-conscious state through the portal of birth.

Reincarnation is the master key that solves most of life's vexing problems.

What is the purpose of life?

Evolution, growth, unfolding of latent faculties. A rising from imperfection to perfection, a gradual advance towards union with man's Inner God, with infinite possibilities for growth when that union has been attained — an ever closer approach to an ever advancing ideal.

Life is a school in which it is never too late to learn. What is mastered in one life will return that much easier in the next reincarnation.

Is this a haphazard Universe governed by blind forces, or is there a plan behind it?

The visible Universe is an embodiment of a portion of Universal Consciousness, which on this plane expresses itself through an infinite variety of life-units or Monads in different stages of development. All these monads are at present advancing their evolution in the various Kingdoms of Nature. They are slowly rising from lower to higher states of existence, those below Man advancing towards the human stage, and Man beginning his evolution towards the Christ-stage.

In this plan, according to the Ancient Wisdom:

> Perfection is the goal.
> Evolution is the method.
> Duality furnishes the working tools.
> Karma is the teacher, and
> Reincarnation provides the time.

The un-self-conscious god-spark or Ray of Divinity, that in the beginning emanated from the Universal Life, has to pass through all forms of life, gain self-consciousness in the human kingdom, then rise higher along the Ray of Divinity until it rejoins its divine source, where, still retaining its identity as a self-conscious being, its consciousness becomes universal.

This marks the end of our present evolutionary period, but not the end of evolution. The Monads that have successfully completed this stage of evolution, then enter a long period of rest, after which they begin a new period of evolution on a still higher plane, thus continuing their ascent to higher and higher states of consciousness ad infinitum.

A subject so vast as that treated of in this volume can not be adequately covered in so small space. It is only presented here as an outline in the hope that it will lead the inquirer to study some of the great works on Theosophy, such as H. P. Blavatsky's *The Secret Doctrine*, G. de Purucker's *The Esoteric Tradition*, *Man in Evolution* and other works by the same authors. They contain the information man needs to understand life and the part he has to play in it.

The following quotations are from the pen of H. P. Blavatsky, the founder of the modern Theosophical Movement.

> The chief point is to uproot that most fertile source of all crime and immorality — the belief that it is possible for men to escape the consequences of their own actions. Once teach them the greatest of all laws, *Karma* and *Reincarnation*, and besides feeling in themselves the true dignity of human nature, they will turn from evil and eschew it as they would a physical danger.*

THE GOLDEN AGE OF BROTHERHOOD

> If Theosophy, prevailing in the struggle, its all-embracing philosophy striking deep root into the minds and hearts of men; if its doctrines of Reincarnation and Karma (in other words, of Hope and Responsibility) find a home in the lives of the new generations, then indeed will dawn the day of joy and gladness for all who now suffer and are outcast. For real Theosophy IS ALTRUISM, and we cannot repeat it too often. It is brotherly love, mutual help, unswerving devotion to Truth. If once men do but realize that in these alone can true happiness be found, and never in wealth, possession, or any selfish gratification, then the dark clouds will roll away, and a new humanity will be born upon earth. Then the Golden Age will be there, indeed.†

---

*The Key to Theosophy, pp. 243-4.
† Lucifer, Vol. IV, No. 21, May 1889, p. 188.